Indian River Lagoon

UNIVERSITY PRESS OF FLORIDA

Florida A&M University, Tallahassee
Florida Atlantic University, Boca Raton
Florida Gulf Coast University, Ft. Myers
Florida International University, Miami
Florida State University, Tallahassee
New College of Florida, Sarasota
University of Central Florida, Orlando
University of Florida, Gainesville
University of North Florida, Jacksonville
University of South Florida, Tampa
University of West Florida, Pensacola

Indian River Lagoon

An Environmental History

NATHANIEL OSBORN

University Press of Florida

Gainesville · Tallahassee · Tampa · Boca Raton

Pensacola · Orlando · Miami · Jacksonville · Ft. Myers · Sarasota

Printed in the United States of America on acid-free paper

This book may be available in an electronic edition.

21 20 19 18 17 16 6 5 4 3 2 1

Library of Congress Cataloging-in-Publication Data
Osborn, Nathaniel, author.
Indian River Lagoon : an environmental history / Nathaniel Osborn.
pages cm
Includes bibliographical references and index.
ISBN 978-0-8130-6161-0
1. Indian River (Fla. : Lagoon)—Environmental conditions. 2. Indian River (Fla. : Lagoon)—History. 3. Natural history—Florida—Indian River (Lagoon) 4. Florida—History. I. Title.
GE155.F6083 2016
577.7'8—dc23
2015031794

The University Press of Florida is the scholarly publishing agency for the State University System of Florida, comprising Florida A&M University, Florida Atlantic University, Florida Gulf Coast University, Florida International University, Florida State University, New College of Florida, University of Central Florida, University of Florida, University of North Florida, University of South Florida, and University of West Florida.

University Press of Florida
15 Northwest 15th Street
Gainesville, FL 32611-2079
http://www.upf.com

Contents

Illustrations

Figures

Table

Acknowledgments

I would like to express my gratitude to Jeff Osborn for generous support and ceaseless encouragement. Thanks to Sandra Thurlow for use of her invaluable sources and warm discussions. I appreciate Marty Baum for allowing me to exploit his encyclopedic knowledge of the region; Guy Bradley lives on in Indian Riverkeeper Baum. Thanks to my colleagues at The Pine School for flexibility in the final days of this project, especially Steve Naumann for technical help with the images. Thanks to Fred and Celeste McFarland for editing help and to Gary Roderick for pointing me to key documents. Thanks are also due to Liz Stebbins for support. To my parents, Bruce and Barbara, many, many thanks for your selfless generosity. My deepest gratitude is reserved for my daughter, Genevieve, and sons, Seth and Benjamin.

More than anyone else, I thank Sarah for patience and love.

Indian River Lagoon

1

Introduction

"It is a wonderful river . . . immensely deep and very fine sweet water," wrote a northern visitor to Florida's Indian River in 1884. "The beauties of nature are here very manifest, in fact it is a wonderland. While I sit here in the cabin of our boat writing [I hear] the croaking of the frogs and the cries of animals and splashing of fish on the stillness of this vast wilderness where probably no human foot has trod."[1] Roughly 100 years later observers described the same body of water as a river of mud that was so polluted that its "stressed-out snook and pompano were developing lesions so wide that their entrails were dragging behind them."[2]

In the intervening years nineteen canals or altered creeks were constructed to flood the most biologically diverse estuarine ecosystem in the United States with freshwater at an average rate of 17,990 cubic feet per second in order to drain the region's agricultural lands.[3] In this period the Indian River Lagoon was also changed by the construction of five permanent inlets and divided by sixteen causeways.[4] Stretching along 156 miles of Central and South Florida, the Indian River Lagoon system is composed of four bodies of water that are connected by nature (or, in the case of the Mosquito Lagoon, by humans). The categorization of the four bodies into one system was formalized in the last decades of the twentieth century. In 1987 the Florida legislature began funding efforts to clean up the bodies by designating the four bodies a single system as part of its Surface Water Improvement and Management (SWIM) program. Two years later, Governor Bob Martinez successfully nominated the river for protection by the federal government. On Earth Day 1990 President George H. W. Bush declared the system a "lagoon of national significance," which led to the formation of the Indian River Lagoon National Estuary Program in 1991. Since that time it became common to refer to the St. Lucie Estuary, Mosquito Lagoon, Banana River Lagoon, and Indian River collectively as the "Indian River Lagoon." Before this slight linguistic change the four interconnected bodies were seldom considered to be parts of a single system, and were referred to individually as "the River" instead of "the Lagoon," which only became common after federal recognition in 1991.[5]

While the Indian River's origins lay in the late Pleistocene Era (125,000 B.C.), humans have inhabited the area for at least 7,000 years. The native Timucua and Ais peoples disappeared within 200 years of Ponce de Leon's 1513 Florida arrival.[6] As an isolated and neglected outpost of a colony that was itself an isolated and neglected outpost of the Spanish Empire, the extreme northern section of the Indian River was inhabited by over 1,000 Europeans in a series of failed British colonial plantations during the 1760s and 1770s. Later, at the end of the Second Seminole War (1835–42) in this newly acquired territory, the U.S. Congress offered free land to settlers in the region. But isolation and continued tensions with the Seminoles ensured that the region remained largely depopulated until the decades following the Civil War, when newspaper accounts of warm, fish-choked waters with near-magical healing properties attracted thousands of northerners to relocate.

These Reconstruction-era settlers were among the first to make significant attempts to alter the ecology of the lagoon system. Increasingly dissatisfied with their reliance on a steamship monopoly to ship their fruit to northern markets and the noxious odors from the area's decaying freshwater submerged vegetation, the settlers dug a cut through the barrier island at the mouth of the St. Lucie Estuary in the southern portion of Indian River Lagoon. These mostly white, northern settlers came to Florida for its "healthy climate," but found that nature needed a hand to meet their conception of health. The scent of freshwater decomposing vegetation did not fit into their conception of a healthy area suitable for healing their ills.

Late nineteenth-century settlers professed to love Florida for its wilderness, and did not see the forest as the Puritans did, as a wicked place to be tamed. Echoing Romantic writers of the previous generation, settlers often spoke poetically about their primeval "fair lagoon."[7] Despite this affection for the "wild," these homesteaders heavily manufactured its environs to suit their ideas. Gilded Age settlers brought with them the ecological ethos of their time, having largely come to the Indian River from the land of the Erie, Ohio, and Pennsylvania canal systems.[8]

Indian River settlers were not merely pioneers of a region, or a zone of cultural interaction, but they were breaking new ground by being among the first to cultivate the idea of modern Florida. These settlers sold an image of an orange blossom–scented paradise and so were among the first to make the Florida of the twentieth century, a concept marked more by dredging, filling, tourists, and citrus than the state's natural features. The region's settlers represent the vanguard of a third wave of peninsular Florida Anglo culture, historically and culturally distinct from the southern inland "cracker" and the Caribbean-derived "conch" of the Florida Keys.

The Indian River has always existed in a state of flux; nineteenth- and twentieth-century human-made developments represented an intensification of earlier natural trends. Historically, the ecosystem was fundamentally unstable. Hurricanes and other severe storms were the primary forces that created and moved inlets, which in turn determined the contours of the barrier islands and lagoon.[9] Late nineteenth- and early twentieth-century human-made changes were "antichanges" intended to stabilize the fluid nature of the Indian River ecosystem. These changes have forever altered the region, but the Indian River system has never known stability. Under natural conditions, the system would experience constant evolution, which can be seen in the sediment layers beneath the area. Instead of a narrative merely documenting decline, this book describes a complex system that has at various times been conducive and hostile to animal and plant health, both before and after humans arrived in significant numbers. Far from being a passive recipient of human actions, the system's larger natural forces with which humans were forced to interact suggest that the lagoon delivered troubles as often as it received harm from humans.

These pioneers adapted to life in a simultaneously fertile and hostile environment. Facing heat, mosquitoes, malaria, interaction with Native Americans, and perhaps most important, near-total isolation from the rest of the world, the lagoon's nineteenth-century settlers adapted by agricultural experimentation, altered the ecology of their environment, hunted nontraditional food sources, and modified traditional boats to meet their needs in this watery environment. The last decade of the nineteenth century saw the coming of Henry Flagler's railroad and, with it, the outside world, ending the isolation that forced the lagoon's settlers to be largely self-reliant. The sweeping changes ushered in with the railroad dramatically altered the industry and culture of the lagoon. Despite their isolation, the Indian River settlers existed on the fringes of (and actively participated in) the transcaribbean world. For example, competition from Cuban imports wiped out the local pineapple industry during the late 1890s, and local economies initially relied on salvaging wrecks engaged in the Caribbean trade.

Chapter 2 offers a narrative of the origins of the lagoon and its early inhabitants. Chapter 5 discusses the region after the Second World War, when the Indian River, like most of the Sunshine State, saw its first major population influx. Chapters 3 and 4, the heart of the book, discuss the ambitions and abuses hurled upon the Indian River by successive generations of schemers and dreamers in the nineteenth and early twentieth centuries. The story of the Indian River in the mid-twentieth century is much like that of its neighboring ecosystem, the Everglades, in that the period's engineers used postwar technology and prosperity to fulfill the dreams of their nineteenth-century predecessors by converting a natural system into one largely manipulated by pumps, canals, jetties, impoundments, and reservoirs. The twentieth-century Indian River was altered by humans by dredging and stabilizing inlets, regulating ocean tides by determining the width and depth of inlets, dredging to prevent formation of natural tidal deltas, and regulating freshwater discharge through dams and locks. Additionally, they altered the lagoon bottom by dredging the Intracoastal Waterway, and building causeways and dredge-refuse "spoil" islands, which all significantly changed the system.[10]

In the late twentieth century came the first attempts to "restore" the region to its "natural" state. This book suggests that such attempts will necessarily declare an arbitrary historical form to be "normal" for the system. There has been no period when the Indian River system was not without shifting barrier islands, cyclically varying freshwater watershed discharge, and dramatically varying salinity levels due to the ocean influx following the opening and closing of natural inlets.

The dualistic portrayal of humans as wholly distinct from the natural world suggests a longing for a mythic past in which nature existed perfectly apart from human actions. It is now widely understood that Native peoples heavily altered the ecology of pre-Columbian America, but, more important, the narrative of decline that permeates much environmental history fails to adequately treat humans as a fundamental and legitimate part of nature. The relationship between humans and the natural world must not be understood as either "natural" or "foreign" but instead something more nuanced.

2

Early Geologic History and Human Habitation to 1842

"The climate of East Florida is an agreeable medium, betwixt the scorching heat of the tropicks, and the pinching cold of the northern latitudes," wrote Englishman William Stork upon his 1765 visit to the newest British colony. "The author . . . asserts that in no part of the British dominions there is found so great a variety of trees, plants and shrubs, as in East Florida, which he conjectures is entirely owing to the temperature of the climate in which the productions of the northern and southern latitudes seem to flourish together."[1]

The biological diversity cited by Stork is due to East Florida's location in the transitional zone between the northern temperate and southern subtropical climates, and flora and fauna associated with each zone are found together in the system. The changing nature of the Indian River also extends along an east-west axis, as it is neither wholly continent nor completely ocean, but an intervening estuarine zone.[2]

Initially named "Rio de Ais" by the Spanish after the area's Ais Indians, the lagoon was later Anglicized to "Indian River." A lagoon is a shallow body of water divided from the ocean by a barrier island. An estuary is a body that has both freshwater inflows and has limited influx of ocean water. Meeting both of these definitions, the Indian River is both a lagoon and estuary, though, despite its name, it is not a river. The defining characteristic of the Indian River system is its relationship with the

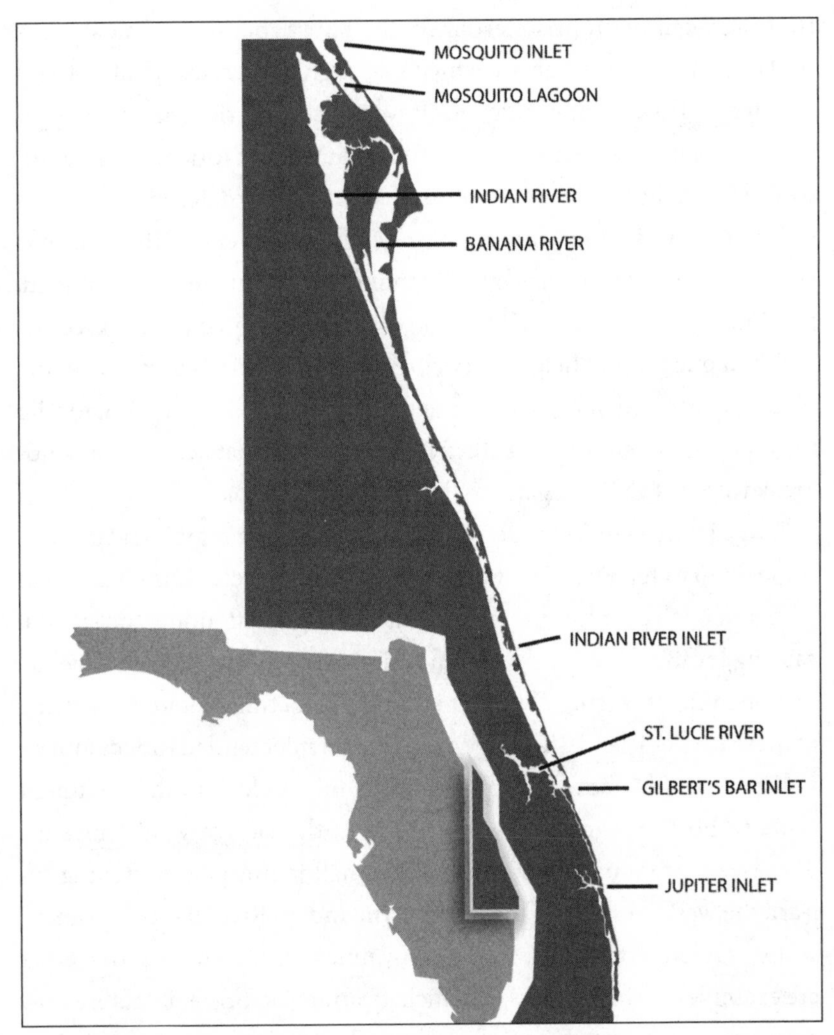

FIGURE 1. Map of the four bodies that compose the Indian River Lagoon system.

sea. Rising sea levels shaped this silvery ribbon, which occupies roughly one-third of the east coast of Florida. The water flow of each section of the shallow system is influenced by rainfall, evaporation, winds, water depth, and proximity to inlets and canals.

The most significant land features of the Indian River are the long, thin barrier islands that limit the transfer of water between the lagoon and ocean, as well as the narrow backbone that runs along the western shore of the lagoon, known as the Atlantic Ridge. One early twentieth-century tourist described the spine as boasting a "most beautiful hammock fringe," above which is a "high, sandy ridge, but sparsely forested."[3] The Atlantic Ridge itself was once a barrier island and provides enough elevation to host most of Southeast Florida's original urban areas, including West Palm Beach, Fort Lauderdale, and Miami, as well as nearly all of the Indian River's early settlements.[4] The lagoon is separated from the ocean by a "wonderfully attenuated strip of land, portions of which are only a few rods wide," and which rarely exceeds a width of one mile or height of twenty feet. "This strip is barren in some places," described one early twentieth-century travel guide, "but for the most part is covered with a sturdy forest growth that serves as a windbreak to curb the fierce gales of the Atlantic."[5]

Large storms could create violent currents in the region and a storm surge of up to ten feet higher than normal water levels. This volatile water could wash over low parts of the barrier islands, flooding the lagoon, causing local freshwater rivers to flow inland and new inlets to develop. The opening or closing of these new inlets sometimes altered the shape of these barrier islands. The lagoon side of an inlet tended to accumulate sediment and become shallow. Upon an inlet's closing, this sediment came to host mangrove vegetation due to the lack of water currents. These vegetated areas developed into small peninsulas stretching toward the western shore of the lagoon. The Indian River has two primary sections referred to as "the narrows" by nineteenth-century settlers that are examples of this process, in which locations of former inlets are now areas where barrier islands are widest. The two primary examples are located between Vero Beach and Sebastian in the central Indian River and between Hobe Sound and Port Salerno in the southern lagoon.[6]

With an average rainfall of just over fifty inches, the mixture of fresh and salt water is the blood of the Indian River circulatory system. Like most of peninsular Florida, the hot, rainy wet season (May through October) invigorates the system, and breeds seasonal hurricanes and storms. The mild dry season (November through April) has historically been punctuated with subfreezing temperatures, at most lasting several days. Water circulation in the system is primarily wind-driven.

FIGURE 2. A short-lived natural inlet in the lower Indian River Lagoon formed by a 1962 storm (Thurlow/Runke Collection, Sewall's Point, Florida).

The tidal nature of the lagoon is limited to a few miles north or south of inlets. This very limited circulation and limited flushing properties make the Indian River very sensitive to fluctuations in land-based water discharge. The slow movement of water to the lagoon is key to the system's health. In the rainy season, wetlands overflow into sloughs, which feed densely vegetated, twisting creeks and rivers, which minimized the speed of water runoff before the remainder was discharged into the lagoon. This slow retention of water ensured that groundwater levels remained high and that the water entered the lagoon relatively clean, having been "filtered" by vegetation.[7]

Although the lagoon's latitude (between 27° north and 29° north) does not extend to the Tropic of Cancer (23° north), the climate of the southern lagoon is one of the few places on earth with a tropical wet climate north of the boundary latitude, according to the widely used Köppen-Geiger classification system. This is primarily due to the effects of the Gulf Stream, which brings warm water from western Cuba to the southeast coast of the peninsula, before it heads offshore for northern Europe. The tropical wet climate of the southern Indian River is characterized by year-round warm to hot temperatures and tropical flora and fauna, such as the native gumbo-limbo tree and exotic mango.[8]

The northern portions of the lagoon are classified in the Humid Subtropical Climate Zone, which covers nearly all of the contemporary southeastern United States. For this reason, the hot summers and occasional frosty winters of the northern Mosquito Lagoon sometimes have more in common with Mobile Bay, Alabama, or Charleston, South Carolina, than with the wet summers and mild winters of the tropical St. Lucie River, which lies near the southern end of the Indian River system. These climate zones are the reason the foliage of many trees in the northern lagoon are deciduous, while the trees of the southern lagoon generally remain green year-round. Similarly, the southern lagoon region infrequently experiences "hard frosts," while the winters of the northern lagoon cannot sustain cold-intolerant tropical species.[9]

For simplicity, this book follows the lead of many researchers by generally using the term "tropical" to refer to what the Köppen-Geiger system labels "Tropical Wet" (found in the southern lagoon) while referring to everything north of Central Florida (including the northern Indian River) as "temperate," due to the hard frosts.[10]

The Indian River averages only three feet in depth, but this has historically varied in different time periods. The narrowest portions of the Indian River barely allowed nineteenth-century steamships to scrape through its mangrove-lined channels, while other parts of the lagoon are as wide as five miles.

The Indian River "is superlatively safe, placid, and beautiful," wrote travel writer Clifton Johnson in 1918. It "is so straight that when one looks along it north or south, water and sky seem to meet. On either side it is fringed by points, harbors, coves, and islands. Near the head of the river are large islands or peninsulas, and at the St. Lucie and Jupiter narrows are innumerable small islands covered with an almost impenetrable growth of mangroves and other tropical vegetation."[11]

The "lagoon" nature of the Indian River is historically due to the very limited natural ocean water influx allowed by the three reasonably consistent natural inlets, Ponce de Leon inlet in Mosquito Lagoon, Indian River inlet near Fort Pierce, and Jupiter inlet at the southern tip of Indian River proper. Both the Jupiter and Indian River inlets currently exist a short distance from their most recent natural location in the late nineteenth century.[12] In the roughly 150 miles between these inlets (which historically were generally open, but not always) are numerous small temporary inlets, which historically opened and closed over the seasons. The often narrow barrier islands allowed natural inlets to form, which would sometimes feebly dribble and other times violently roar. The formation of tidal deltas in the lagoon caused a widening of the islands in areas surrounding the inlets. This process was the primary means of lagoon infilling, and large tidal deltas could be formed in only a few decades. Inlets also were the origins of the lagoon's natural islands, formed by sand deposited from tidal currents and the effects of stormy wave action. Hurricanes were the primary force behind inlet migration, due to the low barrier islands in the Indian River system.[13]

Barrier island sand tended to shift north to south, covering natural inlets, which historically were choked with sandbars. In the twentieth century, jetties thousands of feet long were built to prevent this sand transfer from obstructing the mouth of dredged inlets. Tidal forces prevented some sand accumulation, but each inlet periodically required maintenance dredging to prevent the inlet from closing and reappearing at a new location. Historically, the lagoon's water movement often supported only one permanent inlet. Without periodic dredging, nearly all of the human-made inlets of the nineteenth and twentieth centuries would close due to sand accumulation.[14]

While the Indian River hosted tremendous biological diversity, the region's historic instability also created conditions hostile to many species. During periods of hot weather, an overabundance of nutrients led to rapid algae growth. This causes oxygen levels to become depleted in the shallow water and accelerates additional bacterial growth, which leads to large oxygen-starved "dead zones" with little life, a process known as eutrophication. Similarly, when aquatic animals from the Caribbean subtropical zone of the lower Indian River become exposed to the periods of prolonged cold that can be present in the northern lagoon, there have been many deaths of turtles and manatees. This was also the cause of vast fish kills described by horrified nineteenth-century inhabitants new to the area. Many regional plants and animals were negatively affected or killed by the Indian River's natural substantial fluctuations in salinity following the creation of a new inlet (which resulted in an abrupt injection of salty water) or even prolonged periods of rain (which decreases salinity) during periods when there was no nearby inlet open.[15]

The diversity and vitality of animals and plants in the Indian River correspond with two chief variables: proximity to inlets and location along the region's north-south spectrum. The Indian River's unstable attributes, such as the formation and closing of inlets and storms that caused brief periods of the ocean "overwashing" the low barrier island, ultimately cultivated tremendous diversity. Flora and fauna concentration tended to increase in the southern sections of the system. The most biologically rich areas were located in regions that were both in the system's center or south and in close proximity to an inlet. Species diversity declined in the northern portions of the lagoon. As might be expected, the most biologically productive areas of the lagoon are also the segments where most evidence of pre-Columbian habitation is found.[16]

The Indian River represents the northern limit of many types of vegetation, such as the mangrove and tropical hardwood hammock, which is marked by its many West Indian trees. Sea grasses were the most important element of the Indian River's aquatic vegetation because they serve as a food source, nursery, and habitat for many invertebrates and fish and wildlife species. Sea grasses were historically intensely productive and provide sediment stabilization while being vulnerable to human population increases. Sea grass health and areas of coverage declined considerably in the second half of the twentieth century due to increased waters entering the lagoon that were loaded with nutrients conducive to growing algae and eutrophication. These algae in turn blocked light to the sea grass beds, resulting in the disappearance of much of the lagoon's grasses.[17]

Animal life also benefited from the Indian River's location in two climate zones and dynamic qualities. The thickness (a signal of health) of oyster shells, for instance, is directly related to their proximity to inlets.[18] The lagoon's "bottom for twenty-five miles north is a mass of oyster beds," wrote tourist Amos Cummings in 1874. Speaking of the oysters in the region of the Indian River inlet (near today's Fort Pierce in the southern Indian River), he continued, "I have seen shells fourteen inches long . . . and the branches of mangroves covered with oysters."[19]

While the quality and quantity of flora and fauna populations have declined during the twentieth century, accounts of eighteenth- and nineteenth-century tourists and settlers provide useful descriptions of the region before its significant human-made alteration. Awed descriptions of the region's 2,200 animal species abound. "Thousands of pelicans crowded the island, and the mangroves bent with the weight of their nests," wrote Cummings of the northern Indian River. "The males were dumping bags of fish in to the throats of their setting mates. It was a city of feather inhabitants, with a fish trade that threw Fulton Market into the shade." Before the opening of inlets and canals, "it was common to see great rafts of ducks, 500 acres in extent, packed as close as they could swim. On the approach of a sailboat they rose, making a noise like distant thunder and leaving the water covered with feathers." Settlers also reported "schools of saw-fish in the river chasing other fish; a wicked sight, thrashing their saws from side to side."[20]

The Geological Origins of the Indian River System

The Indian River system of today is a product of long-term geological trends as well as nineteenth- and twentieth-century manipulation. The lagoon passed through four stages in its formation process: submerged marine environment, subaerial environment, brackish water environment, and lagoonal environment.[21]

The region existed originally as a submerged marine environment during the Pleistocene Era, approximately 125,000 years ago. Today's Atlantic Ridge, which runs along the western shore of the Indian River, was itself a sort of barrier island, with the smaller interior mainland ridge serving as the original western coast of the prehistoric system. While the eastern and western borders are clear, the northern and southern edges of this developing system are not.

Until 35,000 years ago, the area had a mostly dry upland climate, due to the period's very low sea levels. The low sea level exposed offshore sandbars and sediments, which turned into Anastasia rock, which forms the basis of today's barrier islands, the Atlantic Beach Ridge. It is this second, smaller ridge that caused the long, narrow barrier islands that fence the lagoon from the sea.

During the glacial period (100,000 to 10,000 B.C.), peninsular Florida was approximately three times its current size and very much drier, as global sea levels were about 300 feet below their current levels. Fluctuating (and ultimately rising) sea levels between 35,000 and 30,000 B.C. inundated the region with seawater, creating the Atlantic Coastal Lagoons, of which the Indian River is the chief segment. The end of the last ice age saw the rise of global sea levels and the creation of the Indian River Lagoon that would be recognizable to the twenty-first-century observer.

Sediment accumulated between 30,000 and 6,000 B.C. gradually formed the barrier island shorelines and hills in their contemporary forms as wind and the ocean shaped the lagoon system as it exists today. As sea levels rose and fell (at times as much as 100 feet higher than contemporary levels), sediment was collected and shaped by wind and waves to create Florida's rock and soil formations. The bedrock of the Indian River, like most of South Florida, is limestone, formed primarily from calcium remnants of sea creatures (especially coral) that were on the Florida shelf as it rose from and sank under the sea over the millennia.[22]

Humans in the Indian River

Identifying when humans first inhabited the region has been a source of contention since the early twentieth century. In 1915 a series of human and animal fossils were discovered while a drainage canal was being dug (one of many built in the era to divert water from wetlands into the Indian River) near the town of Vero Beach. The bones and nearby stone tool artifacts appear to have been related to Pleistocene animal fossils found at the site. Although the human fossils were misplaced before the advent of Carbon 14 dating, some scholars believe that humans lived in the region as early as 15,000 B.C., which would mean that humans lived alongside the lagoon's megafauna, such as mammoths, jaguars, and giant sloth and beavers. Other archaeologists believe that humans first settled in the region several thousand years later (and after the megafauna extinction) and that the Vero Beach bones were simply buried deep among the soil strata of earlier millennia.[23]

In 2006 or 2007 (the amateur fossil digger could not remember) a bone with a carving of a mastodon was discovered in Vero Beach, in the vicinity of the human bones discovered in 1915. Initial analyses indicated that it was not a forgery, which strongly suggested that humans inhabited the region before 10,000 B.C., as had been initially proposed after the discovery of the "Vero Man" bones nearly a century earlier. The mastodon carving was believed to be both the only carving of a mastodon found in the Americas and the oldest piece of American art.[24]

Perhaps the most significant Indian River discovery since the "Vero Man" discovery of 1915 came in 1982 when a backhoe operator building a road for the new Windover Farms housing development in Brevard County found bones in a small pond. A subsequent major excavation of the Windover site found the bodies of 168 Paleo-Indians, 91 of which still had brain matter, a remarkable result of the preservation qualities of the pond's peat. The pond was determined to have been in continuous existence since 10,000 to 11,000 B.C., and the tremendous data provided by the Windover site was evidence that people lived in the area at least as early as 7,000 to 8,000 B.C.[25]

The extinction of the megafauna that once roamed the area (10,000 to 8,500 B.C.) ushered in the Early Archaic period, which is marked by the absence of pottery and presence of the area's first ceremonial burials.[26] The Middle Archaic period (6,000 to 3,000 B.C.) was notable chiefly because it was most likely when small and mobile groups of humans began to intensely inhabit the Indian River area, drawn by the increasing biophysical diversity cultivated by the system's increasing instability.[27] The first pottery in the Indian River region dates to the late Archaic period (roughly 3,000 to 500 B.C.), when fish and mollusks appear to have become a more significant part of the human diet. The coast of peninsular Florida assumed its contemporary lines, and the expanding Paleo-Indian population settled in nearly every part of the state. The chief population trend between 2,000 B.C. and A.D. 800 was for people to move increasingly from inland regions to the coast of the lagoon, where they established the living patterns that would be found centuries later by Europeans. In the period from A.D. 800 to the mid-eighteenth century, most Indian groups experienced an agricultural revolution. However, the Ais, along with the other peoples of South Florida (notably the Calusa and Tekesta), steadfastly remained hunters and gatherers. This is likely a result of the unsuitability of South Florida's hot climate to the temperate crops that were cultivated by peoples in the northern parts of the peninsula. The remarkable abundance of the lagoon's natural fish, oysters, and birds allowed the Ais peoples to meet their needs without participating in agriculture.[28]

In addition to being a zone where two climates converge, the Indian River is also a region of cultural intersection. The Ais occupied most of the Indian River region, which was the junction of Northeast Florida's St. John's tradition and South Florida's Glades culture. The territory of the Ais people extended from Cape Canaveral (although there is some evidence that it did not extend that far north) to the St. Lucie Estuary in the southern lagoon. South of the St. Lucie the closely related Jeaga peoples established villages in the area of the natural Jupiter inlet at the time of European contact. While the Timucuan peoples north of Cape Canaveral had limited agriculture, the Ais's proximity to the highly productive Indian River system enabled them to remain hunters and gatherers. Modern archaeologists have found the greatest quantity of artifacts in tidal deltas that mark the locations of ancient long-closed inlets.[29]

This reluctance to embrace agriculture is consistent with the very elementary pottery culture (simple undecorated bowls are the primary artifacts) found in the Indian River. Just north of Cape Canaveral lay the transitional zone between the Ais and Timucua of northern Florida.[30]

Roughly twenty Indian mounds in the Indian River system were found in the southern edge of Timucua territory, chiefly Snyder's Mound, Turtle Mound, Castle Windy Mound, and Green Mound, all of which are composed primarily of oyster, conch, and clam shells. Turtle Mound (referred to as "Surruque" in Spanish accounts) was abandoned in A.D. 1400 after 600 years of construction, having reached a length of 600 feet. It is about "50 ft. high, situated on the Banana River just at it's [*sic*] mouth. At it's [*sic*] west side it is abrupt, showing that about half of it has been washed away," wrote a tourist from New York City in 1884. "There is also pieces [*sic*] of pottery found in this layer crudely made and having the appearance of being made of sand. Just back of these shell mounds there is . . . generally a burying ground consisting entirely of sand. In these grounds I found pieces of human bone. . . . There has been considerable digging done here for the bones. On top of each grave there are [*sic*] a collection of conch shells, very large size."[31] The need for fill during the construction of route U.S. 1 in the early twentieth century led to the destruction of most of the region's mounds. Each successive Indian River culture bestowed a new name on the site as they discovered the prominent mound. Initially labeled as "Surruque" (after the peoples living there at the time of Spanish contact), the mound's name became corrupted to "La Roque" by the British in 1763, and six years later referred to as "The Rock." In 1790 different descriptions of the feature call it "Mount Velvedere" and "Mount Tucker," in addition to "The Rock." An 1823 U.S. surveyor dubbed the monolith "Turtle Mound," presumably because the site's outline reminded an observer of a terrapin. The prolific bones and other evidence of great feasts suggest that the mounds were occupied intermittently over long periods of time and were located adjacent to the section of the Mosquito Lagoon that offered the easiest access to shellfish. The low and long Ross Hammock midden was located on one of the only segments of the Mosquito Lagoon shoreline that offered direct access to the open lagoon without wading through marshland. The existence of two modest sandy burial mounds adjacent to several shell middens suggests that the shell depositories became central to the culture of the Timucua peoples of the region. So prominent was the nearby Turtle Mound that it was used as a navigation marker by European (and presumably Amerindian) mariners. Europe-bound ships sailing in the Gulf Stream used Turtle Mound as a reference point if they were blown off course.[32] Late nineteenth-century observers marveled at the precision used by Timucua builders ("each shell was placed with precision . . . with the smooth surface facing the sky") as well as the view from the top of the eighty-foot midden ("The view was magnificent. . . . I could see the white capped breakers dashing over the bar at Smyrna . . . [and] hundreds of porpoises").[33] The high, breezy middens and mounds attracted later inhabitants to occupy the same sites, and the first European settlers to occupy the system often perched their modest homes atop the Indian sites.[34]

It is generally understood that the Ais were subject to the more populous Calusa of the southwest coast, but there is evidence that the Ais along the northern fringe of the Indian River had a dependant relationship with the distant Apalachee of Northwest Florida. People in both West and Southeast Florida appear to have shared a common linguistic and cultural Glades heritage, distinct from the northern and central tribes. Because the Indian River Indians (like all Native peoples of South and Central Florida) existed in small, mobile, sparsely populated groups, they were difficult for Spanish missionaries to convert and resisted European political influence.

Spanish Outpost, 1565–1763

While the location of the April 1513 landing of Juan Ponce de Leon is the subject of much debate, it is most likely that he landed somewhere in the vicinity of Cape Canaveral.[35] Ponce de Leon probably encountered the Timucua people, whose territory included the portion of the Indian River system north of Cape Canaveral, and stretched to the Gulf of Mexico and southern Georgia. Ponce's three ships then sailed south, following the southerly countercurrents that hug the beaches of the Indian River region, inside the Gulf Stream, which is generally several miles offshore. The earliest Spanish maps of the region include Cape Canaveral and Turtle Mound, which suggests that Ponce de Leon observed the features. The Mosquito Lagoon was also visited in 1526 by a portion of the Ayllon expedition, which explored the area briefly before establishing its short-lived colony at San Miguel de Guadalupe, in what would later be called Sapelo Sound in Georgia.[36]

Of the six tribes included on a 1675 Spanish document that listed tribes south of Cape Canaveral, four were in the Indian River—the Ais, Santaluce, Hobe, and Jeaga. The other tribes were the Viscayano of Miami and the Matacumbe of the Keys. Of the estimated 100,000 people living in Florida at the time of Ponce de Leon's landing in 1513, only 2,000 lived in the Indian River. The Ais lived by fishing, hunting, and collecting wild plants. Their subsistence was heavily based on the waters of the lagoon, including neighboring wetlands. The Ais population appears to have been concentrated in the northern Indian River, and the reedy salt marsh that once thrived in Cape Canaveral (the modern name comes from *caña*, Spanish for "reed") was able to support the largest regional population.[37]

Each of the ten towns between Jupiter and just north of Cape Canaveral recorded in 1696 had a town leader who was subject to the chief who lived in Jece, near present-day Vero Beach. Due to the system's abundance of fish and game and the sandy soil's unsuitability for corn, the Indian River's Indians lived a transitory lifestyle, with each town existing in two locations on opposite sides of the lagoon, one for the dry season and one for the wet season environment. "Rio d'Ais [Indian River] abounds so much in fish of various kinds, that a person may sit on a bank and stick a fish with a knife, or sharp stick, as they swim by." Inlet sedimentation at inlet locations caused the islands to migrate toward the mainland. For this reason many villages that had been established on the lagoon shore are now located well within the island.[38]

Mosquito Lagoon, the northernmost of the Indian River system's waterways, was inhabited by the southernmost strands of the Timucua people and by the people of the town of Surroque. Surroque is prominently featured on the 1605 map of Alvaro Mexia, who spent eight days in the town while traveling to visit the cacique (chief) of the Ais. Mexia's diplomatic mission resulted in an agreement that the Ais would return shipwrecked Spanish sailors to St. Augustine.[39]

The radically varied cultures and peoples of the Indian River, separated by centuries, tended to settle in the same spots for the same reasons—for example, Ross Hammock, which lies on the Mosquito Lagoon, was one of the only locations along the western shore of the Mosquito Lagoon that did not have a marsh separating dry land from the lagoon. For this reason it became the site of settlement by Paleo-Indians, European contact-era Indians, British colonists, and later American pioneers, all of whom were attracted by the fact that one could access the lagoon without walking through a salt marsh. Archaeologists exploring the site have found Confederate ruins and the remnants of earlier British settlers atop a series of ancient Indian burial mounds.[40]

Like many Indian groups, much of what we know about Florida's original inhabitants comes from the accounts of Europeans. In the words of Jerald Milanich, "to know the [Central Florida group] Jororo existed is to know the Spanish tried to missionalize them. I cannot write about the Jororo apart from their colonial context."[41] Even the names of some Native groups are Spanish in origin, such as the Santaluces peoples, who lived at the natural St. Lucie inlet.[42]

The Indian River's hostile environment and equally hostile inhabitants were not conducive to extensive exploration by Europeans, though the Spanish did send a series of expeditions to the region and established hastily constructed camp-forts at Santa Lucia (located either near the Indian River inlet, near present-day Fort Pierce, or at Gilbert's Bar, south of the present-day St. Lucie inlet). The Spanish established the outpost in the aftermath of the Spanish massacre of French Huguenots at Matanzas inlet, south of St. Augustine. French survivors of the event were taken by the Spanish to another new outpost established in the Indian River, just south of Cape Canaveral. From there, Spanish general Pedro Menendez de Aviles marched down the Indian River and established a fort in the territory of the Santaluces (like the Jeaga, this vague unit was likely a subgroup of the Ais). This voyage down the Indian River led Menendez to believe that the major rivers of the southern peninsula (the St. Johns, Caloosahatchee, Miami, and perhaps the Hillsborough) all were connected with the Indian River and could become a watery highway network for his newly established colony of La Florida. Very little is known about these very short-lived forts and missions, as they existed no longer than several months. The normal functions of such establishments (missionary work among the Indians and the protection Spain's hegemony) likely were secondary considerations. The Spanish forts appear to have been primarily established to protect the Spanish until Menendez returned from Cuba with supplies. In later decades Spanish sentinels regularly patrolled the coast on foot to provide assistance to survivors of the region's frequent shipwrecks, making them the predecessors to the nineteenth-century American Houses of Refuge, which were also lonely outposts along the same (although newly depopulated) coast of Central and Southeast Florida.[43]

The Indian River Indians took advantage of their unique proximity to the Gulf Stream and the frequent shipwrecks it delivered to them and accumulated considerable wealth. Spanish ships returning from Cuba to Spain sailed up the "river in the ocean" between South Florida and the Bahamas, while ships sailing south to Havana had to stay within the three-mile channel along Florida's reef-laden shore to avoid being pushed north by the Gulf Stream. "I desire to speak of the riches of the Indians of the Ais," reported two Spanish wreck survivors, which "were perhaps as much as a million . . . or over in bars of silver, gold, and in articles of jewelry made by the hands of Mexican indians, which the [ship] passengers were bringing with them." The salvaged goods were divided "with the caciques of the Aus, Jeaga, Guacata, Mayajuaco, and Mayaca."[44]

Substantially shortening the time needed for Europeans to return home from the Caribbean, the Gulf Stream passed through the narrow Florida Strait, hugging the coast of Florida from the Keys to Cape Canaveral, roughly half of which was within the Indian River region. The many reefs along this *banda del sur* ("south shore") led to frequent wrecks, especially before ships had internal combustion engines in the early twentieth century. A 1605 agreement between Governor Pedro de Ibarra and the Ais to provide care for Spanish shipwreck survivors was the source of the cooperation between the indigenous peoples and St. Augustine outpost later observed by Jonathan Dickinson.[45] In 1715 thousands of Spanish sailors died when eleven treasure-laden galleons were wrecked along the eastern coast of Florida. Most of them came ashore on the Indian River's barrier islands. Spanish survivors and salvagers of the wrecks were attacked by English pirates from nearby New Providence in the Bahamas, but Spanish accounts also record a pirate base at "Palmar de Ays," which was almost certainly within the Indian River itself. The Spanish salvagers relied on Caribbean Indians to dive on the shallow wrecks. The Indian divers recovered about four million pesos.[46]

The most significant account of the Indian River Indians comes from the widely published captivity narrative of Jonathan Dickinson, who was wrecked along with a small group of other English travelers along the beach in the southern Indian River in 1696. A few hours after their barkentine, *Reformation*, came ashore several miles north of Jupiter inlet, they were discovered by local Jeaga. The Jeaga immediately organized and divided the salvaged goods from the ship, of which a portion was set aside for the Ais cacique.[47] It is from Dickinson that we have descriptions of Indian River dwellings, palmetto-thatched rounded huts built on shell mounds, the height of which made them safe from the Indian River's regular flood events following heavy seasonal rains during periods of inlet closures. Unlike mainland settlements, barrier island settlement patterns were not influenced by access to freshwater. The Indian chief "came to us, who with his hand scratched a hole in the sand about a foot deep, and came to water, which he made signs for us to come drink." What Dickinson observed was the exploitation of thin "lenses" of freshwater that underlie the Indian River's barrier islands. In later years early settlers from the United States also observed this tenuous source of freshwater.[48]

The frequent wrecks in the Indian River region were likely both the cause of the small Ais confederation and their agreement with Spain that all wrecked Spanish sailors should be brought to St. Augustine. It is for this reason that Dickinson and his group claimed to be Spanish. The trek to St. Augustine was accompanied by harsh treatment, and five of the party died en route.[49] Although deeply filtered by his cultural context, Dickinson's journal does give us a useful window into how the culture of the Indian River Indians was adapted to the Indian River system.

The Indian River system's ecological unsuitability to conventional agriculture also cultivated a culture ill-suited for the proselytization of Spanish priests. The groups with which Spanish missionaries had the most success were those who already had long agricultural traditions before European contact, and welcomed new Spanish farming techniques. In contrast, the peoples of the Indian River region steadfastly remained hunters and gatherers. Dickinson observed the Ais selling gathered ambergris, which they collected on the beach, to the Spanish. Ambergris is a by-product of whale feces Europeans prized as a perfume additive. This ambergris exchange was a prime example of the Ais's dependence on their environment to provide for their hunting and gathering culture.[50] Dickinson also provided details regarding the surprisingly sophisticated boats employed in the Indian River. The Ais employed swift-sailing catamarans that were capable of carrying many passengers or cargo and would have permitted significant voyages, including to the Bahamas and Cuba.[51]

Dickinson observed the Indian River Indians in their last days. Within fifteen years the Ais and Tekesta of South Florida together numbered no more than a few hundred, and the Jeaga no longer existed as a cohesive group.[52] In the mid-eighteenth century the remnant Ais joined the few survivors of other Florida tribes and fled the infusion of new Indian peoples from the north, who would become known as Seminoles.[53] A group of Havana-based missionaries arrived in Upper Matacumbe Key in 1743 to establish a mission among the refugee tribes, who agreed to convert to Roman Catholicism and abandon polygamy and human sacrifice in exchange for food and alcohol. The priests reported that many of the men drank themselves to death. Soon after, a smallpox epidemic so ravaged the small group that the missionaries abandoned their mission, which was razed by Spanish soldiers to keep it out of the hands of the English, who regularly passed through the area traveling between Jamaica and South Carolina. It is unclear whether any Indian River Indians were among the group who fled to Havana with the retreating Spanish when La Florida was transferred to the British in 1763. The decision to exchange the expensive, unprofitable peninsular colony for Havana (upon the capture of the Cuban capital by the British during the Seven Years War) was an easy one for the Spanish Crown.[54]

British Experiment and Empty Spanish Backwater, 1763–1821

Upon receiving control of the territory of Florida from the 1763 Treaty of Paris, which concluded the Seven Years War, Britain's chief objective was to populate the peninsula to consolidate British control of the Atlantic coast of North America. After dividing the territory into East and West Florida, at the Apalachicola River, British authorities granted large tracts of land to politically connected gentry. Surveys of the mysterious land were commissioned, and reports began arriving in London speculating that Florida could "produce either rice, indigo, sugar, or any other produce of the West Indies."[55]

The British knew almost nothing about the long series of lagoons snaking down the east coast of Central and South Florida. "Running up the Indian River as I did I could see but little of it, the banks indeed are a true resemblance of its savage name, however in running the two tracts I just mentioned I came upon good back swamps and from appearance of those I'm inclined to think the front of them occasions the river to have a worse carracter [*sic*] than it really deserves, for as to its having been examined by any one is all idea," wrote Frederick George Mulcaster to East Florida governor James Grant in May 1772. "I have seen more of it than any one else and I look upon myself as very little acquainted with it indeed. The country anywhere that I have been is totally unknown." With hopes of repeating the riches made from the colonies of Jamaica and Barbados, British planters poured money and slaves into the colony. "Ross's cane is coming on . . . [the] young plants . . . are green and look well. The frame of the mill is up and the main trial will be in the making as the cane certainly will not be fit to cut till the season for frost is sett [*sic*] in."[56]

One of the largest of the East Florida land grants went to Andrew Turnbull, who planned to turn 40,000 acres along the Mosquito Lagoon into an indigo plantation. Laborers in Turnbull's new colony of New Smyrnea dug an extensive network of canals that crisscrossed the settlement, drained 3,107 acres of wetland, and established a precedent that would characterize the Indian River for over 200 years. The only labor contract that remains from the colony detailed that each head of household would receive 100 acres of land after ten years of labor. The 1,403 indentured laborers Turnbull brought to the settlement from the Mediterranean lived in leaky, dirt-floored palmetto shacks and died at a horrifying rate of roughly 50 percent, primarily due to malaria and scurvy. Only two months after the first ship arrived in 1768, these new settlers fomented a rebellion, but were thwarted when soldiers from St. Augustine prevented the rebels' ship from exiting Mosquito inlet (today's Ponce de Leon inlet).[57]

On a section of land already altered by large Indian mounds and Spanish orange groves, the New Smyrnea settlers laid out fenced fields and buildings in the pattern of South Carolina indigo plantations. Within the first year settlers cleared mangroves from seven miles of shore, and each house was situated 210 feet from the next along the waterfront. They constructed significant coquina and rock structures, including wharves, churches, mills, and canals. Some of these coquina ruins remained prominent in the city in the centuries to come (later spelled "New Smyrna"). Dry hammocks and drained swamps were the preferred location for fields of the easily-planted slender indigo plants, which ensured that "drainage of the rich swamp lands [progressed] in a thorough and scientific way."[58] New Smyrnea's farmers dug canals three feet wide dry around the indigo fields, to keep caterpillars from reaching the crop. So successful was this ambitious agriculture program that the colony was able to ship a large harvest (11,558 pounds) of sugarcane and indigo to Britain in 1771. The settlers made fertilizer by harvesting and burning the lagoon's seaweed to make sodium carbonate. This biological adaptation and experimentation extended to the importation of cochineal insects, which were used in the dye-making process. In dry years these British-introduced insects can still be observed in the region's wild cactus. The ceaseless backbreaking work of digging the extensive canals to divert water from wetlands into the Indian River system was made possible only by a brutal driver system. Because Turnbull did not provide his indentured servants with enough food, they adapted to their new environment by integrating gopher tortoise, oysters, and other seafood into their diet. They fished primarily from homemade canoes.[59] In a letter to colony investor Sir William Duncan, Turnbull discussed the climate of the Indian River and its oranges, which provide "not only a wholesome acid to be used with the fish our People eat, but also one of the best remedies we have for the bilious disorder to which this country, with other hot countries, is subject."[60]

Ultimately, the alterations ushered in by the miles of coquina-lined canals so dramatically altered the Mosquito Lagoon's wetlands' ecology that agriculture was unsustainable. "I observed ye adjacent higher ground which was nothing but sand," reported New Smyrnea surveyor and botanist John Bartram in 1776. "There was indigo planted, but it was thin and poor . . . when the ground & ye roots rotten it may do better but I believe it soon wears out." A drought at this time exacerbated the problem, prompting Turnbull to construct a second series of canals, this time to move water to his agricultural lands. These Indian River irrigation canals still carry water through New Smyrna, more than 200 years after they were built.[61] John Bartram's son, the naturalist William Bartram, returned to the region in 1774 and wrote his famed account of traveling throughout South Carolina, Georgia, and East and West Florida. His brief account of the area described the Mosquito Lagoon as "not above two miles across to the sea beach." Additionally, he noted the remnants of Spanish agriculture. "All this ridge was then one entire orange grove, with live oaks, magnolias, palms, red bays, and others: I observed then, near where New Smyrna now stands, a spacious Indian mount and avenue."[62]

In 1767 London merchant William Elliott began acquiring land (ultimately more than 20,000 acres) in the new colony. Elliott's subordinate, John Ross, of Aberdeenshire, Scotland, selected a tract of sprawling woods along the Mosquito Lagoon and then arranged the purchase of "seasoned" enslaved Africans from Georgia for a price of £3,000. The southernmost plantation in British Florida, Elliott's plantation followed the pattern of other tropical plantations by producing fruits and produce for the plantation itself, and indigo for export. When the plantation failed to produce a profit after several years, manager Ross turned to sugar production. Ross ordered his slaves to dig miles of canals to drain fields in preparation for the new crop. As the first sugar operation in British East Florida, Elliott's enterprise quickly grew to include twenty-eight slave cabins, one large mill, and a boiling and curing building. Two 120-gallon stills produced rum, and a wide assortment of other buildings were also built for the growing operation, including three houses for the British overseers, a chimney, a kitchen, a wash house, and a blacksmith and cooper shop. John Ross claimed to produce "600 weight" of sugar each week, and managed to export 10,000 pounds in 1774, despite an early frost and apparent hurricane that flattened many trees and buildings. The tenuous reliance on the volatile environment of the northern Indian River proved to be a constant source of disappointment for Elliott and Ross, as a sloop full of the plantation's slaves was lost crossing the hazardous Mosquito inlet. The disappointing events of 1774 led Elliott to fire Ross, but the new managers were unable to significantly increase the plantation's profitability. They also failed to stop four horses from being stolen by Indians in 1778 and a 1779 raid by Spanish privateers that destroyed a sixty-acre cane field ready for harvest. This raid caused production to permanently cease on Elliott's plantation, whose slaves were briefly sent to work north of St. Augustine, only to be sold in British Jamaica for £2,282 after Florida returned to Spanish control in 1783.[63]

By 1777 the New Smyrnea colony had failed, and the return of Florida to Spain in 1783 had little effect on the Indian River. With the total destruction of the Timucua, Ais, and Jeaga peoples, the Indian River remained a largely empty region ignored by increasingly impotent officials in St. Augustine. The battles of the First Seminole War, which ultimately led to the 1819 Adams-Onís Treaty, by which Florida was ceded to an increasingly powerful United States, had no significant immediate effect on the Indian River. The Indian River was slowly populated with Seminoles, whose woodland agricultural culture had no marine tradition, as they had come from land that would become later Alabama and Georgia. As such, a modest population of Seminoles traversed the Indian River to exploit its fish and game, but the system would never become a central part of Seminole culture, as it had been for the Ais.

Spain instituted a land grant system to encourage settlement in an attempt to secure its tentative hold on the colony. Large sections of coastal East Florida were granted, including significant portions of the Indian River. The Adams-Onís Treaty stipulated that the United States would honor these grants, which was a source of frustration and legal complexity for later American settlers in the region. "Nearly all the good lands [in the northern Indian River] have been granted away," grumbled one of the first Americans to observe the area in 1823. An example of these prime lands was the Delaspine grant on Merritt Island, because it was reputed to be "free from those causes which produce bilious and intermittent complaints."[64]

In 1803 Georgia planter James Hutchinson received a land grant of 2,000 acres along the western shore of the southern Indian River. Hutchinson sent his family and slaves to the grant to establish a plantation, but claimed that interference from the Seminoles prevented success.[65] In 1807 he successfully petitioned the Spanish governor in St. Augustine to move his grant to the adjacent barrier island, which stretched from the Indian River inlet all the way to Gilbert's Bar inlet, located in what would later be called Peck's Lake, south of the modern-day St. Lucie inlet. "Some negroes were stolen by pirates and wreckers" who used the long island for its proximity to the Gulf Stream. The next year Hutchinson petitioned St. Augustine to provide military protection, but he drowned on the voyage returning to his island. "A beautiful piece of land reaches from the mouth of the narrows four miles. . . . It may contain about 1,000 acres of first-rate hammock, a part of which was cultivated many years since by an old Spaniard named Padre Torre, and more recently was planted by one James Hutchinson, with cocoa nuts, limes plantains, bananas, oranges, &c." wrote surveyor Charles Vignoles in 1823, the same year that the son of James Hutchinson, John, successfully applied to Congress to validate his family's claim to the grant.[66]

U.S. Territory, 1821–1845

Despite mild federal encouragement to settle the new territory, the 1825 census recorded only 317 people living in the entire southern portion of the Florida peninsula. Five years later, the population of Mosquito County, which included all of the Indian River, had grown to 733. The Spanish had introduced oranges to Florida, but there were no major attempts to establish groves in the Indian River, apart from modest plantings in the Smyrnea settlement. This changed in the mid-1820s when Douglas Dummitt purchased land on Merritt Island, situated next to Cape Canaveral between the Indian River proper and the Banana River. Dummitt imported around 100 slaves and established a 3,000-acre orange grove in hopes of repeating the plantation success enjoyed by his family in his native Barbados. One of the region's intermittent freezes came in 1835 and destroyed all of Florida's groves except those of Dummitt, whose trees were insulated from blasts of cold air by the relatively warm lagoons on either side of his grove. His fruit was then sold to other growers to create what would become the famous "Indian River Orange."[67]

In 1823 Charles Vignoles conducted the most significant survey commissioned to assess the new territory. Reports of new sugarcane endeavors "have been uncommonly favorable: several large establishments are about to be erected, and considerable investments are being made for the express purpose of raising the cane."[68] Vignoles's detailed description of the region offered a portrayal of an area that was ripe for easy alteration. "[The Mosquito Lagoon] is separated from Indian River by a narrow isthmus which is only 1980 feet wide, called the Haulover, across which canoes and boats are continually hauled. A canal could be made here at an expense not exceeding one thousand dollars, which would thereby complete a good inland navigation for upwards of two hundred miles."[69]

The same year that Vignoles completed his survey, the United States imposed the 1823 Treaty of Moultrie Creek on the Seminoles, which demanded that the Seminoles move away from coastal areas (including the Indian River) and settle on an interior reservation. In the years that followed the Seminole population became the target of the U.S. Army, which intended to enforce the 1830 Indian Removal Act as well as the 1832 Treaty of Payne's Landing, designed to clear the peninsula for American planters.

Indian warriors resisted removal efforts by attacking the most visible sign of encroaching industry and settlement, the sugar mills that Vignoles had extolled a decade earlier. In 1835 Miccosukee warriors led by King Philip burned most of the mills south of St. Augustine, including that of the New Smyrnea settlement. These acts of resistance, as well as a resounding victory over army major Francis Dade on the west coast, led to the seven-year string of clashes known as the Second Seminole War (1835–42).[70]

On January 2, 1838, a group of army soldiers entered the Indian River inlet in the central Indian River and built a palmetto-log fort on the site of a recently used Indian camp. Named after their commanding officer,

Fort Pierce became the base from which the soldiers marched inland in search of Indians.[71]

"Inadequate are words to express the quantity and quality of fish that abounded in those waters. . . . The finest kind of Sheephead we very soon discarded from our mess tables as noisesome things, in comparison with other fish caught there, and which are unique to these latitudes," wrote Jacob R. Motte, a surgeon who accompanied the unit. Motte marveled:

> As for the oysters; six are a comfortable meal for one person, indeed, without exaggeration, the greatest abundance may be easily obtained. . . . We all of us began to grow so fat upon this good living, that we were afraid that unless something turned up very soon to produce a change in our feliticious mode of life, that we should have to borrow from our neighbors, the Indian their style of dress, for our clothes every day became tighter.[72]

Motte's account of marching westward from the lagoon provides a useful description of the topography of the Indian River region, including slash pine flatwoods, sand pine scrub, and hydric hammock type of still-water swamp, and is an illustration why the region was so eagerly drained by early twentieth-century inhabitants of the region:

> We pursued a westerly course [from Fort Pierce], and after emerging from the dense hammock, we passed through a narrow strip of pine baron, and then entered the famous and undefined Al-pa-ti-o-kee Swamp. A water region indeed! Behind us arose the forest of pine, like a dark wall; while before us and on either side of us, the scene presented to our view was one unbroken extent of water and morass; like that of a boundless rice-field while inundated. . . . The water which covered this immense expanse of savannah was in depth from half-leg to saddle-girth, and extended far beyond the horizon all around.[73]

Although the region had been ostensibly subjected to European rule for nearly 200 years, it was so unexplored that Motte repeated the same mistake as Menendez in his assumption that so much water must be interconnected with the state's rivers.[74] Vignoles's descriptions presaged the boosterism of later decades that would attract settlers to the region. "On the Indian River some of the best hammocks in the Floridas are to be met with, healthy and elevated. The occasioned breaks of pine bluffs are rather advantageous than otherwise as presenting better sites for settlements." Vignoles also observed the inlet at Gilbert's Bar, near the mouth of the St. Lucie, which was apparently partially open. Contemporary maps indicate that the inlet was open, but Vignoles reports that it gave "at sea the appearance of an inlet: on the seashore are the rocks of the St. Lucie directly fronting the mouth of that river," which was at the time blocked by the "money bank: a vessel with coin having been lost here, coin has occasionally been found on the beach."[75]

Glowing descriptions of the nearly empty Indian River ensured that the region would be attractive to proponents of the era's manifest destiny. Foreshadowing the population infusion that would come in fifty years, Vignoles speculated that the "majestic appearance of the St. Lucie River affords at first sight the greatest expectations. . . . [The region's] free circulation of sea air, at once convinces the traveler that on such a place health must reside." The Indian River provides "a variety of places where fruit culture would succeed; a fact which may no doubt hereafter populate this country with a race of industrious whites whom the healthiness of the spot may allure hither."[76]

3

Mosquitoes and Kegs of Manatee Meat, 1842–1892

A series of increasingly desperate and lonely letters were sent between 1843 and 1851 from Caleb Brayton on his homestead along the banks of the central Indian River near Fort Pierce to his wife in Augusta, Georgia. "Why should I be deprived of the comfort and society of my dear wife & children[?] . . . Is it because you dred [*sic*] the accursed mosquitoes? No! . . . Tis true, for months in the year (from June to October) they are almost unendurable here, but the other eight there has never been a more delightful place to live." Brayton continued, "our climate is not surpassed by that of Italy even. We have the finest deer, fish, turtle, Oysters &c imaginable." Brayton pleaded with his wife to join him on the isolated lagoon, though his written disappointments must have negated his entreaties, as Marian Brayton stayed in Georgia until only six months before her husband's death in 1854. For every appealing passage, such as: "I could make you comfortable, if there is any comfort to be taken in a Cabin. . . . Dearest I have now no doubt of ultimate success in this delightful country," and "Did I not once send you a keg of manatee meat?," Brayton included more unsatisfactory sections detailing life in the remote frontier. "I have two cows but they do not give milk now," and "yes dear, the Indians have broken out and killed one of my neighbors & wounded another."[1]

Brayton came to the region because of its reputed healthy climate, but his lonely letters detail his slow decline from consumption. "My cough is rather troublesome & I am thinner of flesh . . . but don't be uneasy for I think the climate will soon strengthen me." "I have been quite unwell since I last wrote to you." "Your letters are getting to be like Angels visits, few & far between, but I suppose your multiplicity of concerns requires your time." "Yesterday was Christmas, but we had nothing unusual here." "I tell you that I fear my life is fast drawing to a close." "I suppose I weigh about 110 . . . my teeth are all loose. What I raise now is the regular pus . . . by the mouthfuls." Eight months before he died in June 1854, Brayton wrote, "You can't imagine how much I need & want you. I can't get any thing to eat and am dying for want of little nice things. . . . I should like to exercise a little sometimes. . . . We have nothing but heavy Negro hoes and I can't use them."[2]

There were two primary waves of Anglo settlement in the nineteenth-century Indian River. The first followed the passage of the 1842 Armed Occupation Act, which was intended to fill the southern and central peninsula with armed white yeomen who would ensure the marginalization of the remnant Indian survivors of the Second Seminole War (1835–42). After this group came a much larger wave of northern settlers in the decades immediately following the Civil War. Agricultural experimentation was the chief means through which these settlers adapted to life in the sandy Indian River system, as well as the alteration of boats to handle the lagoon's shoals and attempts to build an economy based on the watery, isolated environment. Although their numbers were small, these settlers set a precedent for later significant biophysical change by their modest drainage canals and failed attempts to cut inlets.

Nineteenth-century settlement patterns in Central and South Florida did not follow those of the era's other frontiers. The depopulation of peninsular Florida during the Spanish periods and the subsequent Second Seminole War precluded the existence of a frontier of inclusion, in which new settlers mix with indigenous peoples to create a cultural meeting point. The first form of frontier in the Anglo Indian River was a frontier of exclusion. There are, of course, some exceptions. Pioneers

Emily Lagow Bell and Charles Pierce relayed examples of Anglos and Indians displaying good relationships. Pioneers in the western territories did not find a virgin continent, but instead a land heavily altered by the more numerous ancestors of the Native Americans they found. Other frontier regions and processes did exist as zones of cultural interaction between Anglo settlers and decimated peoples who still remained in their ancestral homelands. Nineteenth-century Florida pioneers, however, found a few bands of refugees from tribes who had themselves been refugees who fled the Southeast's rival Upper Creeks less than a century earlier. The Seminole population was simply too small to be major actors in the white sphere of the nineteenth-century Indian River or to establish a dynamic cultural frontier. This is not to deny the agency of the Seminoles. Their limited engagements with the lagoon's newcomers were conscious attempts to balance the preservation of their autonomy with the procurement of goods otherwise unavailable to them. The limited presence of Seminoles in the accounts of Anglo settlers is a result of Seminole decisions to maintain separation from the pioneers. Their real power came perhaps from their popular image as fierce savages, which clearly held sway in the minds of the Anglo settlers. This caricature certainly slowed Anglo immigration to the region (the violent incident reported by Brayton is a prime example). Unlike western "leap-frogging" settlement patterns and earlier eastern continuous sprawling expansion, the tenuous ties of the east coast of Florida to the population center of Charleston created a sparsely populated string of yeomen entrepreneurs who lived largely in isolation and were loosely connected by sailboats instead of wagons.[3]

The 1830 Indian Removal Act cleared vast swaths of the South for an expansion of cotton plantations, which had a ruinous effect on soil and cultivated a permanent state of acquiring new land to replace the quickly depleted soil. The 1842 Armed Occupation Act was an attempt to promote southern settlement patterns that had been disrupted by the persistence of Seminoles in the peninsula and the subsequent Second Seminole War. By offering 160 acres to each single man or head of family who improved land south of Gainesville within five years, the act was designed to open the region to the cotton plantation culture that had recently been imported to northern Florida as well as Alabama, Mississippi, and Louisiana. The quarter sections received by settlers were not enough to establish plantations on the model recently started in Jackson and Leon Counties in North Florida. Instead, the act was a reflection of the period's democratization and official support for the growing power and "masculinity" of southern countrymen. Abolitionists Daniel Webster and John Quincy Adams opposed the act, seeing it as an expansion of slave power. In the words of the bill's sponsor, Senator Thomas Hart Benson, of Missouri: "The peninsula of Florida is now prepared for this armed settlement: the enemy has been driven out of the field. He lurks an unseen foe in the swamps and hammocks. . . . We want people to take possession, and the armed cultivator is the man for that."[4] Southern planters also made efforts to transplant their economies to the vast, empty Indian River. Sea-island cotton and, more alluringly, sugarcane began to be successfully cultivated in the panhandle of Florida at this time.[5] William Peck, a planter from Augusta, Georgia, made a claim under the Armed Occupation Act and brought four sons and a collection of craftsmen and slaves to the lower Indian River in 1843 in an attempt to establish a citrus plantation. South Florida's inability to host significant cotton production meant that the primary crops planted were sugarcane, tobacco, coconuts, plantains, and citrus.[6]

Although the total number of settlers in Southeast Florida, including the Indian River, was small (only nine Armed Occupation Act permits were issued along the waterways of the Indian River), it was expected that the region would follow the lead of Mississippi and experience significant population growth as plantation culture spread west and south. This expectation led to an 1844 U.S. Senate resolution calling for the construction of a railroad across the peninsula, so as to have "direct communication between the waters of the river Matanzas, the Mosquito lagoon, and Indian River at Haulover, in East Florida." The trickle of settlers to the lagoon ensured that this railroad would not arrive until several more decades passed.[7]

In 1849 a small group of young Seminole men attacked the small Anglo settlement of Indian River Colony, in the vicinity of Fort Pierce. The terror spread by this attack nearly emptied the Indian River of the new white settlers. In response to the violence at the recently emptied settlement, Fort Capron was established later that year. The Third Seminole War (1855–58) and the Civil War that closely followed also had suppressing effects on settlement in the region and meant that another generation passed before significant settlement resumed in the area.

As in other frontier regions of the time, the federal government provided the chief incentives for pioneers. After 1842's Armed Occupation Act, the federal government used the Indian River as a watery network to connect a series of forts. Following statehood in 1845, a string of lighthouses came to be built in Florida. Three of these were located on the Indian River (Jupiter, Cape Canaveral, and Mosquito inlet). The completion of the Jupiter lighthouse came on the eve of war in 1860, the same year there was a signed contract to build an improved light at Cape Canaveral.[8] Local settlers, hoping to prevent the Union blockade from closing the inlets to smugglers, disabled the operating mechanisms of the Jupiter and Cape Canaveral lights (the original Mosquito inlet light had been destroyed in 1835 during the Second Seminole War, less than one year after it was built). Like rumrunners some sixty years later, these smugglers crossed the Gulf Stream and took advantage of the Indian River's proximity to the Bahamas.

A modest supply fort was built in New Smyrna on the ruins of the home of Judge David Dunham two years after the home had been torched in the Indian attack that instigated the Second Seminole War. The fort was briefly revived to house goods for soldiers in the series of 1850s skirmishes that are called the Third Seminole War.[9]

Within the first year of the Civil War, the federal government's "Anaconda Plan" to strangle the Confederacy by blocking the importation of goods from Europe (via the Bahamas) with a naval blockade was beginning to have its desired effect. The tiny Confederate navy was no match for the Union fleet, so the Confederate states turned to small, shallow draft private vessels to smuggle supplies. All three natural inlets of the system—the Mosquito, Jupiter, and Indian River inlets—became important to Confederate smugglers who exploited the remote, shallow access points to the sheltered lagoons and creeks beyond, as well as the Indian River's proximity to the Bahamas.

The success of the Union blockade forced the Confederacy to rely increasingly on Florida to supply its armies with beef and salt, crucial in the days before refrigeration. Perhaps as many as 2,500 men worked in Florida's saltworks, most of which were on the Gulf Coast between St. Joe and Tampa. After the destruction of many of these saltworks, the remote northern Indian River system was selected as a location for at least two new saltworks. Boilers, kettles, and drying pans were reused from the Dunlawton sugar mill, which had been burned in the attacks leading up to the Second Seminole War. Water was taken from the Mosquito Lagoon and boiled 100 gallons at a time. The remaining salt was then scraped into boxes or barrels for transport north. The rainy climate of the Indian River region made it impossible for Confederates to use simple solar evaporating pans, which required the construction of the labor-intensive coquina stone wood-fired ovens.[10]

Although it was never the site of fighting, Fort New Smyrna's proximity to the Mosquito inlet made it a useful warehouse for Confederates to store smuggled goods. The standard Union tactic to capture suspected blockade-runners was to send armed landing parties through the inlet, in hopes of capturing the small, swift ships while they sat at anchor in the protected lagoon.

In March 1862 the USS *Penguin* dispatched a unit of sailors at the Mosquito inlet, who located and destroyed a small blockade-runner name *Katie*. On January 5, 1863, the USS *Sagamore* captured the British sloop *Avenger* inside the Jupiter inlet, which was carrying goods loaded in Nassau. Three days later, the *Sagamore* captured another British sloop offshore, ten miles north of the Jupiter inlet, the *Julia*, which was loaded with salt. The next month the *Sagamore* captured a third British smuggler, this time inside the central Indian River, eighteen miles north of the Indian River inlet. The schooner *Charm* was loaded with cotton and on its way to exchange for goods in Nassau. The captain of the *Charm* was Confederate sympathizer Henry T. Titus, who was captured along with his ship in the vicinity of the town that would later bear his name. Smuggling supplies in his Nassau-based ship was only the most recent in a series of adventures undertaken by Titus. As an avowed supporter of slavery and the era's "manifest destiny" military expansionism, Titus had eagerly pursued any adventure that promoted the expansion of slavery. He participated in the filibustering expedition of Narciso López in 1851, which unsuccessfully attempted to liberate Cuba from Spain, with the expectation that the island would follow the pattern of Florida and Texas and become the sixteenth slave state. As an enthusiastic "Border Ruffian" spreading slavery in the "Bleeding Kansas" theater in 1857, Titus met fellow southern filibuster William Walker, who persuaded Titus to travel to Nicaragua to manage men and munitions for Walker's ultimately short-lived takeover of Nicaragua.[11]

Soon after, the *Sagamore* attempted to continue its success when it spotted the masts of another Confederate blockade-runner. On March 1, 1863, the *Sagamore* sent small boats ashore and found that a fire was lit aboard the small schooner *Florence Nightingale*. One Union sailor was killed by a volley of fire from an ambush of between twenty-five and thirty Confederate sympathizers from the area who had been waiting for the Union sailors to attempt to extinguish the fire and capture the vessel. Assuming the *Nightingale* was destroyed, the sailors returned to the *Sagamore* under a hail of bullets. The *Nightingale* was apparently not destroyed in the fire, as it was soon captured by the USS *Octara* and delivered to the Union Key West naval outpost sixteen days after the failed capture attempt by the crew of the USS *Sagamore*.[12]

In July 1863 the USS *Oleander* and *Beauregard* entered the inlet and shelled the most prominent building in the town of twenty-seven families, the hotel of John D. Sheldon, which had been built on massive foundation ruins remaining from Andrew Turnbull's New Smyrnea settlement. The federal troops also destroyed two small schooners, one loaded with cotton for an upcoming run through the blockade.[13]

Although the Civil War had only a negligible effect on the region, at least one settler, German immigrant Augustus Lang, considered it to be insufficiently remote to prevent his conscription into the Confederate military and moved south to Lake Worth Lagoon for the duration of the war. There are no records of Anglo settlers other than Lang in Lake Worth at this time. Lake Worth pioneer Charles Pierce reported that Lang returned to the Indian River upon receiving word that the war was over, more than one year after the fighting ended. There are reports that Lang dug a modest (and short-lived) inlet connecting freshwater Lake Worth Lagoon to the ocean.[14] In 1870 the population of the Indian River region was 1,216 persons, largely due to the 1862 Homestead Act. Settlers could also buy land from the state through the Internal Improvement Fund, established in 1855, or the Board of Education, starting in 1869.[15] "In their hunting, Father saw this land where we still live, investigated, and decided to homestead," recalled one nineteenth-century settler in the central Indian River. "The Government allowed 160 acres of high land, for which you paid $50. High land was owned by the Government and over flow low land belonged to the State. Each child could enter 80 acres. State land sold for $1.00 per acre."[16]

Like other states in the Reconstruction South, Florida emerged financially ruined from the war, and the distribution of its chief asset, land, was rife with abuse. Among the more incredulous and unrestrained descriptions of the era is this hyperbolic description from a New York journalist:

> The great drawback is the State Legislature. This is filled with ignorant negroes and thieving carpet-baggers. They go to Tallahassee with the avowed purpose of making all they can. They have run the State into debt over $15,000,000, and with county and other indebtedness she now owes $100 a head for every one of her inhabitants. The taxes reach about 2 per cent, but they are very unevenly

> divided. The settlers are taxed for the full value of their property, while the owners of the enormous land grants escape without paying a cent. Thousands of acres are covered by old Spanish claims, and these were exempted from tax by the terms of the treaty with Spain when the country was ceded to the United States. Thus the small owners are not only compelled to improve the value of the vast tracts owned by carpetbaggers and others, but are actually forced to pay the taxes of these thieves.[17]

So enticing was the region that some of the workers surveying the land for the federal government were drawn to homestead on the land that they surveyed themselves. In 1877 German immigrant Ernest Stypmann entered the employment of the federal government and surveyed the lower southeast coast of Florida aboard the schooner *Steadfast*. Impressed by the St. Lucie Estuary, Stypmann had a small-scale map made for himself, which showed the location of homesteads and government land, which was for sale at $1.25 an acre, and enticed two of his brothers in Germany to join him in the region.[18]

Stypmann's letter was only one of many written accounts of the region sent to far-flung family members. Northern papers enticed many to move south to the east coast of Florida by publishing alluring descriptions of tropical "song birds, everywhere [s]inging out their heaven-born music [o]n the orange-scented air."[19] The era's newspapers extolled the Indian River's proximity to the warm waters flowing north from the Caribbean in passages such as "the climate along the [Indian] river from October to May is a perpetual Indian summer, seldom interrupted by storms; and most of the time there is a gentle breeze coming inland from the even tempered waters of the Gulf Stream." "Owing to the proximity of this warm ocean current, and the prevalence of the winds from that direction, this locality enjoys the finest climate in Florida, if not the whole world, as these breezes are mild, balmy, and equable to a warm degree the whole year round, yet always free from sultriness and oppressiveness." In light of such alluring prose it is little wonder that the Indian River acquired a reputation in this period as a fertile land filled with "water lilies, hibiscus, pinks, geraniums, roses, poinsettias, salvas [*sic*], cannas, daturas, begonias, and azalias [*sic*]."[20]

In the 1870s and 1880s the Indian River was the focal point of mass marketing that would later culminate in the 1920s land boom and bust. In 1888 New Yorkers lined up to see three manatees caught and transported from the Indian River by the captain of a schooner named *Manatee*. Reporters fanned the Indian River flames with prose such as this account, which claimed that during capture, the exotic manatee "makes desperate efforts for liberty, and with its powerful paddle blade . . . is capable of a severe struggle as long as it has fighting breath in it."[21] Visitors to the Smithsonian Institution in Washington, D.C., were also exposed to many exotic examples of flora and fauna that had been shipped to the museum by the keepers of the lagoon's Houses of Refuge, which had been established by the federal government to provide aid to shipwreck survivors.[22]

Upon arriving in the region, Gilded Age northerners appear to have been satisfied with what they found. "I had long before painted a picture of the Indian River and everything I had pictured was all there, and more," wrote one settler. "The long, hazy, dreamy days spent on a boat on the river or wandering through piney woods or hunting alligators in the marshes of Merritt's Island" were remembered fondly. "To . . . sit on a man's porch surrounded by trees full of ripening oranges and look out at the beautiful blue river was dreamland itself, and *the dolce far niente* (the sweet doing nothing) was emblematic of the paradise I expected to inhabit forever." The Indian River's growing citrus groves and pineapple fields led some Gilded Age northern settlers to romanticize the lagoon in earlier times. The new settlers looked to the remnant of the Armed Occupation Act–era settlers and their "isolated lives lived by a few families of the Civil War 20 years previously, when they were reduced absolutely to their home resources, they said they lived better than they ever had before or since."[23]

Stories written by curious reporters and published in northern newspapers led to a trickle, and then a steady stream of tourists beginning around 1870. Tourists came to the area for their health and initially boarded in the homes of isolated settlers and often accompanied their hosts on sailing trips to hunt and fish. An 1882 discussion of the facilities available in the region recorded that "the boatmen have been overhauling their boats, for excursion parties and visitors are coming with every boat to go down the river on hunting, fishing and exploring parties."[24] Pioneer Lucy Richards recalled that these tourists "all love to sail with 'Cap'n' as they all call Father. He is a delightful companion on a boat, a splendid sailor, always good natured, and full of stories, having traveled a good bit." The region's first hotels opened in this time period, catering to tourists seeking an adventure in an "untamed" wilderness or the restorative effects of the Indian River's climate. Lucy Richards wrote, "We will have quite a few boarders this winter and not a single partition upstairs. We have made quite a few beds of palmetto. It is better than husks for there are no cobs in it. . . . We have a screen on one window now and we really think we are comfortable." In the days before hotels, these tourists were drawn by the possibility of experiencing an exotic wilderness. "I told you Father would bring us a boarder, and sure enough he did . . . a mighty nice man. He wanted to eat a piece of alligator, but did not want to know when he did it. Father got a small 'gator and I fried some of it with a pan of fish and it went down all right." These tourists also published accounts of their visits to the region, which brought others to the lagoon.[25]

As there was no easy way to transport significant lumber to the Indian River, nearly all nineteenth-century settlers used readily available vegetation and built crude palmetto shacks for their initial homes. The hutlike homes described by Jonathan Dickinson vanished from the Indian River along with the Ais and Timucua, to be replaced by nineteenth-century innovations, chiefly the Seminole chickee and the closely related palmetto-roofed shacks (built with open or semienclosed walls of shipwreck lumber or palmetto logs) developed by Anglo Indian River settlers. Housing that was well adapted to the Indian River's heat, mosquitoes, and hurricanes was essential; it should perhaps not be surprising that the same environment cultivated similar houses from such different cultures. "Board lumber was rather scarce on the beach, and some time was spent gathering enough for the attic floor, which was finished first and enclosed in palmetto fans. Shingles were not shipped on sailing vessels at that time and so none were found on the beach," recounted Charles Pierce of the construction of his family's house in the 1870s. Although Pierce's description is of a house built after the family moved from Indian River to Lake Worth, it is consistent with the salvage-and-thatch construction of Indian River settlers. "It was a dry and cool house, but there were others who liked the palmetto leaves also. Roaches, lizards, and small snakes all made their homes in them."[26] Thomas E. Richards's move from New Jersey to the lower Indian River in 1878 was typical of that of the era's settlers. After naming his beautiful waterfront homestead Eden, Richards grumbled to neighbors several days later that it was more like hell.[27] Richards and his son searched the beach for shipwreck lumber to salvage, and the size of his house was dictated by the large beams found. "Father works too hard, he will be an old man before his time," wrote Richards's daughter, Lucy, of his time building their house. "He sails that boat night and day [to load lumber]. Father is so crazy about this country that he does not think much about himself and works so hard."[28]

In contrast to Richards's evident industriousness, New York journalist Amos Cummings reported that the Indian River's climate cultivated laziness. He wrote that a Merritt Island grower named Futch "and his two six-foot sons were lounging around the house. The dwelling was a curiosity. It was a rough board affair, thatched with palmetto. It was so old that the sides of the house in two places had rotted away, leaving holes large enough for a man to enter." Cummings continued, "With characteristic Floridian energy the female members of Futch's family had slapped a couple of small water casks against the inside of the holes. There were no windows in the house. . . . Noticing about a hundred pounds of alligator meat drying in the sun, my guide asked Futch what he was going to do with it. 'Eat it,' was the response." Cumming's apparent distaste extended to the "mansion" of the early Indian River's most successful settler, Captain Douglas Dummitt, which was at this time occupied by his daughter. "The mansion was built of unplaned

TABLE 1. Indian River Population

	Brevard	Indian River County	Martin County	St. Lucie County	Total Indian River Population
1840	n/a	n/a	n/a	n/a	Negligible
1850	n/a	n/a	n/a	139	139
1860	246	n/a	n/a	n/a	246
1870	1,216	n/a	n/a	n/a	1,216
1880	1,478	n/a	n/a	n/a	1,478
1890	3,401	n/a	n/a	n/a	3,401
1900	5,158	n/a	n/a	n/a	5,158
1910	4,717	n/a	n/a	4,075	8,792
1920	8,505	n/a	n/a	7,886	16,391
1930	13,283	6,724	5,111	7,057	32,175
1940	16,142	8,957	6,295	11,871	43,265
1950	23,653	11,872	7,807	20,180	63,512
1960	111,435	25,309	16,932	39,294	192,970
1970	230,006	35,992	28,035	50,836	344,869
1980	272,956	59,896	64,014	87,182	484,048
1990	398,978	90,208	100,900	150,171	740,257
2000	476,230	112,947	126,731	192,695	908,603
2010	543,376	138,038	146,318	277,789	1,105,521

Note: This does not include the population south of the St. Lucie Estuary, which was in Palm Beach County until 1925 and is difficult to estimate. Note the effect of NASA on the population of Brevard County in the 1950s and 1960s, as well as the booming population of St. Lucie County's sprawling city of Port St. Lucie in the 1990s and 2000s.
Source: University of Virginia Historical Census Browser; U.S. Census Bureau.

boards. They had neither paint nor whitewashed, and had become black from the action of the weather. The house contained but one room. The Captain's bed, well protected by mosquito bars, stood in the southwest corner. . . . The walls were neither painted nor plastered, and streaks of daylight could be seen beneath the side boards. There were no windows in the house."[29] Similarly, Michigan reporter Francis R. Stebbins wrote in 1880, "It is a desolate country for any one to live in, but many of the people seem quite contented. Many live in houses sided and roofed with nothing by palmetto leaves. Some have floors and some have not. They live on hog and hominy, fish and venison, and don't seem to care what the rest of the world is doing."[30] Built quickly and cheaply, these homes were constructed of materials plentiful in the Indian River system, were easily repaired, and often took advantage of the cooling effect of prevailing sea breezes. In addition to roofing, palmetto fronds went into the making of broad-brimmed hats and switches to brush off mosquitoes. "Father is so busy making regular trips on the river [for lumber]. It is a big undertaking to build a house of this size and have to go so far for material, but Father says if we have a home large enough to accommodate the people, they will come, and we will soon have some neighbors. . . . [There is] a sandfly bar over his bed. It was a big job making them all by hand."[31]

Tourists trickled into the region in the 1870s and 1880s, lured by accounts of the restorative effects of the Indian River's reputed healthy climate that filled northern newspapers. *Forest and Stream* magazine reported in 1873 that the Indian River "is possessed of peculiar, extraordinary, and little known attractions and resources, which, if properly developed, would make it an unequalled sanitarium for pulmonary subjects." It is little wonder that coughing New Englanders often filled the lagoon's sailboats, in light of claims to have "seen some remarkable evidences of which the benefits of persons of both sexes, having diseased lungs, have received there—benefits that proved lasting—with some yet more remarkable instances of persons so diseased that elsewhere they were in constant pain, yet who were able to lead a prolonged and comfortable life in that singularly equable temperature."[32] "There is absolutely no endemic disease at this place," read a representative 1876 article. "Its mild, genial climate banishes all coughs, colds, and rheumatisms, while a line of hills in its rear effectually intercept the malarial exhalations of the fresh-water swamps of the interior. The chlorinated vapors brought by the trade-winds, which are constantly blowing from the sea, also exercise their powerful sanitary influence."[33]

An 1891 Philadelphia newspaper reported the settlement pattern that developed in the wake of such media attention: "Most of the northern people I find residing here came because of impaired health, and having regained it by outdoor life in this genial clime, are loth to leave it, and so adapting their lives to their surroundings, settle down to orange culture as the most available occupation of their hands. The oranges sometimes fail them, but the climate never does." So alluring were such passages that the population of the Indian River region had climbed to over 3,400 by 1890. The increased social and economic opportunities brought by this growing population only made the lagoon more appealing. "The wealth of restored health rarely fails to come to the feeble ones, amply compensating for all inconveniences, or privations which they may have to endure, and which the rapidly settling up of the country is steadily minimizing, and making the lack of good society no longer an objection to Florida life, or that of needed domestic comforts so greatly felt before."[34]

The attributes that caused the Indian River's climate to be perceived as healthy were portrayed as liabilities by other Florida communities hoping to attract winter tourists and the ill to their region. "Jacksonville and vicinity catch one-third of the winter visitors, and hold them," wrote Amos Cummings in the nascent years of the Indian River's tourist industry.

> After they have been housed for a few weeks, they possibly hear that there are such places as Smyrnea and Titusville, and that they are supplied with hotels. Instantly every native is on the alert. Horrible stories about mosquitoes, bad roads, rotten steamboats, and so on, are dinned in the ears of the visitors. Their wives are frightened, and they themselves settle down where they are, and shell out their money, thanking the liars for their kindness. Up to the 10th of March just four strangers, including myself, had succeeded in reaching [the Indian River].[35]

Like the Everglades, the Indian River's tremendous biophysical diversity is a result of a variety of conditions, only some of which are welcoming to humans. Tourists were often infatuated with the mild winters and warm, palm-lined waters, but less so with the wet season's humidity and mosquitoes. In 1873 Cummings observed:

> Five years ago Dr. Fox came to the Indian River country from Savannah, Ga. He was in poor health, but the climate strengthened him wonderfully, and he was determined to become a permanent resident. So he preempted a lovely palmetto hammock on the border of Mosquito lagoon, a few miles from Dummitt's grove, erected a little cabin and sent for his wife and children. The party spent a year in fighting the mosquitoes, but during the second summer they were compelled to surrender. The insects swept down upon them by myriads, and the doctor tells me that he was forced to take to his sail boat at midnight to escape being eaten alive. . . . So much for the most productive land in Florida. Its only mark is that sickness is unknown. But the natives all have a jaundicy look similar to the complexion of the people in Lower Georgia. An invalid who can't live in any other part of the United States can live in Eastern Florida.[36]

An 1880 visitor observed dryly: "It seems healthy in the winter, but I guess there is a good market for quinine in the summer."[37]

Such dour published assessments of the Indian River's climate did little to damp the power that the mythic qualities of the climate of Florida (and especially the Indian River) held in the minds of many readers. A generation later land developers continued to tout the restorative qualities of the Indian River's environment: "This section of the state [southern Indian River] is entirely free from malaria and possesses a climate which for all the year comfort challenges the world. The average death rate of Palm Beach County is less than one per cent. Per annum . . . the young, suffering from catarrh, bronchitis, tonsillitis [*sic*], or pulmonary troubles, may confidently look forward to a complete cure. Those past middle age find immediate relief—their cough disappears." "Florida is healthy—ten times more so than Iowa or Minnesota."[38]

For the first Indian River Anglo settlers following the Civil War, the lagoon was a place of labor, and fishing was not considered recreation but was only engaged in when needed to obtain food. It would not be until the mid-twentieth century that the lagoon would become inextricably one of recreation and leisure. The rudimentary subsistence economy fostered by the Indian River's isolation from population centers and shallow depth eventually gave way to a growing commercial fishing industry by the end of the century. In 1866 a short-lived cannery was opened on the Indian River for processing sea turtles, fish, and oysters, and a few fishing crews from Savannah and Charleston ventured to enter the treacherous Indian River inlet or Mosquito inlet, but a major commercial fishing industry was only established after the widespread dredging, the human-made inlets, and the arrival of the railroad in the 1890s.[39]

The very limited records of the indigenous peoples left little direct information on pre-Columbian fishing in the Indian River, but the fishing techniques of other Glades peoples were undoubtedly utilized. It is probable that local plants such as Jamaica dogwood and coin vine (found primarily in mangrove swamps) were used as piscicides. Excavations from the west coast's Marco Island have provided detailed knowledge of the palm fiber cords that were the chief material used in the nets of South Florida's original fisheries, which were certainly also used by other Glades people in the Indian River.[40]

Accounts of a lagoon brimming with fish were plentiful. Steamboat captain Steven Bravo was fond of telling visitors that he regularly placed a box under a stern-mounted lantern and just waited for the pompano to jump in and fill it.[41] Amos Cummings wrote of the salty region of the lagoon near the Indian River inlet, "the water fairly boils with sharks. I counted one hundred and twelve within the space of an acre, none of which were less than eight feet long. Indian River people say that they have seen them twenty feet in length. I saw one that measured over seventeen feet. They would frequently break under the bows of our twenty-one foot sailboat, careening her to one side and at times half listing her from the water." These dangers did not keep him from spending weeks on the water in pursuit of prolific fish. After describing a fifty-three-pound bass (redfish), Cummings wrote the "best snapper-fishing is in Indian River, opposite Fort Capron. The inlet is alive with game fish. There are bass, snappers, grouper, jewfish, and cavallo, or 'crevalyea,' as the natives call them, in abundance." From the same spot three years later a visitor reported spearing fifteen to twenty-five six-foot tarpon each day from his small rowboat.[42]

So enticing was this profoundly productive estuarine system that by 1895 over 2,500,000 pounds of fish went to market, made possible by a railroad spur that reached the northern Indian River in 1885. In that year George W. Scobie, of Connecticut, established a fish house in Titusville to take advantage of this new means of shipping freight. By the time Henry Flagler's Florida East Coast Railroad line reached the lower Indian River in 1894, there were nineteen fishing firms established on the Indian River from Titusville to Stuart. That year a hard freeze nearly wiped out the region's citrus industry and led many growers to begin fishing. The 1894 freeze also killed so many fish that year that they would "float by the acres. . . . The east wind would bring them over to the west side of the river, then the men folks would rake them back into the water, and it was so terrible we could hardly stand it." Central Indian River resident Charles Gifford recalled, "Only the mullet and trout didn't freeze, and the buzzards had a great feast; they flocked from everywhere, the trees were full of them, and for a year and a half the stench was still here after a rain. It was the worst freeze on record, but it did good in some ways for it got rid of the catfish and toadfish, which were worthless."[43]

In 1894 an employee of a Titusville fish operation opened a fish house of his own in Eden to take advantage of the nearby St. Lucie inlet, which was cut open two years earlier by local residents. Ransom Ren Ricou had a local boatbuilder, Captain John Miller, build him a fleet of small rowing fishing boats, each equipped with a small sailing rig. So profitable was the Indian River fishery that within twenty years the company had become the largest fish company in the Southeast, with operations from the Keys to Northeast Florida, and Ricou was hailed as the "King of southern fish producers" by the head of New York City's famous

Fulton Fish Market, often shipping five boxcars of fish north daily. In the wake of the railroad and new inlet, dozens of fish houses and several ice plants sprouted along the Indian River. Because of this decentralization, Titusville shipped less than half the fish north in 1895 than it did in 1890, and Fort Pierce's proximity to the Indian River inlet allowed this growing city to become the center of Indian River fishing.[44] It was not uncommon for a goliath grouper weighing several hundred pounds to be placed on the Stuart railroad platform with a card listing the destination address dangling from its mouth.[45] St. Lucie Estuary resident Curt Schroeder recalled that in one haul, over fifty tons of fish were taken, twenty of which were salable. This included 10,000 pounds of stingray, some of which weighed up to 200 pounds each.[46] The tremendous success of the fishing industry in the 1890s attracted legions of recreational fishermen to the Indian River, including President Grover Cleveland, who purchased land in Stuart along the shore of the St. Lucie after sport fishing in the area.[47]

By the 1920s there was a growing consensus that the Indian River's fishery was in decline, primarily due to the overfishing made possible by new technology, chiefly the gas engine, which had a similarly ruinous effect on other Atlantic fisheries. These inexpensive engines allowed fishermen to use the Indian River's inlets, regardless of the weather, to net fish both offshore and within the Indian River, resulting in dwindling stocks. As early as 1897 a congressional committee on fisheries reported that "in some parts of the river the mullet is less abundant than when fishing first began. . . . But an increase in demand for mullet throughout the country, the rapid development of the salted-mullet industry, cheaper express and freight rates, and cheaper ice are possibilities for the near future." A more foreboding observation followed, "the pompano has decreased greatly."[48] The large hauls made possible by mechanized winches for retrieving nets led to legislation limiting seine nets to 1,000 yards, although sometimes several nets were tied together. Such efficient and enormous hauls led to thousands of pounds of undesired "trash" fish being dumped in the river in a single haul after dying in the nets. As the region's pineapple industry declined in the first decade of the twentieth century, many growers turned to fishing. "We all went broke but not hungry. Anyone could get a small sailing cat boat and troll in the river for enough trout to bring in five to eight dollars a day at the wholesale price of three and a half cents per pound. Husky men familiar with the water could join a four man netting crew, at least during the winter months."[49] Curt Schroder pressed the Palm Beach County commissioners to allow the former pineapple growers to use seine nets, after they became banned statewide. Nearly all of the lower Indian River's men began illegally seining after receiving tacit approval from local authorities. Said the Palm Beach sheriff, "Curt, if you rob a bank I will put you in a pen, if you seine, well if I don't see you I can't catch you."[50] In the mid-1920s the Florida Supreme Court also banned dragnets due to increasing fears over the diminishing industry.[51]

The Indian River ecosystem also hosted many green sea turtles, which traveled in the lagoon and deposited eggs in the beach in the spring. The first settlers quickly became eager hunters of the lumbering marine reptiles. Like fish, turtles soon shifted from being a mere food staple for isolated inhabitants to a lucrative commodity. Like growing pineapples, capturing green turtles was an experiment that proved to be an immediate (but short-lived) success in the Indian River. Cape Canaveral settler Mills O. Burnham, like most early settlers, was forced to cobble together subsistence by trying out various enterprises. His most successful experiment was determining how to capture and safely ship the lagoon's green turtles. Burnham stored turtles in watery pens (called "kraals") after capturing them in his newly purchased catboat, *Josephine*. The venture was very profitable for Burnham when his turtles arrived at markets in Savannah and Charleston in good condition because he determined how to successfully tie their flippers and support their heads on small wooden blocks for the journey.[52] The port of New Smyrnea manifest of the schooner *Pearl* in August 1851 provides useful insight into the growing economy of the northern Indian River system. The *Pearl* sailed to New Smyrnea from Charleston with a cargo of slaves and returned to South Carolina carrying a laundry list of products from the Indian River's budding industries, including sugar, molasses, syrup, oranges, and 3,039 pounds of sea turtle.[53]

"Millions of eggs are destroyed every year," wrote Amos Cummings in 1874. "When a settler lives near the beach, his hogs fatten themselves upon the nests. . . . Dr. Wallace gathered 5,000 eggs last year before the season was half over. Of course, he had more than his family could eat. The eggs threatened to spoil on his hands. One night his mules were without corn. He dumped a peck of turtle-eggs in their manger. The beasts seemed to like them better than grain. After that the Doctor fed them eggs once a day throughout the summer, and the animals became as fat as butter."[54] Many settlers recorded how the turtle eggs, unknown in northern markets, quickly became a staple of the Indian River diet. "The boys went hunting one night, and they got a big nest of turtle eggs and also a fine, fat bear," wrote Lucy Richards. "They went to their bunks for a snooze after a breakfast of bear steak, and turtle egg omelet. The rest cut up the bear meat, in steaks and roasts and a lot of it in strips to 'jerk' and the fat they put in the Dutch oven to render into lard. When Dad saw that fat sizzling it put notions in his head. He said 'Great Scott, Bob, let's have some [green turtle-based] doughnuts.'"[55]

At least one regional settler drowned while engaged in turtling when he became entangled in the large mesh cotton nets used in the trade when a heavy nor'easter swamped his sailboat while crossing the Indian River.[56] Emily Lagow Bell recounted the steps taken by her family to protect their increasingly valuable turtles. "In 1886 we had a turtle pen with about 50 of green turtles in it, and it was getting cold. . . . My husband said: 'If the water keeps falling we'll have to bring the turtles out and cover them and build a fire.' . . . So they sat up all night keeping fire, but we lost all but three, the smallest. Over $500 lost in twenty-four hours."[57]

The high price fetched for turtles in northern markets led to intense pressure on the Indian River's turtle population. An 1897 congressional survey of the region noted that the haul and average size of the Indian River's sea turtles had already declined significantly due to overhunting.

In previous years turtles over 200 pounds were sometimes taken, but by 1897 captured turtles seldom reached 100 pounds. The 519 turtles shipped north in 1895 averaged only 36 pounds, which was down significantly from the 50-pound average of the turtles shipped only five years earlier.[58] Poaching of sea turtles continued after the state legislature banned their killing in 1909.[59]

Other animals widely hunted in the Indian River included manatees and alligators. There is some evidence that the lagoon's numerous dolphins were also hunted for food.[60] So intensely had alligators been hunted in the mid-nineteenth century that the congressional committee on fisheries reported in 1897 that their numbers were "very scarce" and unable to support an industry.[61] While manatees were regularly hunted as a source of food, their exotic nature made them more valuable as objects of curiosity in northern cities, with some fetching up to $300. The difficulty of successfully transporting the rotund animals north increased their exotic image and decreased their numbers. Two residents of the lower Indian River caught one in 1874, "intending to send it North for exhibition. The animal weighted [*sic*] over 1,500 pounds. Unfortunately it was tied to the boat so firmly that the rope cut into its flesh, and it died before the party reached the head of the Indian River. The porgies devoured the body." By the 1870s it was reported that "formerly it [manatee] was abundant, but it is now nearly extinct, and becomes more scarce every year. Its meat is greatly relished and tastes like the best Fulton Market beef."[62] The population remained sufficiently robust to become the subject of intense hunting as the Indian River's fisheries began their decline. "Around 1916 young manatees were butchered, pickled and smoked, the meat tasting like pork." In 1897 Indian River settlers transported a manatee with great difficulty to New York. The trip required sinking and floating a skiff under the 2,000-pound animal and lashing additional boats to either side. At the Stuart railroad station, the inhabitants used block and tackle to load the manatee into a custom-made tank on a railway car. "About two weeks later one of the New York Sunday papers told how the brave buyer had captured the monster of the deep at peril of his own life. Of course, manatees are very timid; the only danger lies in coming too close to the broad tail, in deep water a blow with that tail will knock a man senseless," grumbled the manatee's Indian River capturer.[63]

The Indian River's proximity to the Gulf Stream was a steady source of goods for inhabitants of the Indian River. Professional "master wreckers" had been required to be licensed in the state since 1847. The wrecking court (which determined how to allocate salvaged goods) was located in Key West. Between 1847 and 1857, the Key West court processed 499 wrecks valued at over $16 million.[64] Indian River settlers adopted elements of Key West's wrecking culture to take advantage of the many sources of the area's prolific resources. The lower Indian River was considered to be within the sphere of Key West's wreckers, who regularly sailed to the region. The area's nineteenth-century settlers exploited the lumber and consumer goods that were regularly deposited by storms near their new home. For example, the wreck of the 1,343-ton New York–bound steamship schooner *Victor* in October 1871 at the Jupiter inlet was the source of many years' supply of clothing, perfumes, plantation bitters liquor, and butter for a small group of Seminoles who made camp in the area following the wreck, as well as the pioneer Pierce family, who lived at the Jupiter lighthouse. Charles Pierce recounted these two groups racing each other in canoes and skiffs to snatch the floating crates and barrels.[65] An 1886 wreck of the *Panama*, off of the central Indian River, near Sebastian, spilled hundreds of 100-gallon wine casks along the beaches from Cape Florida to Cape Canaveral, which drew wreckers from up and down the coast. "There were hundreds of pounds of [salvage], lard and cases of ginghams," wrote Indian River settler Charles Gifford. "Folks dried the gingham and used it for everything, clothes, curtains, and tablecloths. Everything was alike. Lard and other things that could be sold, were taken to Key West and Atlanta. Men carried it across the island and loaded it on boats. Someone knocked a head in a wine cask and hung up a cup, and folks got drunk."[66] One Indian River family used the enormous iron boiler from a wreck to collect rainwater. In 1873 reporter Amos Cummings colorfully described the nascent Indian River wrecking culture. "The eastern coast of Florida is always strewn with wrecks. . . . Below Canaveral it is fringed with broken coral rocks, which are only visible at low tide." Cummings continued:

> [Wrecks furnish the settlers] with shoes, muslin, calico, buttons, hooks and eyes, and a thousand little necessaries of life which they can get in no other way. A storm arises and a vessel is driven ashore. The sailors wander across the beach to Indian River. They hail some straggler, and are forwarded north in the little cat-rigged wagons. The news of the wreck spreads like wildfire. As the country is flat, the spars of a stranded vessel can be seen at great distance. "A wrack, a wrack," is the cry, and within twenty-four hours Indian River is dotted with winged phaetons, all striving for the nearest point to the ship. The wreckers fight their way through the almost impenetrable palmetto scrub to the beach, and pick up whatever they can find. When the dead bodies become bloated and offensive, they are buried in the sand. Each wrecker piles his plunder in a heap. Some hunt in couples, one man watches the pile, while the other adds to it. . . . At times the water is so shallow that the fleet of cat-rigged sailboats are compelled to anchor a quarter of a mile from shore, and the wreckers have to wade out to them with their plunder on their backs. As fast as the boats are loaded they put for home and return for a second cargo as soon as possible. Some men are weeks in securing all their booty. Occasionally parties build a shanty upon the sand from the driftwood of the ship. They occupy it until the last vestige of the cargo has disappeared. Then they strip the vessel of all the brass and copper they can reach, and leave her for good.[67]

With the announcement in New Smyrnea that the passing ship *Ladona* had been wrecked the day before, the town was deserted within thirty minutes. By the end of that day "there were nearly seventy-five persons at the wreck. . . . The majority of the wreckers stood it out. Some of them went three days and nights without food, and worked all the time like steam engines. When they were totally exhausted they would drop upon the sand in the shade of the ragged scrub and sleep for hours."

The part-time wreckers indiscriminately seized anything that could be used or traded. "One man had small pyramid of rat traps, and another was loaded down with lip salve."[68] Emily Lagow Bell recalled her parents walking "for miles to old wrecks and cut the copper bolts out of them . . . and carry them in sacks on our backs to get something to eat. Capt. Hogg would buy all we could get at fifteen cents a pound. Sometimes we would get fifty pounds, then go back the next day for more."[69]

Gilded Age Indian River settlers were part of a larger trend of northerners moving to southern states in the years following the Civil War. While not culturally southern, these settlers developed a fringe amalgamated society that integrated elements of northern market economies, southern cultural norms, and Caribbean agriculture and salvage. Their adoption of the wrecking culture of the "conchs" of the nearby Bahamas and Florida Keys reflected the transitional nature of the Indian River. Just as the lagoon's ecosystem spanned tropical and temperate climes, so the emerging Anglo culture had one foot in the Caribbean and one in the Reconstruction South. The nearest significant American cities, such as Jacksonville and Savannah, were no more accessible by sailboat or steam than the West Indies. The hodgepodge nature of the Indian River economy reflects the pragmatic stance toward eking out an existence in the isolated lagoon. Although they often professed to love the Indian River for its untamed qualities, settlers to the region universally engaged in environmental manipulation. The importation of agricultural goods from the Caribbean was an example of ecological experimentation attempted by the New Englanders and midwesterners while determining how to produce commercial goods in the Indian River's subtropical climate. Settlers regularly sailed to the Keys, Bahamas, and Cuba. Some ventured as far as Central and South America to bring seeds from "these tropical countries for folks to plant and try out."[70] This second wave of Anglo settlers was not the first to participate in the transnational nature of the Indian River, as the Ais had the sailing technology to travel to Cuba and the Bahamas from the lagoon, and a significant group of black Seminoles fled the region for Andros Island in the Bahamas soon after Florida became a territory of the United

States, which opened the isolated lagoon to the brutalities of American slavery.[71] The lagoon's proximity to the Caribbean and relative isolation made it a popular spot for smugglers, from Civil War–era Confederate sympathizers to Prohibition-era rum runners and, in later decades, those transporting refugees from Haiti and Cuba. In the 1920s the waterfront of West End, Bahamas (the nearest point to the Indian River), was lined with warehouses in which Bahamian women stitched whiskey and gin into burlap packages labeled "hams" in preparation for delivery through the inlets of Florida's east coast, including those of the Indian River.[72] Were it not for the Adams-Onís Treaty of 1819, peninsular Florida would have been considered to be firmly placed in the context of transcaribbean settlement patterns. To the Spanish, the region was an outpost of Havana, and to the British, it was a potential Caribbean-style tropical plantation colony. During the colonial era, "South Florida was far more intimately connected to Havana than it was to St. Augustine."[73]

> In talking with a native to-day he said that a good wreck was very much needed in this part of the country just now. The people were out of clothes, whiskey, and other necessities of life, for which they depended on stranded vessels. He said that he hoped the next wrecked ship would carry a better stock of goods than the *Ladona*. "They were the poorest stock of goods that I ever saw, sir," he said, bringing his fist down upon the railing of the sloop. "The Yankees don't make nigh as good goods as the Inglish. We're really a sufferin' for an Inglish wrack jis now."[74]

With an eye to distinguish the Indian River wreckers from the poor reputation of the Key West wreckers (who were said to lure ships onto reefs with misleading lights), Cummings observed:

> Most of the inhabitants here wear wrecked goods. Even their hats and shoes come from stranded ships. Their wives and daughters have dresses and aprons made of wrecked calico, their tables are covered with wrecked linen, and their beds are spread with wrecked muslin. A good wreck will supply an economical family

> for years. The ship ashore is regarded as legitimate prey. The people are honest and passably industrious, but they will go for a wreck like gulls after a dead fish. . . . In nine cases out of ten a Government official will help himself to the booty, and consequently the wreckers seem to think it a duty they owe themselves and the country to get ahead of him. . . . Ministers, deacons, Freemasons, Christians, and sinners all run a race for the plunder.[75]

The cultural and economic importance of wrecking decreased in the wake of the construction of the Houses of Refuge in the late 1870s and 1880s. After providing aid to wreck survivors, the duties carried out by keepers of these houses included taking control of any wreck to keep it out of the hands of the part-time east coast Florida wrecker.[76]

Like fish, the vast flocks of exotic birds celebrated in early written accounts of the lagoon fell victim to the region's growing commercialization. "The pelican is the prince of feathered gluttons," wrote Amos Cummings in 1873. "I shot a dozen of them on the wing. Sometimes the fish would begin to tumble out of their gullets before they reached the ground. . . . Dr. Fox shot a white one measuring nine feet and one inch from tip to tip, and weighing 19 3/4 pounds. . . . The plumage of the gray pelican is much admired."[77]

Descriptions of fantastic aviary diversity and quantity, such as Thomas Richard's claim to have seen thousands of "parokeets" break tree limbs with their weight, soon gave way to complaints about the flocks' absence. As early as 1880 Eden resident Lucy Richards lamented that "I have seen one [roseate spoonbill] since we reached Titusville. It was stuffed, and in a taxidermist's shop. I said it was a pity to kill it. He had all sorts of birds: ibis, flamingo, pelican and two paroquets [*sic*]."[78] The Indian River's tremendous productivity made it a center for the late nineteenth-century's rapidly expanding plume industry.

Florida's birds could not endure the arrival of market forces that valued plumes more than gold. So prized were the vibrant pink hues of the roseate spoonbill that it is estimated that there were only fifteen pairs in all of Florida the first years of the twentieth century. In 1902 concerned

Audubon Society observers of Florida's recently emptied skies and island rookeries convinced the American Ornithologist Union to hire Lake Worth pioneer (and former plume hunter) Guy Bradley to enforce Florida's scant laws that prohibited plume poaching. Three years later Bradley was murdered in the Everglades by plume hunter William Smith, who was subsequently acquitted at trial. The murder galvanized conservationists, who successfully prodded the state legislature to protect nesting colonies.[79]

In 1886 American Museum of Natural History ornithologist Frank Chapman identified 160 different types of bird feathers on the hats of women while on a single stroll in Manhattan. Of the 700 hats Chapman spotted, 542 were decorated with feathers and plumes of wading birds. Chapman was so outraged that he became an advocate for the protection of the remaining flocks, and beseeched the conservation-minded President Teddy Roosevelt to protect a series of very small islands in the middle of the Indian River near Sebastian. The islands hosted the last significant pelican rookeries in the region, and Chapman argued "birds should be saved for utilitarian reasons—and moreover, they should be saved for reasons unconnected with dollars and cents."[80] It was reported that Roosevelt was so moved that he proclaimed the island to be protected at once. Thus, on March 14, 1903, the Indian River's Pelican Island became the nation's first federal wildlife refuge, before a national wildlife refuge system was created. Five years later, Roosevelt declared the sandbars and islets surrounding Mosquito inlet to be similarly protected for birds and enlarged the Pelican Island preserve to include the surrounding mangrove islands and shorelines.[81]

Ultimately, the market forces that drove the slaughter of Florida's wading birds (an estimated 77 percent of the wading bird population was lost) relaxed pressure on the few remaining birds. By 1917 demand for plumed women's hats plummeted after the fashion was embraced by the prostitutes of New York City. Prices fell accordingly, and plume poachers turned to other endeavors once feathers no longer earned significant money. The population of Florida's wading birds increased to as many as two million by 1940. Soon after, rapid urbanization began to claim the territory of the birds, causing a population decline even more alarming than that caused by the plume hunters, perhaps as high as a 90 percent reduction.[82]

The world of the late nineteenth-century Indian River can only be understood in light of the cultural, economic, and travel centrality of the lagoon's long, narrow waterway. The shape of the lagoon dictated the string of isolated settlements developed along its shores. Jonathan Dickinson recorded seeing Ais using speedy two-masted catamarans, and other Glades peoples regularly sailed to Havana within twenty-four hours to conduct trade.[83] The importance of sailboats on the watery route had not changed when Amos Cummings wrote in 1873 that the

> Indian River is a sort of public highway. Not more than fifteen families live upon its banks. Each family owns a winged wagon, or cat-rigged sailboat. . . . There are but few land roads, and all the trade and business are done in these centre-board buggies. Some of the inhabitants are compelled to sail two hundred miles to reach a store or a church. Others go as far for a doctor. The dead are buried in the garden in home-made coffins. There are no schoolhouses within a week's journey. In some cases it takes four days to go to a post office and return. Everything depends upon the wind. People look for the course of the wind the first thing in the morning. "When do you think the wind will shift?" is a common question. Instead of "How's the weather?" you hear, "How's the wind?"[84]

The shallow water of the Indian River made traditional, full-keel sailboats useless on the lagoon or to cross the natural, shifting Mosquito or Indian River inlet, or the occasionally open Jupiter inlet. After considering an assessment of the Indian River, a British surveyor observed in 1772 that a "large schooner with conveniences to make it comfortable is useless. Boats of little draught of water is what is most wanted consequently to make just surveys and give the country a proper inspection a man must not think much of being exposed to all kinds of weather. Sun, wind, and rain he must be proof against and sleeping in an open boat, the sea, beach, or an oyster bank are circumstances he must teach himself to laugh at."[85] Flat-bottomed, shoal-draft working sailboats called "sharpies" were developed in the mid-nineteenth century for the oyster beds of New Haven, Connecticut. Charles Pierce observed the first-known sharpie in the Indian River while he lived at the Jupiter inlet in 1872. Ten years later there were dozens in the Indian River and its southerly neighbor Lake Worth, as New Englanders recognized how well suited the type was to the shallow lagoon. While not an Indian River settler, Commodore Ralph M. Munroe, of Coconut Grove, brought his thirty-foot *Skipperee* to the Indian River, the first of many sharpie designs he would later draw and build for South Florida's thin waters.[86] In 1884 Dr. James A. Henshall published his observations from a series of trips sailing through the Indian River. "Captain [Mills O.] Burnham, of Cape Canaveral Light-house, was over for a few days with his fine sloop *Osceola*. I found that the quality and accommodations of the boats on the Indian River were vastly improved since my visit three years before, and that my prediction in reference to the introduction of the sharpie has been verified. Skippers Hammon, Bowers, Hendrickson, and Richards have now fine boats of this model of from seven to ten tons, which are admirably adapted to these shallow waters."[87]

Instead of a conventional keel, the new Indian River sharpies had centerboards, which could be raised or lowered as needed in shallow water. Emily Lagow Bell recalled that boats built for the lagoon's shallow waters offended the sensibilities of visitors. "Now, we had one noted man and his wife [visit as boarders], who were English to the bone. . . . She was always swearing at the centerboard boats. She said nobody but Americans would have them." After a sail the advantages of the light, shallow-draft boats were evident, and the woman said, "'Let me buy the boat,' but of course we wouldn't part with it."[88]

Because sailboats were both in short supply and in demand, many settlers converted salvaged lifeboats or purchased and converted rowboats. While living at the Jupiter lighthouse across from the Jupiter inlet, Hannibal Pierce (father of Charles) made a sailing rig for the salvaged lifeboat of the wrecked *Victor*, which he later replaced with a superior skiff he found half-buried on the beach.[89] The largest sharpie in the Indian River was the forty-foot *Illinois,* built by U. D. Hendrickson in 1879. Charles Pierce purchased and later sold the *Illinois,* in order to buy the twenty-eight-foot sharpie *Oriole,* which Hubert Bessey built at the Gilbert's Bar House of Refuge near the St. Lucie inlet.[90] Bessey initially built boats to transport his pineapples to market, but later supplemented his duties as keeper of the House of Refuge by operating a boatbuilding company on the site.

With almost no roads in the region, sailboats were the lifelines of the lagoon's tiny population. Doctors completed their rounds by sailing to docks of their patients, and Captain Walter Kitching's *Merchant* plied the waters from 1887 to 1897 as a mobile general goods store. Kitching "ran it up and down the coast before the railroad came through from Cocoa to Jupiter. . . . He would sell dry goods and food and medicine, and he was a notary public and could marry people if they wanted to be married." With no roads in the region, there was nothing but undeveloped flatwood pine forests and swamps behind the houses that lined the lagoon. "So when they were coming in on this big schooner, the sailboat, one of the mates or the sailor on the boat would blow the conch horn. All the residents and the children would run out to the end of their dock so that they could get all the news up and down the coast and buy whatever they needed to last a month, because it took [the *Merchant*] that long to go back and forth, according to the wind."[91] "Folks went out in skiffs and bought whatever they needed from household articles such as needles, to salt. Practically anything could be obtained from these boats, things you wouldn't expect. The men slept on mats at night, moved on to the next place, and next morning dropped anchor for another day's trade."[92]

Sailboats too served as a primary source of recreation in the system, and the central event on the (sparse) social calendar was for many years the Washington's Birthday Regatta held off of the town of Jensen.[93] "You could tell a man many miles before he reached the dock by the cut of his sails or the rig of his boat," recalled one early settler.[94] Indian River settlers became adept at building boats. John Miller, of Eden, built hundreds of rowing, sailing, and steam-powered boats and became so proficient that he was able to build a twenty-four-foot sailboat every thirteen days.[95]

The unreliability of sailing goods to market ensured that the region remained isolated and depopulated, despite its tantalizingly fertile climate. Amos Cummings observed:

> I believe that the Indian River hammocks contain the richest land in the United States. Capt. M. O. Burnham, of Cape Canaveral, has raised sugar cane that will average over two quarts of juice to the stalk. One cane alone produced a gallon, a quart, and a pint of raw syrup. I saw a stalk that had fifty-two joints, averaging four inches to the joint. . . . It produced immense crops for seven years, without manuring or putting a hoe to the ground. But the Captain's nearest neighbor is twelve miles distant, and there is neither doctor, school house, post-office, or church within thirty miles. His only way of reaching them is by a cat-rigged sailboat, and he is entirely dependent upon the caprice of the wind. . . . I went to his house at Cape Canaveral, and his good wife declared that a lady in our party was the only woman who had visited them in four years. The Captain has a wonderful sugar field and a rare orange grove, but there is no way of getting sugar or orange to market.[96]

Because the natural inlets were generally very shallow and unstable, the first civilian steamboat to ply the Indian River was the *Pioneer,* which arrived through the Haulover Canal from the Mosquito Lagoon sometime around 1876. Six years later the first concerted effort to make a profit from a scheduled steamship route along the Indian River came with the *Cinderella.* Upon seeing this new ship for the first time, settler Emily Lagow Bell recalled, "Now every house was astir. It was four in the morning when we saw her bright light. She blew her whistle . . . and the echo sounded from one side of the river to the other. Oh, how light out hearts were. I knew we could ship out turtles to a good advantage—not lose so many."[97] Unfortunately for Indian River residents, the deep draft *Cinderella* left the region within a year, after having run aground

FIGURE 3. Steamship *St. Augustine* in Rockledge, northern Indian River Lagoon, in the late 1880s (Florida State Archives, Florida Photographic Collection, Tallahassee).

regularly. In 1884 the ninety-foot steamship *Indian River* began a successful career traversing the lagoon. Having been designed specifically for the Indian River, it was modeled "somewhat like a New Haven sharpie. Nine miles per hour. Twelve staterooms aggregating 24 berths."[98]

In 1886 the Jacksonville, Tampa and Key West Railroad established the Indian River Steamboat Company to provide access to its Tropical Trunk Line, which terminated in Titusville, in an effort to connect its network to the rest of the lagoon. Within several years the company deployed a growing fleet of steamers named after some of their stops in the far reaches of the lagoon, including the *Rockledge, Santa Lucia, St. Sebastian,* and *St. Augustine.*[99] The 130-foot *Santa Lucia* was the pride of the fleet, and, like the earlier *Indian River,* was built "with exceeding light draft and just suited for the peculiar waters she was built to navigate.

FIGURE 4. The large volume of mail and freight carried by the *St. Augustine* and *St. Sebastian*, built with shoal-draft hulls for the Indian River Steamboat Company, convinced Henry Flagler that there was enough demand in the southern Indian River Lagoon and South Florida to sustain an extension of his Florida East Coast Railroad line. This railroad competition ended the steamship companies, which then allowed the two ships to slowly deteriorate on the banks of the Loxahatchee River (pictured), near the Jupiter inlet (Florida State Archives, Florida Photographic Collection, Tallahassee).

Her captain, Bravo by name, knows his business and is a great favorite along the river."[100] Regular steamship service of the lagoon spurred the U.S. Department of Lighthouses to establish regular navigation markers along the newly dug channel. "There were Beacon Lights on the river for steamboats to run at night. There were lights on each shoal," recalled Charles Gifford, of the central Indian River. "Father filled six lights each night. He filled them every other day and got $10.00 for each light from the Government."[101] An 1891 federal survey of the lagoon noted, "The present facilities for navigation are insufficient. Owing to the slight depth available the traffic must be carried on in vessels of very light draught. To obtain the necessary tonnage they must be broad and of broad beam. . . . Vessels of this character have slight hold on the water and are difficult to manage in the brisk winds which prevail throughout the year in this river, so close to the ocean."[102]

The *Santa Lucia*'s captain, Richard Paddison, started a competing steamship company in the lagoon in 1889. In 1890 the Indian River Steamboat Company sued Paddison's new firm, the East Coast Transportation Company, which had recently begun running its elegant 134-foot steamer *Sweeney* in the northern Indian River, between Rockledge, Titusville, and New Smyrnea. The region's newspapers reflected the nation's emerging antimonopoly populism (this was the same year that the Sherman Antitrust Act was passed) when they urged Indian River growers to support the new East Coast Transportation Company's steamships to ensure that the Indian River Steamboat Company would not have a monopoly. Because their competitor, having prior access, blocked access to the docks in Titusville, the steamers of the East Coast Transportation Company had to dock in distant New Smyrnea to unload freight. In 1891 the Florida Supreme Court ruled that the new East Coast Transportation Company could not be prevented from use of the docks. The smaller company responded to this victory by announcing an expansion of service to the whole length of the lagoon to take advantage of the growing pineapple business along the St. Lucie Estuary and lower Indian River.[103]

The first company to significantly dredge the Indian River was the Florida Coast Line Canal and Transportation Company, incorporated in 1881. George Miles became connected with the new Florida canal company (having previously been involved in a company that hoped to dig the Cape Cod Canal), whose state charter required the company to dig a channel fifty feet wide and five feet deep running the length of the shallow waters of the Indian River. In exchange for creating a 134-mile canal from Haulover Canal to Jupiter, the company would receive 345,972 acres of valuable land from the state Internal Improvement Fund, which was nearly the only asset available to the cash-strapped state government.[104]

In 1896 Miles formed a new company, the Indian River and Bay Biscayne Navigation Company, to take advantage of the mostly opened waterway recently built by his other venture, the Florida Coast Line Canal and Transportation Company. Rather than design new ships, Miles purchased the briefly abandoned steamboats *St. Sebastian* and *St. Augustine* from the recently bankrupted Indian River Steamboat Company. The purpose-built shallow-draft sharpie hulls were used to establish a significant link between Miami and the North in 1896, the same year that Standard Oil magnate Henry Flagler brought his Florida East Coast Railroad to the city. Flagler's railroad would ultimately fundamentally transform the society, politics, and economy of Florida's east coast. Although none of the magnificent hotels built by Flagler were in the Indian River Lagoon, thousands of winter tourists were introduced to the lagoon as they traveled its entire length. Ice plants, citrus-packing plants, and cities sprung up along the shores of the Indian River once the Florida East Coast Railroad offered easy access to northern consumers. Despite the might of Flagler's railroad, it was not immediately clear that the (brief) era of steamship dominance was over. For several years the competition between the railroad and new steamship company was intense. The new steamship route inside the lagoon was viewed by Indian River growers and farmers as "a deliverer from the clutches of a monopoly," and the Indian River growers promised "their strong support as long as we give them a fair service." "The new company's steamer had even been beating the new Flagler railway by as much as twenty-four to forty-eight hours in transporting crops to New York markets, by using the Jacksonville, Tampa and Key West railway. If the *St. Augustine* was delayed for any reason, the Jacksonville, Tampa Railway even ran a special train to ship the pineapple crop."[105]

A single, reliably deep waterway running the length of Florida's east coast was completed when the Florida Coast Line and Transportation Company finished cutting a canal between Jupiter and Lake Worth. This new link allowed the Indian River and Bay Biscayne Navigation Company to offer cheaper freight rates to South Florida, which the U.S. Army took advantage of to transport war goods en route to the Spanish-American War. In May 1898 the steamboat company charged $2,500 ($6,500 less than the west coast's new competing line built by Henry

Plant) for the *St. Sebastian* to carry a forty-ton mortar from the rail station in Titusville through the Indian River to Key West.[106]

The age of the palatial steamers on the Indian River was over within twenty years. In December 1911 George Miles started another short-lived steamship company, the Florida Inland Coastal Navigation Company. But the well-established competing passenger service afforded by the Florida East Coast Railroad (which was about to reach Key West) ensured that business was too lackluster to ultimately support the company's four enormous, aging steamers.

In the first decade of the twentieth century, small gas engines began to appear in the Indian River, and the rigs of many sailboats were removed to convert to the new, faster technology. Gas-powered boats and ships did not carry significant freight from the region, as the industry by that time had become inextricably reliant on the rail line. Gas-powered boats did, however, immediately increase the hauls of local fishermen, and hastened overfishing in the lagoon.

By the time the Indian River had become famous for its citrus in the early twentieth century, the region's Anglo settlers had several decades of experience experimenting with all sorts of northern, southern, and tropical agriculture in the region's sandy soil and humid climate. Armed Occupation Act claimant Mills O. Burnham first introduced pineapples to the region in the 1840s when he planted a small number alongside subsistence citrus and vegetable plots. Upon arriving in the region, Thomas E. Richards, of New Jersey, sailed across the lagoon and met a hermit called "Old Cuba," who had fled the Caribbean island to live in isolation on the lower Indian River. In broken English, Old Cuba instructed Richards how he had planted a small pineapple plot in Hutchinson Island's inhospitable hammock.[107] The pineapple (touted as "king of the bromeliads") became the backbone of the Gilded Age Indian River economy only after Thomas E. Richards successfully introduced the sweet fruit in his new homestead of Eden. Richard's narrow field running along the Atlantic Ridge, just north of modern-day Jensen Beach, was the first commercial pineapple operation in the United States.[108]

Encouraged by the economic potential of this exotic plant, Richards enlisted the help of a group of a small band of Seminoles to clear his homestead. Richards sailed to Key Largo (which had in turn imported them from Cuba) and returned with 43,000 pineapple slips. The 40,000 slips planted on Hutchinson island fared poorly, but the 3,000 Richards planted in his fields on the western shore thrived.[109] The sloping eastern face of the Atlantic Ridge, stretching to Richard's long dock (equipped with a sail-powered rail cart), was an ideal environment in which to grow the fruit. "Pineapples grow best in sandy fields that are well drained. The fields are plowed and furrowed and suckers or slips are planted in rows 20"–30" apart. Planting is done in July, August and September. They flower in midwinter and in the late spring or early summer harvesting begins. The fruit is put in baskets very carefully so it won't get bruised and spoil."[110]

The pineapples grown at Eden were sailed by Richards to Titusville, then transported overland to the St. Johns River, where they traveled by steamer to Jacksonville. Even working among the sharp plants was a relief to young Lucy Richards, who spent most days cooking on an outside stove or washing laundry in the freshwater lagoon. "I'm helping trim the slips. It tears up one's hands, and I don't like the scorpions and other critters that are among the plants, but anything for a change."[111] Two years after clearing his land, Richards built a mill and began to grind pineapple juice from which he made and bottled "Pinapin," a popular pineapple "wine" and digestive cure.[112] Each two-to-four-foot-high plant produced a single fruit, and "great care is requisite in its cultivation to produce fruit that is delicate and richly flavored. Without such care it is insipid and fibrous." The pulpy juice was fermented, bottled, and warmly praised by the small number of other settlers in the region.[113]

The reputation of the Indian River pineapple-laden Eden built by Richards spread far, thanks to the ceaseless boosterism by the family, who built a considerable fortune in the process.[114] In addition to forming the Indian River and Lake Worth Pineapple Growers Association in 1892, Richards wrote dozens of letters to local and northern newspapers

FIGURE 5. Indian River Lagoon pineapple field, 1909. A house atop the Atlantic Ridge is visible in the distance (Florida State Archives, Florida Photographic Collection, Tallahassee).

extolling the economic possibilities of the Indian River. "It beats all how fast the country is settling up, and with such nice people. It is because of the pineapple business. [We write] articles and they are published in the papers, copied from one to another, and the boarders we have go away and talk about us and our place and our work."[115]

The establishment of the Indian River Steamboat Company was a considerable improvement over the slow and unreliable method of individual growers sailing their crop to Titusville. "We have [brought our crops to market] to much better advantage than we have in former years, thanks to the Indian River Steamboat Company and the RR who have given us good and reasonable rates. . . . We are certainly encouraged now with steam, for there is no satisfaction in the sailboat shipping perishable goods," wrote Richards in a letter published in the Titusville-based *Florida Star*.

> But with steamers one can send one crate or one hundred and you know just when they will go. We have a crate now that suits our pines first-rate, and will until we learn to grow them larger, which we will shortly. We do not know it all yet, but we are learning very fast. We cannot do our work as they do it at the Keys or Bahama Islands. We have had to work out our own way, and it has been with fear and trembling.[116]

In addition to finding themselves engaged in growing and trading tropical fruits, the effects of tropical politics came to pineapple growers of the Indian River. The Indian River settlers looked forward to the expected benefits of any future Caribbean conflict, being both influenced by the era's jingoism and located on an obvious water route to any future war with Spain in Cuba.[117] Soon after the brief 1898 war it became apparent that the primary effect of the clash on the Indian River would be increased competition from Cuban pineapples, which enjoyed new access to American markets and very low freight rates from the Florida East Coast Railroad. This new competition coincided with a voracious pineapple fungus that rapidly spread among the genetically homogenous planted fields.[118] Henry Edwin Sewall covered his tiny peninsula in the lower Indian River with pineapple fields and claimed that the region's pineapple growers paid 74.5 cents to ship a crate of pineapples to New York while Cuban pineapple growers were charged only 39.5 cents.[119] At its peak, the Indian River pineapple industry produced one million boxes of product annually and dominated culture and the economy from Stuart in the south to Merritt Island in the north.[120] "The pineapples hide the earth on the ridge next to the river for miles and miles with their prickly green leaves. In places the plants are under slatted sheds acres in extent."[121] A brutal freeze in February 1910 ensured that the Indian River pineapple industry would never recover from its peak of several years earlier, although the industry continued. The cry for protective measures to guard against the menace of competition from Cuban fruit would continue to resound from the era's growers and populist politicians for several decades.[122]

The nearly frost-free sultry climate of the southern Indian River was the region's primary draw to potential growers and simultaneously laid the groundwork for future agricultural failure. Growers often enjoyed between five and ten years of mild winters only to find their crops ruined by a single hard frost. Judging rightly when to ship crops north each year to best take advantage of the southern Indian River's winter growing season was the subject of much discussion. The introduction of regular steamboat service in the region made this process much easier by largely removing the unpredictabilities of sailing. "It is very probable there will be a good many tomatoes grown next winter," wrote Thomas Richards. "For now we know that they can be got to market; and as we know we can grow them, there will be a good many planted. We want to grow all we can to help build up the steamboat line, and if there is plenty of freight for the boat, or more than one boat can handle, why the company will put on more."[123]

The Mighty Indian River Orange

So valuable was the reputation of the Indian River orange that in 1930 the Federal Trade Commission ordered growers from other regions to stop labeling their fruit "Indian River." Native to East Asia, the first oranges in the region were planted in small numbers by Spanish settlers. Indigenous and Seminole Indians later spread the golden spheres in far-flung clusters to provide food while traveling through the area. Planter Thomas Dummitt moved from Barbados to establish a sugar colony manned by at least 100 slaves in North Florida's Tomoka River region in 1824, one of the last attempts to create a sugar slave colony modeled after those in the Caribbean. It was from here that Thomas's son Douglas visited the Indian River and purchased property on Merritt Island, between the Banana and Indian River Lagoon proper. The roots of the famous Indian River citriculture are found in Douglas Dummitt's hybridization of the remaining gnarled orange stock left from Andrew Turnbull's British-era groves in the northern Indian River with sour orange buds that he purchased at Orange Mills, near Palatka. Turnbull's New Smyrnea settlement, in turn, had propagated sour orange groves that had been established by generations of Spanish colonists. The cold weather–moderating effects of being situated between the twin estuaries allowed Dummitt's grove to survive the first major freeze (1835) since the advent of Indian River agriculture, which wiped out the region's infant industry. Suddenly finding himself the owner of the area's only oranges, Dummitt used his oranges to rebuild the tiny industry and lived to see his fruit hailed as the world's finest in the markets of New York as well as by the second wave of Indian River Anglo settlers, who were the first to export the fruit in large quantities.[124]

"The 'orange fever' did not fully break out until the fall of 1858, but the few who were stricken had it bad, and my comrade and I were among the early victims. Reports of enormous returns from small investments in orange groves reached us from time to time, and fired out ambition to 'go and do likewise,'" wrote settler Andrew Canova in the wake of Dummitt's success. Canova continued:

> We cleared about an acre in the hammock, where the soil was blackest and deepest, and grubbed leisurely along, until we had

> prepared ground for about two dozen trees. We found a wild grove not far away, and transported them to where we thought they would do the most good. But when the leaves began to have the rich, golden hue which the ripe fruit possesses, and speedily turned into so many dry, withered sticks, we gave up, in despair of ever making an orange grove.[125]

The orange balls became so entwined with the culture and economy of the Indian River that they sometimes played a role in the courting process. Emily Lagow Bell recounted that her future husband, James Bell, "came out and brought me out a fine box of choice fruit—100 of golden beauties. Say, my heart beat three times too fast, so I thanked him so much for them." "Of all the fruits, we declare the orange *queen*," wrote one enthusiastic Massachusetts observer. "Its culture may not only be considered a *fine art*, but as a *Divine art*."[126]

Northern journalist Amos Cummings described the aged Dummitt as lazy, a trait he attributed to the lagoon's heat and the fact that its fertile climate provided ample food with little effort. "The Captain never looks for a purchaser (for his oranges). The purchaser must look for the Captain. . . . 'Dummitt works for no man—not even himself,' is a common saying on the river."[127] Cummings described the pattern of laying out an orange grove emulated by Gilded Age homesteaders:

> The groves are about a mile long and a quarter of a mile wide. The trees are about twenty-five feet apart. The ground beneath them is kept entirely free from any vegetation. . . . The climate and the soil is such that Capt. Dummitt [*sic*] says that he has raised oranges every month in the year. The Captain's black razor-backed hogs appeared to have a good time of it, for they roamed about the grove fattening upon the ripe oranges as they fell from the trees.[128]

After the Civil War, Dummitt's groves followed the trend of many southern plantations, and he turned to cultivating and harvesting his yield by sharecropping. In contrast, however, Dummitt's will allocated the small plots to each of his sharecroppers, who had once worked the same ground while enslaved.[129] In 1873 Cummings wrote: "Dummitt's Grove has produced 600,000 oranges this season. He says he will raise a million next year. Three or four years ago the trees were nearly destroyed by insects, but they have fully recovered and look finer than ever. This grove is celebrated throughout the State. It is looked upon as a kind of Mecca by the orange producers of Florida." Reflecting the growing northern population and economic intrusion in the Reconstruction, Cummings claimed, "in the hands of a shrewd Yankee possessed of Dummitt's experience," the grove "would turn in an income of from $50,000 to $70,000 a year."[130]

It was not until the early twentieth century that the bulk of the region's citrus industry moved from Cape Canaveral to the central lagoon, away from the more common frosts in the Indian River's northern, temperate climate. The introduction of regular steam and later rail service was a boon to the region's agriculture, especially oranges.

With the exception of the nearby Timucuan peoples, the first organized agriculture in the region were the fruits planted in Turnbull's New Smyrnea colony, other than small-scale gardens that surrounded the Indian River's fleeting Spanish settlements. Many early Indians, Spaniards, and Anglo residents of the lower Indian River all learned to process the indigenous coontie plant, from which a starchy flour was made.[131] The mildly successful efforts of the Armed Occupation Act settlers failed to successfully import significant southern labor systems, but did determine which fruits could be cultivated on the shores of the lagoon system. Although pineapples and oranges were by far the most successful of the Indian River's agricultural experiments, bananas, coconuts, guavas, mangoes, and sugarcane were also successfully transplanted to the Indian River's sandy soils, most initially for family subsistence farming, and, with the advent of reliable steam and rail transportation, as a commercial enterprise. Captain Mills O. Burnham named the lagoon on the other side of Merritt's Island the "Banana River" after the exotic bananas he found when exploring what had previously been assumed to be an untouched area.

Glowing accounts of a prolific and fertile lagoon regularly appeared in northern newspapers, such as this exchange between the writer and an Indian River farmer:

> "[You use] no manure at all?"
> "No, none whatever. We never use any. The soil is rich enough without it."
> "What is garden land worth . . . ?"
> "About $1,000 an acre," he replied. "The land there is all gardens."[132]

The soil was not as productive as was assumed by many settlers, and hardwood ashes were needed to increase yields.[133] Amos Cummings was disappointed to find that reports of the region's productivity were grossly exaggerated.

> The truth is that no farmer in the enjoyment of good health has any business in the Land of Flowers. A farmer in poor health can barely earn a living here, and that is all. Half of the land is composed of shells and sand. Sometimes you will strike what seems to be a rich black muck, but give it a kick with the toe of your boot, and the inevitable sand will appear. The hammocks which dot the immense sandy scrub like oases in a desert are unusually rich, but neither grain nor hay can be raised upon them. . . . I have seen a dozen farmers from Wisconsin, Iowa, and Michigan here this winter, but I have not seen one who has located a farm. The first look at the soil frightens them.[134]

"John's Island . . . was rich and being nearly free from frosts was a mecca for vegetable growing farmers," recalled a resident of the narrows located between Vero Beach and Sebastian. "The vegetables were shipped by boat until the railroad came, and then were brought over to the railroad by boat to be shipped. This grew to be quite a chore and gradually was abandoned."[135] Peaches were unsuccessful, as was honey (due to the lagoon's common beach-roaming black bears), but as early as 1844

Caleb Brayton reported that his pineapples "look better and bear larger fruit than any in the West Indies."[136]

An indication of the primacy of citrus and pineapples is found in an 1882 federal survey of the region that reported that 2,000,000 oranges and 50,000 pineapples were shipped the previous year, dwarfing the harvest of bananas (500 bunches), sugar (400 barrels), and early vegetables (1,000 crates—mostly tomatoes). Only eight years later the number of pineapples shipped had exploded to an estimated 691,250, while crates of oranges jumped from 14,000 to nearly 70,000.[137] By 1906 the amount of citrus (overwhelmingly oranges) had reached 1,000,000 crates. So powerful was the allure of the name "Indian River" in the mind of orange-buying northerners that growers along the Mosquito Lagoon (and the Hillsboro River, which flows into it) successfully petitioned the state government in 1901 to officially rename their waters "Indian River North."[138]

In the days when only sailboats plied the lagoon's waters, Cummings dismissed the feasibility of exploiting the Indian River's riches. "Both Irish and sweet potatoes thrive well in winter, but it would cost a fortune to get them to New York. Peas, beans, cauliflowers, asparagus, turnips, beets, radishes, cabbages, strawberries, and innumerable other vegetables ripen along the Indian River in December, January, and February, but they might as well ripen in the moon so far as market is concerned."[139] The dredging of the Indian River and steamships and railroads made it possible to reliably bring the region's goods to market, but the Florida East Coast Railroad's monopoly allowed it to charge high freight rates. It was claimed that the railroad's monopoly allowed it to charge $4.13 to ship an item from Jacksonville to the Indian River settlement of Jensen, while it charged only $1.02 to ship the same goods from New York to Jacksonville. Farmers in the Midwest became politicized after they voiced similar complaints about the abusive practices of the railroads, which led to the Grange and Populist movements. The Army Corps of Engineers rejected the appeals of residents of the lower Indian River to deepen the St. Lucie inlet (in hopes of opening a new route for freight), which they themselves had dug in 1892.[140]

A brutal freeze in 1894–95 betrayed the myth of the (almost) frost-free Indian River. Nearly the entire harvest of settlers in the northern and central Indian River was lost, but the crops of the subtropical southern Indian River fared (a bit) better. Recognizing the need to build up demand for its trains, the Florida East Coast Railroad distributed fertilizer and seed to the region's farmers.[141] Smaller freezes in 1897 and 1898 failed to end the image of the Indian River as an agricultural mecca.

Other enterprises enjoyed some success in the Indian River, most notably oysters, which were common in the central and northern Indian River but had an uneven presence in the lower lagoon. Because they require an environment with salinity between two and twenty-five parts per thousand, oysters did not exist in the lower Indian River in and around the St. Lucie Estuary for most of the nineteenth century, because the lack of open inlets ensured that it was thoroughly freshwater at the time. The region hosted freshwater manatee grasses, which were killed with the opening of the St. Lucie inlet in 1892, allowing for the formation of substantial oyster beds. These beds were killed in the years following the completion of the Okeechobee waterway in 1923, which flooded the system with freshwater.[142] The large oyster mounds in both the lower and northern Indian River are remnants of eras when inlets were open in the regions. "If the winter visitors continue to flock to the region and eat oyster[s] freely, in the course of time the vicinity of the resorts will become a mountainous country (from the oyster shells)," quipped a nineteenth-century visitor.[143] An oyster cannery was established in Fort Pierce, which was the southernmost extent of the oyster beds observed in an 1897 federal survey of the lagoon system.[144]

Instead of appropriating wholesale the fishing technologies employed by the region's indigenous people, the first and second waves of Anglo settlers in the region slowly developed avenues of exploiting the riches of the vast and isolated ecosystem. Gilded Age homesteaders in the Indian River were part of a larger wave that established a pattern of settlement that would build an environment dedicated to leisure, fishing, and orange blossoms, an image that they had created. Despite agricultural experimentation, commercial fishing, and importing and refining sailing technology to suit the lagoon's demanding conditions, these settlers were for two generations simply too small in number to significantly alter the system itself. These isolated settlers, however, found themselves deeply changed by the environment around them.

4

Atlantic Gateway to the Gulf of Mexico, 1881–1941

In 1844 a long, sweaty day of digging a new inlet was followed by a terrifying evening for the resting workers.

> "Life or death! Life or death!" [shouted the first digger to awake on the beach], with all his strength, as he snatched up a spade and ran from tent to tent. Striking each with the blade of the spade as he ran, and startling every sleeper from his repose. . . . Life or death, men! The ditch is cut through from river to sea, and you have but an instant to save your lives! Up all! Out! Out!" All were out, and all were up and in safe position, very quickly—but not in time to save two of the tents, beneath which the undermined sand sank almost while their terrified tenants were scrambling from them. The two tents were quickly engulfed by the river torrent and swept to where freshwater and saltwater waves were battling victory.[1]

Because their tents were pitched next to the tiny cut they had just dug, the "imminent peril of some of the sleepers was increasing each instant,"[2] and the men were vulnerable to falling into the rapidly growing cut as the sand beneath them washed away. Such was the dramatic scene of the violent reaction of the lagoon's hydrological forces to attempts of lower Indian River settlers to dig an inlet in 1844. Although the Gilded Age second wave of Anglo settlement in the Indian River was the first time that the Indian River was subject to major human-made change, the small population of settlers who followed 1842's Armed Occupation Act also took (modest) steps to create a built environment. The inconvenience of sailing south to Jupiter or north to the Indian River inlet (nearly twenty miles each way) from his newly established plantation just south of the St. Lucie Estuary prompted William Peck to organize a party to dig a cut through the narrow barrier island adjacent to his claim. Peck's account of opening the short-lived inlet is a useful window into the difficulties faced by the isolated settlers in the years immediately following the Second Seminole War. After a long day of digging, Peck and the men went to sleep on the beach because "all were very weary for all had hoped to complete the affair before sunset that they might behold the expected rush of opposing waters by daylight, and had labored most industriously. All knew that the scene would be grand, and desired to see its beginning in full light of the sun." Because the primary method of water circulation in the lagoon was the wind (except in areas in close proximity to inlets), Peck feared that a change in wind would increase the lagoon's water level and flood sand into the nearly complete cut. "Were the wind to change, and blow from the west or northwest, the water of the river would certainly rise, sweep aside the sand heap in the river mouth of the ditch, plunge into the ditch and deepen and widen it to the peril of all who might be sleeping near the edge of the excavation." The enslaved men who were tasked with keeping watch to announce a change in the wind fell asleep. As feared, a shift in the wind increased the lagoon level, and "the river waves began to lap over it into the ditch and to flow seaward with swiftly increasing force and volume."[3]

The settlers successfully sailed through the new inlet until the southward movement of sand created a small ebb tidal delta, which filled it after several years. Not long after, nearly all of this first wave of Anglo settlers abandoned their claims in the wake of the 1849 bloodshed at the Indian River colony recounted by Caleb Brayton. In that incident several rogue Seminole young men attacked Anglo settlers in the Indian River and the Peace River region, near the west coast of the peninsula. The unstable nature of the hydrologic system was evident when the lagoon's water had reverted to being fresh due to lack of ocean water influx and freshwater infusion from the nearby St. Lucie Estuary by the time the second wave of settlers arrived in the years following 1862's Homestead Act.

After playing leading roles in establishing the peninsula's citrus and tourism industries, Gilded Age and Progressive-era Indian River settlers were among the first to construct a built environment marked by dredging and filling that would define much of the twentieth-century Sunshine State. Even in an era of unprecedented national ecological change (the colossal Los Angeles Aqueduct and northern California's Hetch Hetchy Dam are examples of the period's other ambitious Progressive-era projects), the Indian River was integrated into a larger human-made transformation that forever changed the face of the southern peninsula (chiefly the many attempts to drain the nearby Everglades). By 1890 the lagoon had a population that was large enough (over 3,400) and, more important, armed with technology and the mindset to implement what would become the first of three significant stages of major human-made change in the Indian River system.[4] Within one generation of the dredging of the Intracoastal Waterway and digging of the St. Lucie inlet, the lower Indian River experienced dramatic salinity variation after tremendous saltwater infusion following the 1892 new St. Lucie inlet (the first stage), and then unprecedented land-based freshwater discharge through the newly dug 1920s St. Lucie canal (the second stage), which became part of a post–World War II movement that made the Indian River system the recipient of drainage from Central Florida's Kissimmee valley and Lake Okeechobee (the third stage). These major human-made changes to the Indian River's physiography included the creation of inlets at St. Lucie, Fort Pierce, Sebastian, and Canaveral; the construction of hundreds of miles of mosquito impoundments; the expansion and stabilization of the Jupiter inlet; and the closing of the natural Indian River inlet. Additionally, the Indian River's naturally small watershed expanded greatly, and the narrow, shallow lagoon received a tremendous infusion of freshwater from extensive channelization designed to drain the wetlands (and provide irrigation to the newly dry areas) that had been previously firmly separated from the Indian River system by the Atlantic Ridge. Within two generations the Indian River system would become connected with both the St. Johns River and Lake Okeechobee through a complex, heavily managed network of canals, locks, and pumps.

The Indian River's Ais peoples constructed a causeway in the Indian River, which is consistent with the actions of other groups within the Glades tradition, such as the Calusa, who dug networks of canals in the Pine Island area of Florida's southwest coast. Although Amerindians and Anglos both engaged in environmental manipulation, the small-scale Native canals built to accommodate canoes were qualitatively different from massive American projects that fundamentally altered the structure of the system.[5] Because the natural state of the Indian River is one of flux in which migrating barrier islands enclose a body of water that regularly transitioned from fresh to salt, it is difficult to identify precisely which inlets were open at specific times or what flora and fauna thrived or suffered at a specific historical point. While Native cultures responded to lagoon instability by moving villages with seasonal rhythms, later Americans battled the forces of wind and sea in an effort to make the Indian River's shorelines stay in place.

The Second Seminole War brought hundreds of American soldiers through the lagoon, and convinced many that the watery highways were insufficient for the new American territory. "The difficulties which I experienced when directing the operations against the Seminoles in the campaign of 1837–38 in supplying the division of the Army operating south of the Haulover," wrote Quartermaster General Thomas Jessup, "enable me to speak with positive certainty as to the necessity of improving the inland communications from St. Augustine to Key Biscayne."[6]

Spurred by pleas such as Jessup's, on June 15, 1844, Congress allocated $1,500 to the U.S. Army Corps of Engineers for surveyor Lieutenant J. E. Blake to assess the narrow isthmus (known as the "Haulover") that separated the Mosquito and Indian River Lagoons. In 1852 there was an additional $5,000 appropriation for cutting a canal at the location for "boats carrying supplies to the United States troops stationed at various points on the east coast of Florida."[7] Because it had to dig through the coquina rock underlying much of the Indian River, the tiny cut was only two feet deep and eight feet wide. The Mosquito (later called Ponce de Leon) inlet was only thirty-two miles from the canal, while the northern Indian River proper has no inlets closer than the central Indian River's Indian River inlet, near Fort Pierce, a distance of some ninety miles. Heavy summer rains raised the water level (and dramatically decreased the salinity) of the Indian River Lagoon, while the inlet drained rainwaters from the Mosquito Lagoon, maintaining the lower water level. Combined with the winds that are the Indian River's primary cause of water circulation, the difference in water level was at times as much as two feet, creating a current for months at a time that prevented passage from the Mosquito Lagoon to the Indian River. This problem led the surveyor to suggest one of the first examples of the massive hydrological system manipulation that would mark the system in the mid-twentieth century. "For relief . . . it would be better to open a cut from the end of Banana river to the ocean . . . and allow the water to escape."[8] Improvements to the canal did not come until 1891, despite an earlier federal survey that recommended improving the canal to a depth of four and a half feet and sixty feet wide because the region's growing citriculture, consisting of 240 groves, was forced to sail its oranges to Titusville, then transport them overland to Lake Poinsett, then down the St. Johns River to Jacksonville aboard a steamer. It was observed that the Indian River settlers at this time "are compelled to employ all their available capital in rendering their lands productive, and have little to spare in establishing routes of communication."[9] Ambitious plans to eliminate the need for the Haulover Canal by building a fourteen-mile canal to connect the Indian River with inland Lake Harney on the St. Johns River were first made in the 1850s and considered again in 1909, in 1946, and in the 1960s to complement the Cross Florida Barge Canal planned to the north.[10] Reconstruction-era Republican politician William Gleason promoted a similar scheme to make a connection between the water bodies the centerpiece of his new central Indian River settlement of Eau Gallie, via Elbow Creek and Lake Washington, built by his Southern Inland Navigation and Improvement Company. After constructing a single building to house an agricultural college, Gleason's planned Indian River city and canal were never constructed, victims of the loss of power experienced by Gleason's Republicans at the end of Reconstruction.[11]

While the light dugout canoes of the Indian River's pre-Columbian peoples were generally sufficiently portable to haul from one body of water to another, proposals to connect the various rivers, lagoons, and estuaries that twist and flow along the east coast of Florida into one protected inland route existed as long as there have been written records of the region. An 1861 survey of the area recorded that there only existed a channel of "barely three feet water, leading to Fort Pierce and Fort Capron, established during the Indian Wars."[12] William Gleason "had a project in his head to connect the whole series of internal rivers along the coast with Biscayne Bay."[13] So shallow was the bottleneck between the Mosquito and Indian River Lagoons that a schooner was built in 1876 for the purpose of sailing freight up and down the Indian River, but "in order to pass through the canal at the haulover, [small skiffs had to] be stationed there to relieve her freight and convey it through the canal to the other side, where it [was] restored to the schooner after she passe[d] through."[14]

"Florida is more highly favored by nature for a system of canals and inland navigation than any other state, both by climate and the natural topography of the country," wrote Gleason in 1877. Gleason's unfulfilled grandiose (and corrupt) plans included receiving vast stretches of land in exchange for digging seven drainage canals in the region, including two to connect the west coast's Caloosahatchee River with Lake Okeechobee and another between the lake and the St. Lucie Estuary (this canal was eventually completed in 1923). "Indian River and the streams lying adjacent to the eastern coast and flowing into the Atlantic, are mere inland waters which should be connected with the harbors of Fernandina and Key West," wrote Gleason. "In fact, a general system of canals should be inaugurated for the improvement and development of the state." Gleason portrayed his plans for a unified inland water route through the peninsula with populist zeal: "Water communication has the advantages of not being controlled by a monopoly, as railroads are, and freights by water are always cheaper per mile than by railroad." Gleason formulated his elaborate plan for an inland waterway because he was convinced that the inlets of Florida's east coast would always be too unstable to support regular shipping. At the time of his writing, there had been no successful human-made inlet created along Florida's east coast. Wrote Gleason:

> The bars at the mouth of the St. John's and at the entrance to St. Augustine and New Smyrnea, and the other inlets along the Atlantic coast, are ever shifting and changing, and there is no possibility of ever making any permanent improvement in the entrance of these harbors. The bars are not formed from the debris which flows down from the interior, but from the ocean sands, which are thrown upon the coast by heavy northeast gales, together with the polar current which washes the entire Atlantic coast, consequently the jetty system, which has been adopted for the improvement of the Danube and Mississippi rivers cannot be applied successfully to the improvement of the harbors upon this coast. No system of engineering can be adopted to overcome the force of the northeast gales, and prevent the outlet of the channels from being filled with the ocean sands.[15]

Gleason's plan amounted to little, but following soon, in 1882, was the Florida Coast Line Canal and Transportation Company, which began dredging what would become a continuous waterway from Jacksonville to Miami, a distance of some 340 miles. Although the canal would be plagued by delays and financial troubles, the company's 1882 prospectus exuded confidence in the ease with which it expected to construct the route. The company boasted that its dredge "will easily attack" the formidable coquina rock that separated the Indian River and Lake Worth. The firm also speculated that dredging through the turtle grass beds of the shallow sections of the Indian River "can be rapidly and cheaply done" and (in an effort to contrast its project from the era's notorious corrupt public works schemes and boondoggles) promised to exercise the utmost efficiency by ensuring that every dollar raised "will be economically expended in cutting the canal, improving the existing channels, and building the necessary dredges and two flat bottom stern wheel steamers of light draft." Upon completion of this reliable watery route, the company boasted that "a large emigration will flow into Southern Florida . . . to take advantage of the equable climate, and the fertile lands with a view of producing oranges, lemons, pine-apples, cocoa-nuts, and other tropical fruits for the winter and early spring markets of the north." The company anticipated no reason that an Indian River conveniently connected with other regions "should not compete with the Bermuda and Bahama Islands in the early vegetable trade." Steamships loaded with tourists would soon flood the lagoon and Lake Worth and Biscayne Bay because this was "the only portion of the United States not affected by frosts, and purely tropical in its characteristics, the climate being similar to that of the West Indies."[16]

Rather than being "easily attacked," the alternately muddy, sandy, and rocky bottom of the shallow Indian River sub-basins required the new dredging company to abandon its original simple bucket-type dredges and adopt more costly clamshell, dipper, and suction dredges.[17] Although the company exhausted its initial capital within two years (after dredging only twenty miles, all still within the St. Augustine area), it still anticipated an easy task ahead after securing investment from a group of New England entrepreneurs, who formed the Boston and Florida Atlantic Coast Land Company to sell the 100,000 acres they received from the state in exchange for their investment in the beleaguered canal company. By the spring of 1889 the company had managed to excavate almost one million cubic yards of sand, mud, rock, marsh, and shell between St. Augustine and the Jupiter inlet, although large sections remained prohibitively shallow. The company anticipated that oceanic exchange currents from future inlets along the route of its canal would keep the channel free from "rank vegetation, grasses and other freshwater plants."[18]

"Some company or other is trying to make a canal along the entire east coast of Florida," wrote a dismissive *New York Times* correspondent in 1889. He presciently observed: "Of course, the Indian River covers the greater part of the route, and here they only have to dredge. I took pains to learn nothing whatever about the company, for if a man once begins to get on the track of the endless Florida improvement companies he is forever lost and mixed up." The only way this company can complete the canal is with a government subsidy, which "strikes me this would be a first rate way of relieving the bursting treasury to dig a canal through the pine woods parallel with the Atlantic ocean and five miles from it!" scoffed the paper's reporter. The only expensive boondoggle more useless than this would be "that Florida scheme of building a railway from one key to another, connecting Key West to the mainland," which would "be of no earthly use to anybody but to Cubans who make cigars at Key West."[19]

The government subsidy anticipated by the *Times* reporter arrived in 1891 when the federal government assumed responsibility for maintaining the Indian River section of the new canal-within-a-lagoon. In exchange for public maintenance, the canal company removed the chains that it had installed across several points of the lagoon in order to collect tolls from passing boats.[20]

By the time the private corporation stopped operations in 1912, the waterway had been completed, and the company had received over one million acres of choice waterfront land along the east coast of Florida, at a rate of 3,840 acres per dredged mile; 345,972 of those acres were awarded in 1890 in exchange for dredging the Indian River from the Haulover Canal to Jupiter inlet. The newly completed route was not considered to be sufficiently reliable to meet the shipping needs of the growing population of the Indian River, Lake Worth, and Biscayne Bay. An 1891 proposal to build a pier into the Atlantic capable of receiving large oceangoing freighters at Cape Canaveral, connected to the Indian River system by a short railroad, was met with alarm in Jacksonville, which stood to lose the profits gained from the Indian River freight that passed through en route to northern markets. The *Jacksonville Tribune* thundered, "This Indian River country is rich and productive, and is rapidly becoming more so. Its trade, naturally, come[s] to and through Jacksonville; but here is a desire intimated to divert that trade." The newspaper argued that the only solution to ensure that Jacksonville remained along the most efficient route for the produce of the east coast of the central and southern peninsula was for the city of Jacksonville to revive the failed plan of William Gleason and support the construction of a new canal to connect the Indian River with the St. Johns River. "The plan is feasible, the distance is short and the amount of capital required would be very small when compared to the great benefit it would do to the Indian River country and to the future prosperity to our city."[21] The unfeasible, long, and prohibitively expensive canal never materialized. The negative ecological effects of diverting freshwater from the St. Johns to the northern Indian River, many miles from an inlet, would have been considerable.

In 1926 the Army Corps of Engineers released an enormous survey of the Florida east coast waterway network and recommended that the federal government assume ownership of the entire system in response to the decade's land boom, which had caused a "great increase in population and the extensive building operations have placed this section of the state in a position where it is badly handicapped for transportation facilities." The report also portrayed the Florida canal as an important part of the larger inland water route running along the east coast of the United States, and called for increasing the size of the canal through the Indian River to seventy-five feet wide by eight feet deep.[22] Before the federal government would assume responsibility for the new, enormous canal (much deeper and wider than any previously approved by the Florida state legislature), the communities along the canal route were required to provide rights-of-way and locations to deposit dredged sand and dirt for the federal government. In response, the Florida legislature created the Florida Inland Navigation District (FIND) the next year. FIND purchased the canal from the Florida Coast Line Canal and Transportation Company for $776,266 and transferred ownership to the federal government in 1929.[23] The next year Congress authorized funding for the Florida canal to be widened to 100 feet. By the end of the 1930s the enlarged new canal had been initially constructed, and regular maintenance to prevent shoaling over much of its length began. The sandy bottom of the Indian River, dredged to enlarge the canal, went directly onto salt marshes, submerged sea grass beds, and mangroves to form the system's first spoil islands.[24]

Just as the east coast canal was dug to accommodate freight-hauling ships along a protected inland route to northern markets, so inlets were created in the lower Indian River to provide an offshore route for the region's produce to reach buyers. The Indian River system naturally had sufficient energy from intertidal oceanic exchange and freshwater "scour" to keep between three and five inlets open at any time, but seldom in the same location. These growing and shrinking inlets migrated up and down through the region. Each human-made inlet opened robbed energy from other inlets. This reduction in hydrologic energy allowed sand to accumulate and close in other inlets (as happened at the Indian River inlet), or required regular dredging to keep them clear, as would be necessary in each of the six permanent Indian River inlets in subsequent years.[25]

The second wave of Anglo immigrants to the region (during the Gilded Age) often occupied the abandoned claims of their Armed Occupation Act predecessors and resolved to create a permanent, reliably open inlet in the region and to construct a hospitable tropical frontier environment that suited their northern sensibilities. In November 1880 Lucy Richards wrote in a letter to a friend:

> Father keeps worrying about getting an inlet dug down the river. He says it will kill all of the grass in the river and make it more healthy here. We have, none of us, been sick, but the smell of the decaying grass is very unpleasant. They have been down several times to look the land over. Father does not want to make the inlet where old Gilberts Bar was, but farther south where he is sure it will keep open. They all met there last week. The Baker brothers,

> Old Joe, Jensen and the man from the House of Refuge. They talked it all over, and as they were in favor of the old cut, Father and Harry gave in and they will start digging soon.[26]

Selecting a site about two miles north of the Peck inlet, newly arrived Hubert Bessey organized a digging effort in December 1885.[27]

> Out of the boats, into the jungle of mangroves and mud we went and mowed the mangroves down with our bush hooks. Day after day, in mud and sand, we worked vigorously, nourished on sow-belly and grits, until we were almost ready to open the last barrier which, when cut through, would bring the then brackish waters of the St Lucie and Indian River to the salt of the ocean. The nucleus for an inlet eventually was read and, once opened, the high wash coming down from the St Lucie would do the rest to make the approach navigable.[28]

Just before they completed their work, Lucy Richards visited the workers and invited them to spend Christmas at nearby Eden. "Mr Bessey warned against leaving the work unfinished at this critical time; the St Lucie River was running strong for a successful opening. However, who could blame the hungry, youthful group of adventurers after their hard work? We quickly overruled the leader, with visions of refreshments and pineapple wine, and even dancing on the floor of the captain's new packing house; who could have resisted the prettiest girl on the river?"[29]

The settlers' experiment created a small-scale version of the hydrologic forces that had established the geomorphic shape of much of the biophysical system, when their cut created a small delta-shaped formation that began stretching from the island toward the western shore of the lagoon. "While we were enjoying ourselves at the Richards home, a fierce southeaster sprang up. By the time we returned to our inlet, our great ditch was sanded up from the river to the ocean and our work of weeks was completely demolished. Furthermore, the sands, no longer dammed by the fence of mangroves we had cut through, had piled up some 100 feet into the Indian River."[30]

Seven years later there was another attempt to open an inlet near the St. Lucie River, and it stayed open permanently. A group of prominent local pineapple growers and boatbuilders cited three reasons for opening an inlet through Hutchinson Island across from where the St. Lucie flowed into the Indian River proper. They resolved to improve the local fishery by bringing more saltwater fish to their region, just as they were plentiful around the Indian River inlet less than twenty miles north. They hoped to create a new avenue for boat traffic to the area, to bring in tourists (John Jensen had recently completed the forty-room Jensen Hotel in the area), and to ship their produce to northern markets apart from the Indian River Steamboat Company. Removing the "rotting stench of river vegetation" was the last cited reason for digging the cut.[31]

The high salinity of the northern Indian River fostered considerable marine life at this time. In the words of Amos Cummings: "The water of both Musquito [*sic*] Lagoon and Indian River is much more salt than the water of the ocean. This is owing to the action of the sun and the shallowness of the water."[32] In contrast, the subtropical lower Indian River was choked with freshwater manatee grass. The odor and density of this freshwater submerged vegetation did not conform to the settlers' perception of the healthy nature of the lagoon's climate. Said Sewall's Point settler H. H. Sewall:

> The river was very grassy then. They spoke of it as the meadows and called it the hay field, for the river was full of grass as far up as Ankona and it grew out 600 feet from the shore was [and] awfully hard to get through. The river bottom was only two or three feet below the surface and the long flat bladed grass lay six feet or longer on top of the water and was full of iodine, mosquitoes, and snakes. And when it got ripe and the wind blew it ashore and it began to decay, it would turn a white house black in a night and it was no use to paint a boat and expect it to look any better than an old weather-beaten hulk.[33]

This seasonal stench was difficult to reconcile with the supposed healthy nature of the Indian River climate. After the failure of the 1885 inlet attempt, Lucy Richards complained: "We will continue to smell that decayed grass. There is so much iodine in it that it turns the silver black and our rings too."[34] An 1891 Army Corps of Engineers surveyor included Sewall's argument in his report, which recommended a stabilization of the lagoon's liminality: "As the inlets to the ocean close from time to time, and as free tidal circulation is necessary for keeping the channels open, as well as for the preservation of health, provision should be made for a small amount of dredging from time to time for this purpose."[35]

In April 1892 a work party of local growers and fishermen was convened to clear a strip of palmetto across the narrow barrier island at a point directly across from Sewall's Point and the mouth of the St. Lucie Estuary.[36] After four days of working, the roughly 100 workers succeeded in opening a four-foot-deep, eight-foot-wide channel. The settlers initially were very pleased with the effects of the oceanic exchange, but the southerly movement of beach sand closed the inlet within four months. A dredge that had been commissioned by the Army Corps of Engineers to improve the natural Jupiter inlet was found to be currently idle, and an agreement was reached by which the settlers would pay the dredge operator $2,000 to dig a cut sixty feet wide and four feet deep through the Anastasia limestone rock that underlies the barrier islands of Central and South Florida. Thomas E. Richards solicited donations from other local growers, whose growing pineapple profits enabled them to donate liberally. Neighboring cabbage palm trees and other vegetation fell into the widening inlet after an 1893 hurricane opened the inlet to 400 feet and created a sand spit stretching into the lagoon.[37] Were it not for regular maintenance dredging, this sand spit would have turned the new St. Lucie inlet into another large delta-shaped protrusion in the lagoon.

"What the outcome will be we cannot tell," proclaimed Thomas Richards at an October 1892 fish fry held to celebrate the digging of the St. Lucie inlet.

> But of one thing we must be assured, our freight will not be raised, nor will our complaints of rough handling of our fruit be met as

heretofore with a "what are you going to do about it." The grip of the Indian River Steamship Co. is broken. The arrogance of monopoly will be exchanged for the courtesy of competition. Yes, neighbors, I rejoice with you, as I feel we are released from the tyranny of transportation companies.[38]

The prospect of opening "a new gateway to the old ocean" through Hutchinson Island near the mouth of the St. Lucie Estuary was the cause of much "jollification." Having grown dissatisfied with the service provided by the region's only steamship company, and reflecting the growing agrarian unrest and antimonopoly populism of the era, Richards and his lower Indian River neighbors hoped the new, convenient route to the Gulf Stream would allow them to build seagoing boats larger than their current Indian River–bound sharpies to sail their pineapples to northern markets by themselves. "We are released from the tyranny of transportation companies. Hereafter, we can do our own fighting. We know how to build schooners and sail them. It is, in fact, no new business to us."[39]

Richards spoke only three months after the new Populist Party called for the nationalization of all railroads, "in the interest of the people," which had been appropriated from 1890's Ocala Demands. The "Demands" were a foundational document that detailed the grievances of the nation's rural communities in response to the economic abuses of the Gilded Age's mighty trusts, such as Andrew Carnegie's U.S. Steel and the Standard Oil Company of John D. Rockefeller and Henry Flagler.[40] The enthusiasm of the beach fish fry faded when it was soon realized that the shallow, unstable inlet dug could not support significant commercial ocean shipping. The arrival of the Florida East Coast Railroad to the lower Indian River two years later bankrupted the Indian River Steamboat Company, as the railroad established a shipping monopoly of its own. An 1898 Army Corps of Engineers survey of the inlet observed, "the topography and water flow in this vicinity have changed a great deal since the inlet was opened." Within two years the width of the new inlet had expanded to 1,000 feet from its originally dredged 60-foot span and had grown to 1,700 feet after six years. "The peninsula on the south, formed by the inlet, has entirely disappeared for a distance of 8,000 feet. . . . The hydrography in the lower end of the Indian River has changed considerably. The shoals have become more shallow and have increased in area; the channel leading from Indian River to the inlet has deepened to a least depth of 6 feet at mean low water and has become wider." In addition to providing a modest shipping outlet to the sea, the cut provided an outlet for the St. Lucie's freshwater discharge, which historically had accumulated in the surrounding lower Indian River. The new inlet also caused wetlands to be exposed and exploited for agriculture in the upper reaches of the St. Lucie (now a tidal salt estuary), as much of the water that had been in the system now ran directly into the Atlantic, lowering the water level. Decades before drainage canals expanded the watershed of the Indian River to support orange groves well inland from the lagoon, supporters of deepening the new inlet hoped to achieve the same end. "It would drain and bring in to use thousands of acres of rich muck land which are now useless. This grade of land is well adapted for the cultivation of rice, tobacco, and sugar cane."[41]

Henry E. Sewall celebrated the killing of the freshwater vegetation that had filled the area and wrote that the new inlet had "destroyed all the malarious conditions existing in this region before its opening, making this one of the healthiest parts of Florida."[42] The vast flocks of ducks that had annually enticed hunters by filling the freshwater lagoon ceased to return soon after the freshwater vegetation was killed by saltwater intrusion. The water where once Lucie Richards and her friends "rinsed off in the river to get rid of some of the salt" after swimming at the beach was now thoroughly salty.[43] The Scobee Company of Titusville established a fish house adjacent to the new inlet, Manatee Pocket, within one year of its opening to take advantage of the dramatically altered saltwater fishery developing in the lower Indian River.[44] The new inlet had a maximum depth of seven feet but was subjected to considerable wave action, which made the inlet safe to traverse by sail "not more than ten days" during the eight-week visit of an army surveyor. There are "few days during the year when passage across the bar is safe, even for vessels of very light draft, owing to the high seas that entirely break across it." Despite this dour assessment, the area's boosters who hoped to improve the inlet claimed that "[it] has proved a great benefit to small vessels and yachts, and is used by them continually passing in and out to sea."[45]

The 1898 survey did not lead to dredging in the inlet, although it suggested that a jetty on the northern edge would be necessary. "There has been some apprehension that the St. Lucie inlet might close in the same way. There is little danger of this," because the flow through the inlet was two or three times greater than what passed through Gilbert's Bar. "A breakwater would insure the permanency of the opening."[46]

Although many natural inlets have opened and closed through the effects of storm, tide, and wind over the centuries in the Indian River, there were only two open when nineteenth-century settlers moved to the area, Jupiter inlet in the extreme south of the system and Indian River inlet in the central lagoon.[47] Gilded Age tourist Francis R. Stebbins described the defining characteristic of the Indian River system's dynamic forces when he observed the Indian River inlet's instability. "Yesterday we sailed over to the Indian River inlet for a little fishing . . . and we found a wonderful change there from last year. A new inlet has been formed by the washing out of a sandbar," wrote Stebbins in 1883. "This beach and piece of land is all gone, and the sea waves and tides are breaking over its whole extent. Similar changes in many places recorded along this coast. We visit places where not many years ago the sea rolled in through an inlet into the lagoon. Any heavy storm is liable to close the present inlets, and open new ones."[48]

The first attempt to stabilize an inherently unstable Indian River inlet came in 1892 after Pennsylvania senator Matthew Quay secured a $75,000 appropriation to dredge the Indian River inlet, which lay just north of Fort Pierce, and was one of only three natural inlets that existed in the late 1800s (the others were Mosquito inlet and Jupiter inlet). In addition to making the inlet accessible by larger boats, Quay reputedly opened the cut further so that his home on the Indian River's western shore opposite the inlet (in a settlement called St. Lucie) could have a view of the ocean.[49] The closing of this natural inlet within several years was blamed by some on Quay's dredging and by others on the 1892 opening of the St. Lucie inlet, less than twenty miles south, which diverted flowing water from the St. Lucie Estuary that would have otherwise run through the Indian River inlet.

The construction of the St. Lucie canal and St. Lucie inlet fundamentally changed the natural environment with regular freshwater infusion and inlet flushing that bears close resemblance to many other estuarine systems. The temperate northern Indian River, however, is separated from significant ocean water influx and is a largely closed system.[50]

Gilded Age settlers in the Indian River found only three open inlets connecting the lagoon system to the Atlantic (Jupiter, Indian River, and the Mosquito). Several settlers in the second wave of Anglo settlement in the years following the Civil War attempted to open an inlet in the central Indian River to make the region more attractive to other settlers. A retired Methodist minister from Detroit named Thomas New established a homestead and post office named New Haven along the southern side of the Sebastian River in the central Indian River sometime around 1881. It was about that time that he cut a tiny inlet through the barrier island across the lagoon from his claim, despite his advanced age. "Toiling all day, beating against a head wind, we have made slow progress, and we come to anchor off 'New's cut,' where old Mr. New has been trying to open an new inlet to the ocean, where the crossing is not over two hundred yards," observed Francis R. Stebbins in 1885. "We found the old gentleman at work on his cutting in the sand. He is very sanguine of success, and expects eventually to have a ship canal from here to the gulf of Mexico; Mr. New is seventy-five years old, but looks hearty and rugged."[51] New's modest cut only afforded the smallest boats clearance over the shallow sandbar, which ran across the narrow inlet.[52] Within a short time the inlet had closed, but less than five years later David Gibson had purchased the peninsula between the Indian River and Sebastian River (and much of the surrounding area, including part of the barrier island) and made another attempt to establish an inlet at the same location as had Thomas New.[53] Gibson's team of volunteers, recruited from the thin ranks of other local settlers, gave up the task before they finished hand digging through the narrow barrier island. Ten years later the inlet successfully opened, only to be closed by a storm the next season. In 1887 Francis R. Stebbins observed the same phenomena at the extreme southern end of the Indian River: "Another surprise meets us at this point. Jupiter inlet is closed—where we last year sailed out into the ocean surf, there is now a wide sand beach of acres in extent."[54]

As the 1910s movement was under way to dig a replacement inlet at Fort Pierce for the closed Indian River inlet and to make improvements to the new St. Lucie inlet, residents of the central Indian River also hoped to establish ocean access for their area. An engineer in Melbourne named R. D. Couch led the charge to establish a substantial inlet at Sebastian with a coquina stone jetty to prevent the frustrations experienced by the earlier builders. In 1916 he oversaw a project that used a six-inch power dredge to open the cut successfully. Within a year the inlet had closed again during another storm. The Progressive-era residents appealed to Florida senator Duncan U. Fletcher, who secured an emergency permit to open the inlet based on his dubious claim that the unrest related to World War I required access to the region's agricultural production, which was locally believed to one day become vital to the nation. Couch also succeeded in persuading the Florida state legislature to establish the Sebastian Inlet District Commission in 1919. Bonds were issued (as they were in Martin County for the same purpose in 1925) to secure $100,000 to reopen the inlet. Two substantial coquina jetties were built, and a storm sped up the project's progress by opening the inlet.

This inlet remained open until 1941, when the regular "maintenance" dredging ended in order to close the inlet to potential use by German U-boats. Jupiter inlet was also closed at this time for the same reason.

At the extreme northern end of the Indian River system lay Mosquito inlet, which had supported the failed New Smyrnea colony.[55] In his 1823 survey of the new territory of Florida, engineer Charles Vignoles described the inlet as narrow, but deep enough to allow ships drawing up to ten feet to pass safely through. Other than highlighting the nearby

FIGURE 6. Sebastian inlet, 1943. Note the sedimentation accumulated in the Indian River and the development of a delta-shaped protrusion created by the ocean water influx that did not exist at the site in the years immediately following the opening of the inlet. A row of newly created spoil islands can be seen on the left side of the image (University of Florida, "Aerial Photographs of Indian River County—Flight 1C [1943]," Map and Imagery Library, Gainesville, Florida).

tall Turtle Mound, Vignoles's survey indicates that he was unimpressed with the lagoon near the inlet, as it was generally narrow and "shut out from the sea breezes by the cluster of mangrove islands out front."[56] As the only Indian River inlet located north of Cape Canaveral, the dynamic oceanic currents shift sand differently than at the other Indian

River inlets. At Canaveral inlet (completed in 1954), as well as Sebastian, Fort Pierce, St. Lucie, and Jupiter inlets, the southward movement of sand along the beaches of the barrier islands has been the primary cause of periodic shoaling and regularly scheduled maintenance dredging. Mosquito inlet has at various times experienced both northerly and southerly accumulation and erosion of sand.[57]

If the 1892 opening of the St. Lucie inlet ushered in the first major human-made change to the Indian River's hydrologic system in recorded history, then a second (and much larger) wave of changes occurred in the 1920s. Instead of a smattering of newly established pineapple growers who cobbled together funds to hire a single modest dredge (as happened in 1892), the nearly 16,000 residents of the Indian River in the third decade of the twentieth century unleashed on the lagoon millions of dollars and the machines of America's growing industrial might. This ten-year span witnessed not only the creation of the Fort Pierce inlet and its neighboring deepwater port but also a significant expansion of the St. Lucie inlet, the dredging of a major anchoring field near the mouth of the St. Lucie Estuary, the improvement of the Sebastian inlet in the central Indian River, and the opening of the St. Lucie canal (part of the larger Everglades drainage plan), which would prove to be the system's most significant alteration.

In 1918 the Fort Pierce Inlet District was created by an act of the state legislature to fund and maintain the new inlet cut in the area in 1920. After years of having no inlet in the central Indian River, the new cut was dredged south of the natural Indian River inlet, at that time blocked by sand after much of the water flow through the inlet was diverted through the 1892 St. Lucie inlet. Named for the growing city it was created to serve, the Fort Pierce inlet was dredged by the Army Corps of Engineers in the 1920s to provide stable ocean access, replacing the natural inlets in the region that historically not only opened and closed but also migrated north and south through the tidal sedimentation process. Extended jetties and other improvements increased the ultimate cost of the inlet from $88,000 to more than $500,000.[58] Anastasia limestone rock exposed during the cutting process became inhabited by sabellarid worms, which created a reef at the location similar to the region around the St. Lucie inlet where the Anastasia rocks naturally were exposed (site of the Gilbert's Bar House of Refuge).[59] The Fort Pierce inlet brought reliable ocean access to the central Indian River for the first time. This new inlet created a permanent hydrological flushing effect in the Indian River system that had historically existed only during periods when storm-based tidal surges had washed over the barrier islands, creating natural inlets.[60]

The end of isolation of the Indian River in the 1890s created a new wave of settlers to the region who arrived on the new Florida East Coast Railroad. Canals built in the Indian River were part of a larger peninsula-wide trend in which settlers clamored for drainage in their regions, and the state legislature and Army Corps of Engineers generally heeded these local calls for the canalization of natural streams. For example, North Florida's Ocklawaha River Basin was subjected to drainage canals to permit agriculture in the region, and in 1919 the Winter Haven Lake Region Boat District was established to build a navigation canal through the Winter Haven chain of lakes. Progressive-era settlers expressed enthusiasm for the potential agricultural development of the Indian River region and frustration at the persistence of largely infertile vast wetlands that remained separated from the lagoon by the Atlantic Ridge. As early as 1854, engineers had proposed creating canals through the Atlantic Ridge to drain the wetlands (inaccurately called by settlers "the savannahs").[61] In the early twentieth century canals were dug through the ridge to drain these wetlands, which increased the size of the watershed that flowed into the Indian River. These early ambitious drainage schemes were dwarfed by the scale of the complex network of drainage canals that were built in the years immediately following World War II.

The impetus for the massive increase in the size of the watershed of the Indian River was the 1916 Drainage Act, which established taxing districts to drain land for flood control and agriculture. The miles of canals and ditches that followed this legislation rerouted and canalized meandering small creeks, effectively increasing the naturally small watershed

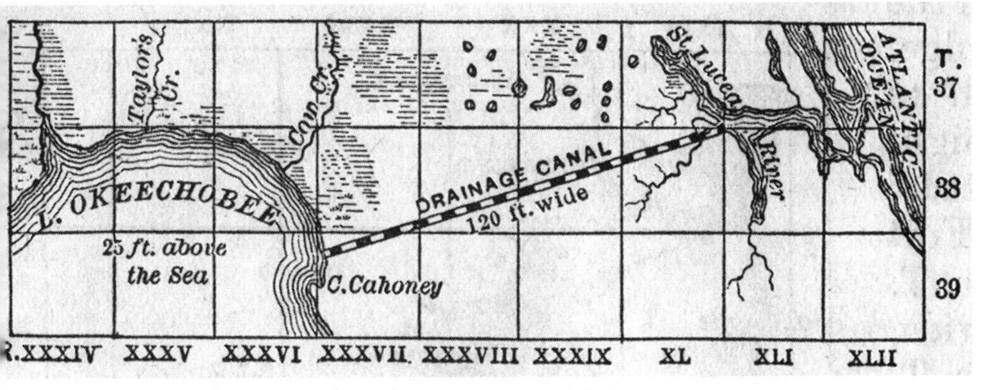

FIGURE 7. An 1884 map detailing the planned St. Lucie canal, which would not be built for some forty years (University of South Florida Special Collections).

of the Indian River to include much of the wetlands that were historically separated from the Indian River. These canals lowered the groundwater table in the Indian River, connecting the lagoon's sub-basins and leaving vast stretches of wetlands dry for most of the year. The purpose of lowering the groundwater was to prevent damage to the root systems of trees (primarily citrus), a goal accomplished through the simple process of digging a sloping ditch. As long as the bottom of the ditch was lower than the groundwater table, the ditch would automatically drain a significant area by whisking groundwater into the Indian River after it seeped into the ditch. It was in these newly drained lands that the region's famed citrus industry grew in the early twentieth century. By the last decades of the century much of these lands were the site of urban development that would come to characterize the region in the later years.[62] As the wetlands of the Indian River were drained, the names of land features shifted over the decades to reflect their changing form. Today's "Allapattah Flats" near the St. Lucie Estuary is undoubtedly a postdrainage name for the same feature listed on nineteenth-century maps as "Halpatta Swamp" or "Alpatiokee Swamp," but the lowered water table has left the area no longer resembling wetlands. Surveys of the lands west of the St. Lucie Estuary in the decade before the completion of the St. Lucie–Okeechobee canal suggest that the land was covered with standing water for eight to ten months of each year. In the years following the post-1916 Drainage Act canalization, this drained region (like much of the Indian River) became citrus groves, the town of Palm City, and the post–World War II development of Port St. Lucie.[63]

The most ambitious example of Progressive-era planned agricultural development in the Indian River was that of Fellsmere, located several miles west of the central Indian River town of Sebastian. In 1896 the Cinncinatus Glades Company built a railroad spur, the Sebastian and Cinncinatus Farms Railroad, from the Florida East Coast Railroad line at Sebastian to 118,000 acres of wetlands that the corporation purchased and named Cinncinatus Farms, with an aim of attracting midwestern farmers (especially in Ohio) to buy small agricultural plots. The company hoped to quickly drain the standing water that covered the region for much of the year by diverting it primarily to the nearby Indian River (separated from the wetlands by the Atlantic Ridge) instead of building much longer (and costlier) canals along the route of its natural, slow connection to the St. Johns River system. While the drainage for the purpose of developing agriculture was initially a failure, the canal network significantly increased the effective watershed of the Indian River and introduced considerable freshwater infusion to the central lagoon network. Within ten years the company had sold hundreds of lots, had dug thirty-four miles of canals, and had successfully drained a portion of the land, which was divided into five- and ten-acre segments. The drained lands flooded after severe rains in 1907 and 1908 collapsed a number of the new dikes.

Being unable to recover from this event, the Cinncinatus Glades Company sold its land and railroad to developers E. Nelson Fell and Oscar T. Crosby on June 6, 1910.[64] So lucrative were sales of the lots after the new developers successfully redrained these wetlands that the Florida East Coast Railroad added Sebastian as a regular stop so that the railroad could better handle the influx of northern visitors who visited Fellsmere. In 1913 the Fellsmere Farms Company announced that it would create three master-planned communities named "Grassland," (which was never built), "Broadmoor," and "Fellsmere," a precursor to similar city-scale developments that were built in much of the peninsula

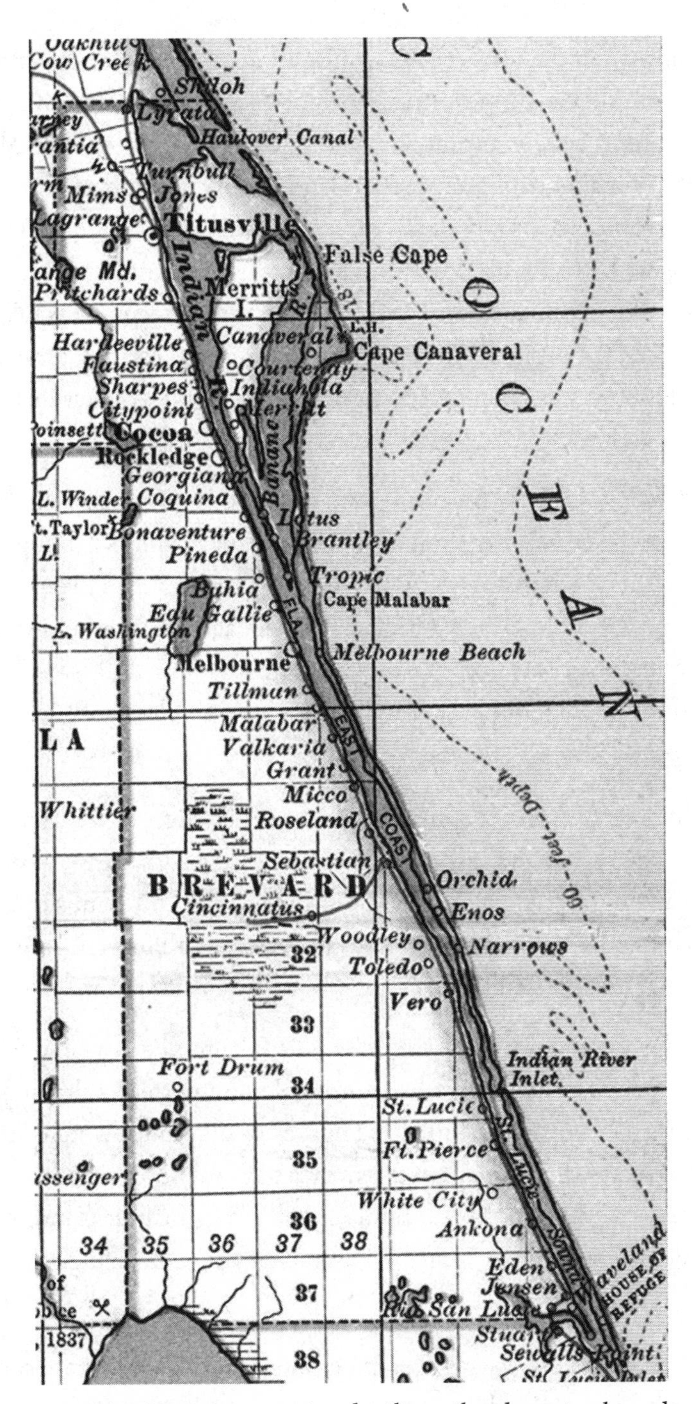

FIGURE 8. An 1897 map section detailing railroad spur to planned agricultural development of "Cinncinatus," located in the wetlands in the center of this figure (Exploring Florida, University of South Florida).

(including the Indian River) following World War II. Sales of residential and commercial properties in Broadmoor were brisk. Negative publicity of unscrupulous promoters abounded in northern newspapers, and grossly inadequate drainage left land buyers disappointed to find their newly purchased farm land still under several feet of water. "I have bought land by the acre, I have bought land by the foot but, by God, I have never before bought land by the gallon," bemoaned one Everglades land buyer of the period.[65] In response, the Fellsmere Farms Company's promotional literature sought to assure potential buyers that its lands would be arable:

> [Fellsmere Farms is the] only one large body of muck land in Florida, which is being drained as a whole on a carefully thought out plan, and where the work is sufficiently far advanced to enable the land seeker to closely estimate the date at which his land will be ready for occupation. . . . It is scarcely to[o] much to say that upon the success of Fellsmere the success of all Florida reclamation projects now depends.[66]

So easily was agriculture spurred by the introduction of the fertilizer found in the region's soils that the Fellsmere Farms Company boasted that "a skillful farmer can play with his crops as a skillful musician on his instruments."[67] Fellsmere soil was promoted with fevered language describing its supposed near-supernatural fertility and absurd value:

> In order to render this vast storehouse of Ammonia available for plant food, the land must be thoroughly and perfectly drained. The prize is worth the effort; the figures of the values which can be derived by the drainage of this tract are almost beyond imagination. . . . The value of the Ammonia contained in the muck lands of the Fellsmere Farms Company . . . reaches the astounding figure of $632,100,000.[68]

While the Fellsmere Farms Company constructed significant canals in the area, it was "the duty of the farmer to supplement this drainage work by a proper system of farm ditches and by the proper treatment

FIGURE 9. Fellsmere Farms canal dredge, 1912 (Florida State Library and Archive).

of his land." With Progressive flourish, the company assured potential buyers that everyone who farms the region "can feel he is acting in the spirit of the true American and contributing by his skill and energy to the happiness of the toilers of the world by opening to them the road to independence."[69] By 1916 the new city was destroyed when several buildings (including the post office) were washed away when the poorly drained land was inundated with heavy rains, a repeat of events in 1907. The tremendous demand for agriculture products generated by World War I prompted the company to drain the land once again, and sales of the wetlands resumed during the land boom of the next decade. In the following years the land was used to mine the area's peat for fertilizer components, as well as for growing sugarcane and citrus. Neither the major canals dug by the developers nor the small secondary "V" canals dug by individual farmers off of these central canals successfully drained the land sufficiently to develop the planned robust city of independent truck farmers. The Fellsmere Farms Company underestimated the extent of the area's wetlands, and the flooding that overwhelmed the relatively small drainage canals regularly consumed the region, including the paved streets of Fellsmere.

The 1920s Florida land boom ushered in an unprecedented wave of optimism about the potential for tourism and schemes for agricultural and residential development of the southern peninsula. The decade saw the first significant drainage-induced declension of the Everglades, and other ecosystems (including the Indian River) were similarly altered. A major component of Everglades drainage was the need to divert the sheet of water that slowly flowed south from Lake Okeechobee through the Everglades to Florida Bay. A series of drainage canals were cut through the east coast's narrow Atlantic Ridge to divert this sheet flow to the Atlantic. In 1905 the state legislature established the Board of Drainage Commission, which was soon replaced by the Everglades Drainage District. This new agency was permitted to dig canals and levy taxes on properties within new drainage districts. Governor Napoleon Broward charged the new Everglades Drainage District with diversion of the natural southerly flow of freshwater from Lake Okeechobee. This stream was fed by the Kissimmee River as well as by smaller creeks and rain, which flowed through a canal to the Caloosahatchee River on the west coast of Florida and the south fork of the St. Lucie River on the east coast.[70] As early as 1907 area newspapers were filled with advertisements for land and boasted of Broward's imminent canal that would bring fame and importance to the St. Lucie Estuary and lower Indian River. After the state legislature appeared to lend support for the canal in May 1907, the Fort Pierce–based *St. Lucie Tribune* reflected the jubilance of a region that expected to be the site of the world's next great canal. "From Gulf to Atlantic . . . Enormous Possibilities of Water Transportation Through Florida's Most Productive Region" boasted the tiny newspaper.[71]

Construction of the vast drainage canal began on May 28, 1915. On June 13, 1923, water from Lake Okeechobee began flowing through the canal into the St. Lucie River. Efforts to deepen the drainage canal to speed the rate of drainage and to make it navigable for ships or yachts continued for the next five years. The dredges of the Everglades

MARCH 1, 1907.

NOW is the Time to BUY LAND

The Everglades will be Drained

A route has been surveyed and the canal from Lake Okechobee to the St. Lucie river will be dug, and **Stuart-on-the-St. Lucie,** near the canal route, is attracting the attention of the homeseeker and investor. Unexcelled bathing and boating, launch trips up the river and to the ocean, and fresh and salt water fishing offer more than ordinary inducements to the tourist and health seeker. Hotel and boarding house accommodations for all at most reasonable prices.

WE ARE ON "THE SPOT"

Real Estate is the only Safe Investment

I have secured some of the most desirable and best locations at **Stuart-on-the-St. Lucie** and on the St. Lucie river that are to be had. If you anticipate buying here, NOW is the time, and you should call or write for further information at once. Stuart people realize the future importance of of this section and, as a rule, are making no effort to sell property, but some desirable locations can be had through this agency. Every courtesy will be show our customers.

Send for list of properties for sale.

W. A. BALL, Land Agent, Postoffice Building
STUART-ON-THE-ST. LUCIE
Dade County, Florida

FIGURE 10. Representative advertisement from developers in Stuart, which found itself along the proposed route of the Okeechobee waterway (*St Lucie Tribune* [Fort Pierce], March 1, 1907, 6).

Drainage District labored to dig through miles of limestone throughout the 1920s and ultimately removed seventy-nine million cubic yards of dirt and rock until construction was completed in 1928, at a cost of over $6 million. Water flow through the new canal from Lake Okeechobee increased after the construction of the earthen Herbert Hoover Dike around the shores of the lake in response to the more than 2,000 deaths in the catastrophic hurricanes of 1926 and 1928, both of which caused the lake to overflow a small dike that had been built in 1910. The hurricanes led to a major increase in flood control projects of the Army Corps of Engineers, the largest of which was the Hoover Dike, which would eventually be enlarged to nearly forty feet tall in places.[72]

The St. Lucie canal was only one of many canals dug by the Everglades Drainage District in the 1920s, which boasted that its new canals had made 100,000 acres of wetlands suitable for farming.[73] Historically, the regions of the Indian River system have received land-based freshwater from relatively small areas dictated by the soil, elevation, and vegetation of the area. Artificially enhanced watershed limits greatly increased the land area of the Indian River watershed. Before the infusion of freshwater from twentieth-century drainage canals, the salinity of the Indian River was already vacillating due to the natural opening and closing of inlets and rain. The first human-made increase in the size of the watershed was the modest drainage canal network of the 1760s Turnbull colony in New Smyrnea. The most significant period in which the watershed size increased was the 1920s. The canalization of this decade was part of a trend that ultimately increased the size of the watershed 61 percent, from an estimated 558,000 acres to 1,460,000 acres. Dramatically varying salinity levels were often invisible to the human eye, and the carnage inflicted on the system's flora and fauna was sometimes difficult to grasp. If there had been severe changes in the ratio of oxygen to nitrogen, settlers would have understood intuitively the scale of change that was taking place beneath their hulls. Because the Indian River itself is somewhat divided into separate drainage basins, it is useful to examine briefly changes to each of these sections.

While the northern portion of the Indian River system (roughly north of Melbourne) received little canalization in this period, the lower lagoon was subjected to significant 1920s canalization efforts that increased water flow. The Melbourne-Tillman Drainage District (formed in 1922) drained lands west of Melbourne (which historically drained into the St. Johns River) into the Indian River for the purposes of lowering the groundwater table to facilitate agriculture and urban development.[74] Other bodies that built canals for drainage include the Fellsmere Farms Water Control District (established in 1919, it built 300 miles of canals), the Sebastian River Water Control District (established in 1927), and the Indian River Farms Water Control District (established in 1920). The cities built on the land drained by these projects in turn constructed storm-water drainage systems, further increasing the freshwater discharge into the lagoon. In the southern Indian River the watershed extends deep into the interior of the state, thanks to the St. Lucie–Okeechobee canal. The canal linked together the distant Kissimmee River basin of Central Florida, which fed Lake Okeechobee. In addition to this canal, others of this era were built to drain much of western St. Lucie County into the north fork of the St. Lucie Estuary. The North St. Lucie River Water Control District (established in 1917) ultimately dug 200 miles of canals to facilitate an expansion of the region's famed citriculture on over 62,000 drained acres. This district dug the vast C-25 canal, which dumps into the lagoon through Taylor Creek in Fort Pierce, and the C-24 canal, which drains into the north fork of the St. Lucie River and allowed the building of the vast postwar development of Port St. Lucie. The neighboring Fort Pierce Farms Drainage District created fifty miles of canals to drain 13,000 acres.[75]

By the 1920s support for the Gulf-Okeechobee-Atlantic Canal became obligatory for the state's politicians looking to cement their progressive credentials. In his unsuccessful 1920 campaign for the U.S. Senate, Florida governor Sidney J. Catts boasted of his support for the canal ("I am in favor of the Cross-State St. Lucie-Okeechobee and Caloosahatchee Canal. . . . Why is it Florida is so barren of everything the

FIGURE 11. The St. Lucie canal under construction in 1921 (Florida State Library and Archives).

United States should have done for her, such as helping the Great Everglades Drainage District, as has been done in the western states?") alongside his other populist qualifications, including his opposition to the "Catholic toe kissers of the Pope" and "big corporate [railroad] interests," and his support of Prohibition by fighting "the whiskey crowd." Boasted Catts of himself, "Not long ago a citizen of Florida said that the poor man in Florida had but three friends-Jesus Christ, Sears Roebuck and Sidney J. Catts."[76]

Prominent residents of the towns along the Okeechobee waterway established the Gulf, Okeechobee and Atlantic Waterway Association in 1914 (originally called the Cross State Waterway Association) to promote deepening and widening the planned drainage canal to accommodate freight-hauling ships from the St. Lucie inlet on the Atlantic to Fort Myers on the West Coast.[77] "The plan is to utilize the Caloosahatchee River to LaBelle, canalize to Moore Haven on Lake Okeechobee, across the Lake and by way of the St. Lucie canal, Indian Town and the St. Lucie River, proceed by way of Stuart to the Atlantic."[78] They pushed the Everglades Drainage District to make the St. Lucie canal navigable for ships (or at least yachts) as part of a larger plan to support a deepwater port at the St. Lucie inlet. The meeting minutes of this group bristle with passages of unbridled optimism of a land boom–era Florida as they fought to ensure that no other cross-state canal would be built, which might divert boat traffic. The group hoped to "get the state to rush the 'easy engineering' of the St. Lucie canal at the earliest possible moment and then direct our efforts to direct the Federal Government to improve the waterway" to create "at least a barge canal" that was twelve feet deep.[79]

In the context of exploding land values, the era's canalization, and an anticipated population increase, the members of the Gulf, Okeechobee and Atlantic Waterway Association made increasingly absurd comparisons to the Panama Canal and optimistic claims such as "the world will appreciate the saving of distance of the arduous trip encountered by going around the Keys of Florida and also the eliminating of the hazard encountered in these states which in turn would reduce the expense of insurance, which would soon pay for the building of this canal." Association member Stanley Kitching, commodore of the Stuart Yacht Club, told the group that he could send 250 yachts through the canal were it deepened, each of which would lavish money in the towns along the waterway.[80] The group pushed Tallahassee to speed up the canal improvement by using increasingly frantic claims, including that the canal was also necessary to drain the region's "four million acres of back country, the richest in the world. . . . The time is coming when that body might have to feed the whole United States of America, and that it was capable to doing so." Undaunted by estimates of the Interstate Commerce Commission that the Okeechobee waterway would not lower freight rates for the region's growers, members of the association claimed that the canal would "starve the railroads and those who represent them into submission," and then "you will see industries spring up. Then we will settle up this country with actual settlers who will make the land productive."[81]

The 1923 opening of the St. Lucie canal dramatically altered the salinity of the lower Indian River's St. Lucie Estuary, an intensification of the process begun by the previous generation with the 1892 opening of the nearby St. Lucie inlet. While the inlet's opening had introduced salt water into what had been (at the time of the post–Civil War settlement) a wholly freshwater environment, the opening of the canal introduced much larger and more regular infusions of nutrient-laden freshwater than occurred naturally in the system's tributary creeks. Within several years of the 1923 opening of the St. Lucie canal, muck soil from Lake Okeechobee began to enter the St. Lucie Estuary. Nineteenth-century surveys of the system record average depths in the St. Lucie River of fourteen to sixteen feet. Within several years the saltwater sea grass and white sand that covered the bottom of the system were covered with vast quantities of Lake Okeechobee muck, and the depth of the estuary decreased significantly.[82] The volume of water released from Lake Okeechobee into the St. Lucie (and the Caloosahatchee on Florida's west coast) increased after the 1929 creation of the Okeechobee Flood Control District. This new entity assumed responsibility for the canal and shifted the focus from draining the Everglades below Lake Okeechobee to maintaining the level of the lake low enough to prevent it from spilling southward and high enough to irrigate the newly created Everglades Agricultural Area south of the lake, and to ensure that the canal was navigable for the barges that were expected to use the cross-peninsula shortcut.[83]

In addition to the St. Lucie–Okeechobee canal, there were efforts made to drain the lands west of the southern Indian River by constructing canals to divert water to the north fork of the St. Lucie Estuary. By the late nineteenth century there were already small vegetable farms along the "sluggish streams" that naturally compose the system's watershed. It would not be until the mid-twentieth century that significant canals were built to drain the "low-lying swamplands."[84] In 1925 a small, privately built drainage ditch diverted water to the north fork of the St. Lucie Estuary and quickly created a one-mile sandbar across the natural waterway, leaving only eighteen inches of water over which boats could pass. This sandbar was blamed for preventing the southerly flow of water from the upper north fork, causing annual flooding among the few modest vegetable farms upstream.[85]

The construction of the Okeechobee waterway added momentum to earlier plans to establish a deepwater port in the lower Indian River where the St. Lucie Estuary meets the Indian River (next to the St. Lucie inlet). The opening of the 1892 St. Lucie inlet failed to bring a viable shipping alternative to steamships or the Florida East Coast Railroad after it reached the lower Indian River in 1894. There were efforts in the first decade of the twentieth century to entice the Army Corps of Engineers to improve the St. Lucie inlet, but the agency instead decided to support the deepening of the small deepwater port at nearby Fort Pierce. Therefore the agency saw little need for another deepwater port at St. Lucie, only eighteen miles south. In 1909 the Army Corps of Engineers endorsed a proposal to spend the estimated $1,400,000 needed to complete the dredging, as well as the $5,000 anticipated for annual maintenance. This plan's approval came partially in response to the claims of local residents that such an inlet would provide the only harbor of refuge along the 600-mile coast between Key West and Jacksonville for distressed ships that drew more than twelve feet. The simultaneous wrecks of the freighters *Georges Valentine* and *Cosme Calzado* at the foot of the Gilbert's Bar House of Refuge (one mile from the shallow St. Lucie inlet) only four years earlier lent credibility to this claim.[86] The twelve-foot depth demanded by the region's pineapple growers, according to the Army Corps of Engineers' estimate, seemed to be needlessly deep for the lagoon's established shoal-draft steamboats and not deep enough for oceangoing freighters. Such an inlet would therefore

FIGURE 12. A 1926 arch that reads "Stuart: Atlantic Gateway to the Gulf of Mexico," built to promote the town's proximity to the new Okeechobee waterway to passing "tin can tourists," as it appeared in 2014 (photo by author).

probably not lower the region's "excessive freight charges which they are now compelled to pay." In response, the federal engineers called for a minimum depth of eighteen feet because "the Indian River is being rapidly developed and the annual shipment of fruits is assuming considerable magnitude."[87]

In an attempt to speed up the construction of the canal expected to connect Lake Okeechobee with the St. Lucie Estuary, pineapple growers of the lower Indian River established the South Florida Navigation Company in 1907 to dig the canal themselves. The group estimated that within ten to fifteen years of the canal's completion, the 80,000 acres of "fine hammock and muck land will be producing thousands of crates of fruit and vegetables" in the vicinity of the canal. Hubert Bessey, the company's president, claimed that the combination of the canal and improved inlet would save the region's growers $334,900 annually in freight charges. The boosterism of the region's growers so influenced the federal engineers that their report echoed some of the residents' more outlandish claims, including the exceedingly dubious assertion that the inlet would get fruit to northern markets faster than transporting it by railroads. It "is confidently expected that there will be very much less loss by water shipment than by rail, as it is believed that a vessel direct from this point to New York can deliver its fruit in less time than the fast freights of the railroad."[88] Because the shallow inlet proved to be an unsuitable avenue to ship fruit and fish to northern markets, there were plans to establish a deepwater port at the site. Deepening the inlet would be of little use if the lagoon itself were too shallow to host deep draft ships.[89] The Army Corps of Engineers began to plan an elaborate and complex design for the deepwater port, including a turning basin 400 feet by 800 feet in which the anticipated freighters could anchor or tie up to wharves. This basin would be connected to the new inlet by a major channel 200 feet wide, "with the dredged material deposited along the south side, so that the spoil bank, built well above the height of the storm tides, would provide a training wall for the current through the channel." Bisecting this channel would be a 200-foot opening to allow north-south passage of boats traveling the previously constructed canal running the length of the Indian River. The increasingly complicated proposal included "two parallel jetties be built out to deep water" at the inlet, to be constructed with coquina rock, which would require a modern dredge more powerful than any yet introduced to Florida. This complex network of inlet, canals, and turning basin connected with the railroad and Okeechobee canal represented a preview of the heavily engineered environment, sculpted by dredging and filling, that would reshape much of twentieth-century Florida.[90]

Within a few years, Congress was persuaded by the 1909 report and the region's economic boosters to appropriate a modest $100,000 for dredging in the St. Lucie inlet in 1913 (part of the Rivers and Harbors Act), but this digging halted after only $26,689 was spent due to the prohibitive hardness of the Anastasia rock that forms the basis for the

Indian River's barrier islands. This wave of dredging was sparked by the region's increased population and by the fact that the lagoon's natural inlets in 1920 were especially unusable. In 1920 both Jupiter inlet and Indian River inlet had been closed for some time, and the Mosquito inlet at the extreme northern edge of the system was nearly so. This left only the St. Lucie inlet to provide all Indian River access to the ocean, and it was only four feet deep at low tide.[91]

Local papers during the 1920s Florida land boom were filled with articles that decried the high freight rates charged on the region's oranges, vegetables, and pineapples.[92] This perceived obstacle to growth was despised in the midst of the booming state, which led many Florida settlers to expect that nearly every fishing hamlet would become a metropolis. This was especially true in Stuart, whose location on the St. Lucie Estuary and proximity to the new Okeechobee waterway and St. Lucie inlet led its residents to expect that the city would become a significant center of commerce. The new deepwater port planned for the region would serve as a shipping point for the area's growing citrus industry as well as a point of transfer for goods being shipped along a proposed canal that was envisioned to connect the St. Lucie Estuary with Lake Okeechobee. The canal and port were considered to be so significant that the northern portion of Palm Beach County and a southern portion of St. Lucie County, from Jensen to just north of Jupiter, became a new county, named for Governor John Martin in a successful effort to enlist his support for improvements to the St. Lucie inlet.[93] The leaders of the new county immediately issued municipal bonds to raise money to improve the inlet without the aid of the Army Corps of Engineers. Between 1926 and 1929 residents of the lower Indian River raised and spent $850,000 to build a 3,300-foot jetty along the north side of the inlet, as well as another (failed) attempt to deepen the cut to a depth of eighteen feet.[94]

The era's newspaper headlines reflected the enthusiasm of the residents of the lower Indian River. "Voice of People Is Almost Unanimous in Election to Complete Inlet and Channel," boomed the *Stuart Daily*

SOUTH FLORIDA DEVELOPER—The Newspaper About Florida — Tuesday, December 29, 1925.

PORT OF STUART

Florida's New Gateway

The Opening of the St. Lucie Inlet

THE GREAT STUART HARBOR AND NAVAL BASE, ST. LUCIE INLET

St. Lucie Ship Canal Locks

FIGURE 13. Excerpt from newspaper *South Florida Developer*, December 29, 1925. The left photo is labeled "The Great Stuart Harbor and Naval Base, St. Lucie Inlet," neither of which was actually built (Thurlow/Runke Collection, Sewall's Point, Florida).

News as the county issued bonds in 1926 to build a protective jetty and deepen the "million dollar" St. Lucie inlet. "Every Effort Is Being Made by the Inlet Commission and Contractors to Open the Harbor for Ocean-Going Traffic During 1927."[95] The county used its new funds to build the large jetty on the north side of the inlet (to block the natural southward movement of sand along the barrier islands), but the end of the land boom caused a number of banks to fail, including those that held the new county's money allocated for the new inlet. After this fiscal fiasco the inlet's depth was still only about six feet (again, due to the underlying Anastasia rock reef that ran across the inlet) and remained much too shallow for the envisioned major port.[96]

The collapse of the Florida land boom in 1926 ended dreams of a major port city growing at this strategic crossroads of the Okeechobee waterway, Indian River, and deepwater St. Lucie inlet. Streets had been already plotted for the "Golden Gate" residential development in Stuart, and a Spanish revival arch spanned the new Dixie Highway (used by the era's "tin can tourists") to highlight Stuart's location as the "gateway" to the new cross-state canal. Developers laid out enormous plots of land for anticipated truck farms that would develop in the region, including a finger of water near the mouth of the St. Lucie Estuary called Manatee Pocket. It was here that developer Benjamin Mulford made plans for a grand development of "Salerno" on the cove, which at the time hosted little more than a few fish houses. Mulford's promotional literature bubbled with feverish descriptions of the supposed fertile environment of the lower Indian River and boom-era zeitgeist. Mulford claimed that only five acres of this "poor man's paradise" would bring up to $5,000 a year because four harvests of fruits and vegetables could be enjoyed year after year on the inexhaustible sandy soil.[97] Other developers of the region focused on the freight-hauling opportunities expected upon the opening of the St. Lucie canal. Developer George Kline lured investors into his Salerno Development Company with the same imagery used to attract the company's land buyers. Images of winter vegetable riches were all but assured because Salerno would be the "nearest and most accessible market" for the "vast territory of fertile land" opened by the St. Lucie canal. In the fevered prose of the company's literature, land that the previous year sold for $3.50 per foot of waterfront was now selling for $12 per foot. Developers boasted of the region's planned massive ecological innovations, which guaranteed success for the area due to the "the Ship Canal being completed this summer, the hard surfaced road, from Ship Canal Lock via Salerno to the Ocean Beach which has now been authorized by Board of County Commissioners and the best ocean inlet on the East Coast."[98]

The boosters of the lower Indian River attempted to distance themselves from the growing negative publicity received by unscrupulous developers of the nearby Everglades (and the slow progress of the Everglades Drainage District) by greatly exaggerating the elevation of the area and highlighting the well-drained nature of the lots in Salerno. "The land is high and dry, being eighteen to twenty feet above tidewater, lying as it does in the valley of the St. Lucie River, and separated from the Everglades Drainage District by a high watershed; hence is separate and distinct, having nothing in common with other Florida lands, but is clearly in a class by itself." Breathless descriptions of the environment's "unsurpassed" suitability for cattle litter the literature for "Salerno Lots and Grove Lands," which are "Both Sure Winners" in the judgment of "thoughtful, far-sighted makers of history."[99]

Attempts to turn the Indian River from a liminal biophysical system marked chiefly by its unstable inlets (which at any time may have hosted roaring waves, feeble ebbs, or firm sand dunes), shifting coastlines, and fluctuating salinity into a stable environment suitable for the demands of a market economy forever altered the lagoon.

Despite the increased size of the Indian River's watershed, due to the canalization of western lands that had historically been separated from the system by the Atlantic Ridge, there was insufficient hydrological exchange to scour the inlets created by late nineteenth- and early twentieth-century residents. The initial speculation was that engineers would be able to carefully construct a stable, self-sufficient system out of the Indian River's intolerable instability. "It has been predicted, after such improvement, [the construction of inlets and canals will cause] the natural effect of the tides from the sea, through the 'inlets' remaining open and the accumulation of waters flowing into the sounds from the interior [would] increase the depths of the channels of the sounds [along Florida's East Coast]."[100] The new inlets at Fort Pierce and St. Lucie introduced significant salinity in the lower Indian River and had to be regularly dredged to prevent shoaling. Decades before the Everglades would become heavily altered, the lower Indian River had become a managed system requiring permanent human actions to maintain the desired built environment. From the ceaseless opening and closing locks of the St. Lucie canal to release water from Lake Okeechobee to the "maintenance dredging" of the system's new canals and inlets, the

Indian River remained a system in flux and could not be wholly stabilized. The large scale of dredging in the system, including that done by the Florida Coast Line Canal and Transportation Company, the Fellsmere Farms Company, and the failed deepwater port at the mouth of the St. Lucie Estuary, established a pattern that would define and reshape the peninsula in the twentieth century.

5

From Labor to Leisure, 1941–Present

"Port St. Lucie is a fun, carefully planned, progressive community—built in a setting of great natural beauty," boasted the General Development Corporation regarding its newest creation in the lower Indian River in 1961. "The lovely St. Lucie River which winds through the property, is one of the most picturesque in all of Florida. And as you drive through the countryside, you will marvel at the beauty of the green and gold citrus groves and savor the sweet scent of fragrant orange blossoms." Descriptions of the region's balmy tropical environment lured northerners of the mid-twentieth century just as successfully as had those of the nineteenth century. "The climate is wonderful—cooled in summer and warmed in winter by prevailing trade winds from the Atlantic Ocean. Here you can enjoy your favorite outdoor sport—raise tropical fruits, vegetables and gorgeous exotic flowers throughout the year."[1]

While the lagoon itself was the center of all economic and social activity in the region until World War II, the urban growth in the following decades made the water increasingly peripheral to a new affluent culture built on highways, subdivisions, and strip malls. Although it would remain a beautiful component of the region's economy, the Indian River became largely invisible to inhabitants of the region, who were attracted by national advertisements for cheap bungalows and shuffleboard clubs rather than by the lure of laboring in exotic pineapple fields or orange groves.

In the decades immediately following World War II, the Indian River received a significant portion of a new northern population influx, which has been described as one of the great population shifts in U.S. history.[2] The seeds of a sun-drenched culture planted in the decades following the Civil War blossomed into hundreds of rapidly urbanizing decentralized retirement communities. As the chief among the booming Sun Belt states, Florida's post–World War II population infusion created vast expanses of strip malls and suburbs built on land that was dredged and filled at an astonishing rate. Although there were areas of the peninsula more heavily altered in this period than the Indian River (the megasprawl of Dade–Broward–Palm Beach on the east coast and Pinellas through Lee Counties on the west coast are the most obvious examples), the environment of the Indian River region continued to draw the elderly and sick, as well as the young and ambitious. The backyard orange trees and plastic pink flamingoes that festooned multitudes of trailer parks and retirement duplexes expressed the tiki-torch kitsch of Florida into which a new generation of retirees and ex-servicemen bought. The severe housing shortage that followed World War II was answered across the nation by building low-density sprawling houses on former farmland, from Levittown in New York to Port Malabar in the central Indian River.

Just as Paleo-Indians tended to build villages near inlets, so would later Americans, both groups attracted to the prolific fishing the inlets offered. The inlets were largely transformed from places of labor and productivity to sources of recreation. Only one of the Indian River's five inlets of the twentieth century (Fort Pierce) would be used for significant commercial freight. The remaining inlets would be regularly dredged and maintained at great expense for the pleasure and convenience of sport fishermen. Instead of dangerous gauntlets to be crossed in the course of sailing cargo to market, inlets in the mid-twentieth century transitioned into tame sources of leisure and continued to attract wealthy northerners who built their mansions along the surging currents of the narrow barrier island gaps.

While the climate of the Indian River had long been celebrated as a haven for the sick and snow-weary, nineteenth- and early twentieth-century settlers perceived it as a place of work. Though it was the site of several large Gilded Age hotels for winter vacationers, it was not until the years following World War II that year-round residents perceived the lagoon as fundamentally a place of recreation instead of labor. In this period the fish houses of Titusville, Fort Pierce, and Jensen Beach were shuttered and demolished in the wake of depleted fisheries. The value of the cottages, mansions, and swimming pools built on their locations came not from a utilitarian proximity to commercial fish stocks but instead from the commodification of leisure and beauty.

Midcentury public works projects converted the perennially shifting and liminal Indian River into a fixed managed system of canals, pumps, dikes, seawalls, and fill. The comparatively modest drainage projects completed through the 1920s paled in comparison to the prosperity and industrial might unleashed in the wake of World War II. Over 100 new small spoil islands were created in long, straight lines inside the lagoon, with the dredging of the canal running its length to a new depth of twelve feet in the 1950s. In the 1960s the vast wetlands drained in the early twentieth century found a new use when thousands of acres of Indian River orange groves were plowed under to make way for mile after mile of sprawling residential construction, part of a movement that was familiar to residents of the booming cities surrounding Orlando. Canalization of historic creeks and rivers continued in the years immediately following the war, which increased the watershed of the shallow lagoon system from roughly 550,000 acres to 1,500,000 acres by the late twentieth century and firmly connected the shallow coastal lagoon system with the Okeechobee and St. Johns River system. Complex pumping stations and schedules managed the drainage of agricultural and residential lands into the Indian River and provided irrigation in the dry season for thousands of front yards carpeted with brilliant green (and thirsty) St. Augustine grass.[3]

The Progressive-era bird conservation efforts of the first decades of the twentieth century expanded in the late twentieth century into a full-blown national environmental movement, which recognized the importance of preventing pollution in the lagoon. The population flood (the 5,000 residents who lived in the Indian River in 1900 had exploded to over 1.5 million 100 years later) of the mid-twentieth century plagued the water quality of the system, despite the fact that many careless polluting activities were curbed by the mid-twentieth century. For example, outhouses and oil-change shops built on docks and designed to deposit waste directly into the lagoon were largely removed, only to be replaced with leaky septic systems and fertilizer-laden lawns.[4]

By the late twentieth century more than 70 percent of the mangroves in the Indian River had been separated from the larger lagoon through small, dikelike impoundments as a result of widespread mosquito control efforts, and more than fifty wastewater treatment plants discharged an estimated twenty-six billion gallons of sewage annually into the fragile system.[5] These local trends coincided with nationwide indiscriminate spraying of the pesticide DDT that resulted in plummeting bird populations. Large fish kills and massive algae blooms occurred periodically as a result of pesticide- and nutrient-laden land-based water infusion (much of it from Lake Okeechobee through the St. Lucie canal) and the construction of large causeways spanning the Indian River, effectively segmenting open water and disrupting the natural wind-based water circulation.[6]

Increasingly ambitious and aggressive flood control measures came about in response to the natural flooding that followed hurricanes. The most significant step in the establishment of the Indian River as a managed system came with legislation passed in the wake of a hurricane in September 1947 that damaged citrus in the Indian River and other agriculture in the drained lands south of Lake Okeechobee.[7] To prevent more flooding, Congress passed the Flood Control Act of 1948, which called on the Army Corps of Engineers to tame the inland waterways of South Florida. In response, in 1949 the state legislature established the Central and Southern Florida Flood Control District (CSFFCD) to manage the project.[8] This new body assumed and enlarged the duties of the Everglades Drainage District (which initially dug the St. Lucie canal) and the Okeechobee Flood Control District (which was itself established in the wake of the 1928 hurricane). Within several years, hundreds of miles of canals and gigantic pumps moved water among wetlands, reservoirs, lagoons, and lakes. An area of over 16,000 square miles, including the watersheds of the Everglades, Indian River, Kissimmee River, and St. Johns River, were connected and permanently damaged during this period. The Kissimmee River was canalized between 1962 and 1970 (officially named the C-38 canal) and straightened from its historical meandering 108 miles of oxbows and twists to a short 58 miles. Without the filtering effects of the oxbows, the Kissimmee became a major source of nitrates and other pollutants streaming into Lake Okeechobee, which in turn flowed into the Indian River. Six years after the completion of Kissimmee's canalization, researchers determined that the new canal had already contributed significantly to the eutrophication of the lake.[9]

Previously constructed canals, such as the St. Lucie canal (officially designated the C-44 canal), were enlarged and deepened, which nearly doubled the volume of water drained from Lake Okeechobee.[10] The CSFFCD divided the Everglades system into sub-basins, segmented from (and restricting the water flow to) the new Everglades National Park (dedicated in 1947), and constructed a massive levee, roughly from West Palm Beach to Homestead, to separate land west of the Atlantic Ridge in the southern part of the peninsula from the Everglades. This enabled the modest cities of West Palm Beach, Fort Lauderdale, and Miami to absorb the region's tremendous population infusion and sprout dozens of sprawling suburbs, which would come to spread westward and fill all available land between the western levee and the beach.

Historically, rain was the primary source of water entering the Indian River system. Land-based water was of very limited volume and entered the lagoon only after a slow, meandering path through sloughs and wetlands, whose vegetation removed much of the nutrients and ensured a high water table. Twentieth-century canalization changed this. Efforts to reduce the water table resulted in a managed system in which water was diverted from a very large area of western land and immediately deposited into the lagoon, along with agricultural by-products such as fertilizer and other human-made additives.[11] Discharge from this greatly enlarged wetland created conditions of dramatically varying salinity as the sloshing storm water runoff from each summer rainy afternoon was quickly channeled from fertilizer-laden suburban lawns directly into the lagoon. Historically, new storm-created inlets also changed salinity quickly by introducing tremendous amounts of salt water. Storm events in the twentieth century now discharged enormous amounts of land-based freshwater containing suspended solids, which have greatly decreased water quality in all sections of the lagoon. Conversely, during the dry winter months, the pumps and locks regulating the now thoroughly controlled system severely restricted water discharge into the system to ensure sufficient agricultural irrigation.[12]

In the midst of a growing environmentalist movement, Congress passed the 1970 Clean Water Act, and progressive Florida governor Reuben Askew called a conference on water management. This meeting led to the Waters Resources Act of 1972, which reorganized Florida's flood control agencies into five water "management" districts, each structured around a historical water system. The Indian River found itself spanning the newly created South Florida Water Management District (SFWMD), which includes the Kissimmee River and Everglades, and the St. Johns Water Management District (SJWMD).

As a natural connection between interior wetlands and the Indian River, the north fork of the St. Lucie Estuary has always been a major recipient of land-based water discharge. Twentieth-century drainage efforts exploited this watery route through the Atlantic Ridge. Three major canals were built to drain the surrounding lands for agriculture (the watershed became a hub of the region's famed citriculture) and, after World War II, St. Lucie County urbanization. These three canals (C-23, C-24, and C-44) collectively increased the St. Lucie's watershed to more than four times its historic size (from 187 square miles to 821 square miles).[13] In 1922 (as the St. Lucie canal was being constructed a few miles to the south) there was dredging on the north fork of the St. Lucie Estuary to make the body navigable for boats to provide market access to the new agriculture industry being built on the freshly drained

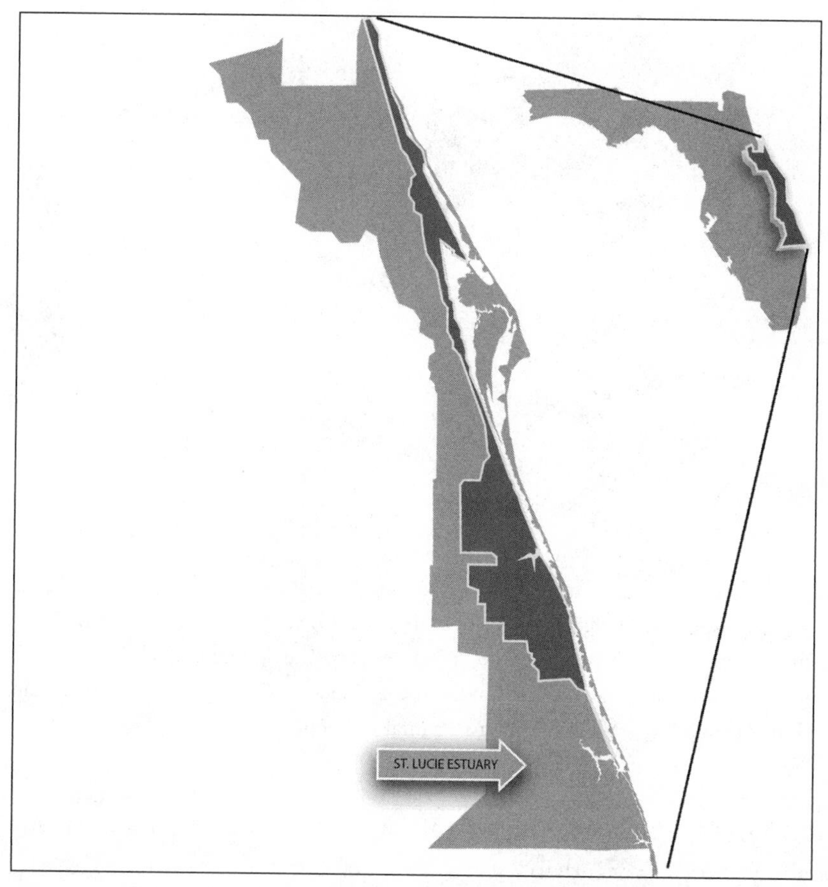

FIGURE 14. Enlarged modern Indian River Lagoon watershed (dark-shaded areas). Notice westward expansion in the central lagoon. This map does not show the watershed of the St. Lucie Estuary. The light-shaded areas roughly correspond with the political boundaries of counties along the Indian River (M. T. Brown).

lands. To this end, historic twisting oxbows were cut off in the straightened north fork, and high earthen embankments were constructed with the fill from the river bottom, a canalization pattern used in many rivers in Florida, most notably the Kissimmee River. These embankments separated the system's historically small floodplains and came to host nonnative vegetation. These alterations dramatically increased the amount of water entering the St. Lucie during the wet summer months and decreased the water discharge in the dry season.[14] So successfully did these canals remove rain water from the marsh and swamplands in

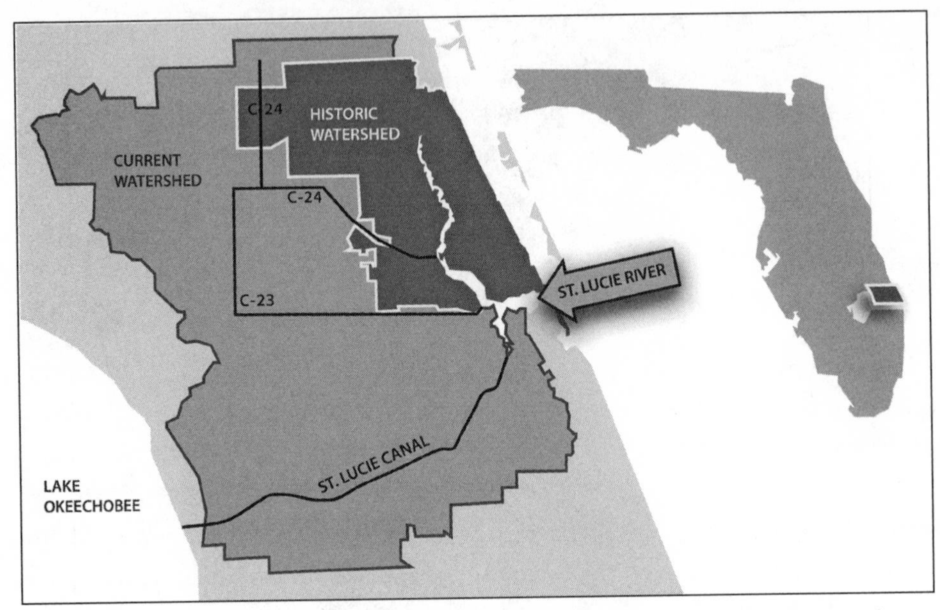

FIGURE 15. The historic watershed of the St. Lucie Estuary is a fraction of the size of the watershed established in the twentieth century. The St. Lucie canal/C-44, which diverts water from Lake Okeechobee, is the primary reason for the watershed expansion (Florida Department of Environmental Protection).

which water had previously accumulated that the region's newly dry soil allowed the lower Indian River's citrus acreage to double in the six years after 1959.[15] The levees and canals built in the 1950s deluged the estuary in the wet season and attempted to store water for irrigation during the dry season.

Thus the St. Lucie (and, by extension, the whole of the lower Indian River) underwent a conversion into a managed and regulated system. This postwar manipulation was merely a branch of larger trends happening throughout the Kissimmee and Everglades, to which the Indian River was historically only loosely connected by wetlands, but was now firmly yoked due to the St. Lucie canal. The three primary canals that flow into the St. Lucie drained Lake Okeechobee when the lake's water level exceeded 15.5 feet to prevent the enormous body from overflowing its dike and threatening the newly drained agricultural fields to the south.[16]

Like the rest of the Indian River, the St. Lucie Estuary has experienced varying levels of salinity historically as inlets have periodically opened and closed in Hutchinson Island, the nearby barrier island. The periods in which salinity plunged following releases from Lake Okeechobee or salinity increased during the dry season following an abrupt end to releases were much more volatile than the (generally) slow forces of nature.[17] While the northern Indian River has experienced prolonged periods of very high salinity and heat that were inhospitable to many species, the process of achieving this cyclical state was not rapid. The very abrupt infusion of enormous quantities of Lake Okeechobee fertilizer-infused freshwater often overwhelmed the resilience of the fauna of the lower Indian River. Increasingly clear and public signs of decline following releases prompted the SFWMD to institute "pulse" releases through the St. Lucie canal in 1991, in which water was released from Lake Okeechobee in a series of small portions, instead of all at once. The program (termed "Run 25") was designed to loosely mimic the natural infusion of water following a rain event and prevent the salinity of the system from plunging due to the massive discharge of freshwater.[18]

This very modest change failed to prevent the St. Lucie Estuary from becoming a notorious example of late twentieth-century pollution. *Stuart News* editor Ernest Lyons was a prominent critic of the SFWMD's efforts to direct freshwater to the St. Lucie Estuary, which surrounds the city of Stuart on three sides. Lyons was a vocal opponent of the canalization of the Kissimmee River (begun in 1962), silt from which came to flow into Lake Okeechobee, then through the St. Lucie canal to the St. Lucie Estuary. Instead of remaining in the twisting oxbows of the Kissimmee, this silt largely filled in the St. Lucie, greatly reducing its depth.

Where nineteenth-century visitors described a deep, clear river with a sandy bottom, the St. Lucie of the late twentieth century had become a shallow, muddy morass. By the late 1970s the previously deep water surrounding the Palm City Bridge, which crosses the south fork of the St. Lucie River between Stuart and Palm City, had become so choked with silt that the muck formed significant islands and permanent large mud flats. Longtime *Stuart News* reporter and columnist Joe Crankshaw lamented that he could now nearly walk across what had been a deep river in his youth.[19] While canalization has increased siltation in other rivers, such as the growing and shifting soil at the wide mouth of the Mississippi River, much of the silt in the St. Lucie River never left the small estuary and merely accumulated. The narrow St. Lucie inlet is simply too far removed and too small to spit out most of the canal's silt and muck into the Atlantic. Tourists and snowbirds in the decades following the CSFFCD's canals found a river that bore little resemblance to that described by engineer Charles Vignoles in 1823: "the majestic appearance of the St. Lucie river affords at first sight the greatest expectations." Vignoles's breathless description of the region also foreshadowed one of the causes of its eventual decline. St. Lucie is "of a good quality and affords a variety of places where fruit culture would succeed."[20] The canals that carried muddy, fertilizer-laden water were constructed largely to accommodate the citrus industry. Like the St. Lucie, other Florida waterways were subject to the "improvements" that accompanied a population and agricultural influx in the years following World War II. For example, in 1955 the Peace River was declared by the State Board of Health to be "suffering severely from organic and chemical pollution." Similarly, Boca Ciega Bay on the west coast of the peninsula was nearly completely filled in with causeways and spoil islands, each bristling with tidy rows of tiny retirement homes.[21]

The impact of the CSFFCD C-23 and C-24 canals on the St Lucie became increasingly clear, even before the capacity of the flood control (and later irrigation) canals was doubled in the 1960s. As early as 1953 sport fishermen in the lower Indian River reported having to travel three to four miles offshore to find water not tainted by canal runoff pollutants. The freshwater discharge threatened to revert the St. Lucie into a shallow, mucky version of its freshwater state, which it was in the period before the 1892 opening of the St. Lucie Inlet. While large, desirable sport and commercial saltwater fish such as snapper, grouper, jacks, and tarpon had earned fame for the Indian River (and especially the St. Lucie) as a fishing center in the first decades of the 1900s, the new flood control canals dramatically restructured the fragile ecosystem, from its smothered benthic organisms to the loss of its once-prized goliath grouper and tarpon.[22] Soon after the completion of the St. Lucie canal the new canals began draining vast areas of citrus and urban lands in St. Lucie County into the St. Lucie. The city of Stuart soon rebranded itself as the "sailfish capital of the world" and a center of *offshore* sport fishing because the inshore fish stocks of the St. Lucie (on which the city was built) had become so depleted.

In the last decades of the twentieth century the decline of the St. Lucie was increasingly apparent. Damage to the small estuary in the southern Indian River system had become increasingly visible. Devastating algae blooms and fish kills had periodically swept the St. Lucie following releases of freshwater from Lake Okeechobee, as well as through the C-23 and C-24 canals, which flow into the estuary's north fork. Following the 1998 El Niño event, large, toxic, bright green algae blooms were found throughout the water body, caused by the inundation of the supernutrient agriculture runoff released into the estuary through drainage canals created earlier in the century.[23] Particularly egregious instances of these phenomena also occurred in the summers of 1984, 1991, and 2013.[24] The nutrient-rich water was the perfect incubator for the microalgae *Cryptoperidiniopsis*, which ate mucus off the fish of the estuary and left them vulnerable to other parasites.[25] In the spring of 1998 researchers found that nearly 40 percent of the striped mullet caught in the estuary and over 30 percent of the sheepshead had lesions.[26] Thousands of lesioned and deformed fish littered the banks of the newly brown waters following significant releases (such as storms) through the agricultural canals that deposit into the estuary. Scientists found high levels of copper and other pathogens used as antifungal agents in citrus production in the enlarged watershed in the beginning of the twenty-first century. Other than copper, the lower Indian River experienced little chemical contamination. Instead, a muck composed of a dark organic matter filled the small estuary. The rich black muck found at the bottom of Lake Okeechobee and the Everglades was thought to be very fertile for agriculture and contributed to the 1920s Florida land boom. In addition to disappointing a generation of would-be truck farmers, the muck that flowed into the St. Lucie created hypoxic conditions that suffocated many plants and animals by removing oxygen from the water.[27]

Along with reduced water quality, loss of habitat due to urbanization was the primary reason that dozens of the Indian River's animals were listed as endangered by the end of the twentieth century, including the manatee. Scientists reported finding an outbreak of *fibropapillomatosis* (a virus that caused bulbous skin tumors) in Indian River green turtles and the serious fungal skin infection *lobomycosis* in "epidemic" numbers among many bottlenose dolphins in the southern Indian River.[28] In the second half of the twentieth century there were significant declines in the population of many of the Indian River's roughly 700 species of fish, including those of commercially valuable fish and shellfish. Catches of spotted sea trout, for example, declined by 50 percent. Unlike most fish in the Indian River, the spotted sea trout lives within the lagoon its entire life, which suggested that its decline was indicative of systemic ecosystem deterioration. The significant inshore fisheries, such as the very successful shark fishery exploited by lower Indian River fishermen in the 1930s and 1940s, had declined so significantly that by the late twentieth century commercial fishing had ceased to be a major industry in the Indian River.[29]

The declining commercial utility of the lagoon coincided with an unprecedented northern population influx. Indian River developers continued to publish siren songs of tropical warmth in northern periodicals, but descriptions of water-skiing, sunbathing, and recreational fishing had replaced an earlier era's boasts of agricultural abundance. Instead of healing tuberculosis, the warm climate of the Indian River was hyped as a beautiful golf and fishing-infused backdrop against which to spend a new American innovation: the modern retirement. Thanks to postwar economic affluence and the Social Security Act, the Indian River was no longer seen as a way to secure food for the table but instead as merely one more venue to enjoy the Sunshine State's growing number of attractions.

Stress on the Indian River increased as it absorbed its share of Florida's booming population. The 303,000 residents of the Indian River in 1970 increased to an estimated 1.54 million in the early years of the twenty-first century.[30] In 1990 the Environmental Protection Agency (EPA) designated the Indian River an "estuary of national significance," the same year that the Florida legislature passed the Indian River Lagoon and Basin Act, which required that all discharges from wastewater treatment plants be phased out. The act did not limit industrial discharge, which continued in over fifty locations, including the St. Lucie Nuclear Power Plant (which began operation in 1976 in the southern Indian River on Hutchinson Island) and concrete batch plants.[31]

Because sea grass is perhaps the most important plant in the ecosystem of the lagoon, the Indian River's dwindling sea grass communities were an especially alarming example of decline. The most significant sea grass losses occurred in the central Indian River between Palm Bay and Cocoa, where more than 70 percent of the lagoon's sea grass beds disappeared between the 1940s and the early twenty-first century.[32] In the central lagoon areas immediately surrounding Turkey Creek, the Eau Gallie River and Crane Creek saw more than 80 percent of their sea grass beds disappear due to urban runoff and huge amounts of sediments that were deposited in the lagoon from the rivers.[33] Favored by fish and manatees alike, the system's sea grass fields declined by more than 80 percent in regions near urban centers, but remained relatively robust in isolated areas, such as the waters surrounding Cape Canaveral. Sea grass loss is largely a result of the water-clouding effect of pollutants, algae, and sediment, although single-celled phytoplankton, which thrive in runoff introduced into the lagoon, also block sunlight, killing grasses. Without sufficient clarity to provide ample light, roughly 20 percent of the whole lagoon's sea grass beds have disappeared.[34]

The relatively healthy sea grass beds and mangrove-lined shores of the Cape Canaveral region in the northern Indian River are a result of events far removed from the east coast of Florida. After being subjected to World War II–era practice bombing raids and the dredging and widening of waterways to accommodate PT boats, Cape Canaveral became the site of a series of early Cold War–related activities, including the Joint Long-Range Proving Ground, the Banana River Naval Air Station (later renamed Patrick Air Base), the Cape Canaveral Air Force Station, and, most important, the Kennedy Space Center. While the rest of the lagoon experienced the ill effects of a population boom, the vast stretches of mangroves in the northern Indian River remained undisturbed and healthy within the newly established Merritt Island National Wildlife Refuge and the Canaveral National Seashore.[35] Like sea grasses, mangroves are a critical component of the ecosystem because their submerged roots provide food and shelter for many species and support complex food webs.[36] Like other key elements of the Indian River, mangroves have historically varied from periods of healthy vitality to naturally occurring periods of significant decline. For example, St. Lucie Estuary resident Curt Schroeder reported that every mangrove in the Indian River died in the days following the agriculturally catastrophic freezes of 1894–95.[37] While accounts of twentieth-century decline were accumulating in the rest of the system, in the last decades of the twentieth century the system's cleanest water was consistently found in the vicinity of the Kennedy Space Center.[38]

Isolated Cape Canaveral was selected by the federal government to be the center of the nascent space program. Wide expanses of scrub fields and remote pioneer cabins were bulldozed to make room for quickly built launchpads. The 1950s saw an array of increasingly large and complex rockets, from the July 1950 launch of a V-2 rocket to the satellite *Explorer I* of January 1958, quickly hurled skyward in response to the Soviet *Sputnik*, launched four months earlier.[39]

These institutions and related support industries swelled the region's population fivefold between 1950 and 1960, to over 200,000, which briefly made Brevard the fastest-growing county in the nation.[40] The National Aeronautics and Space Agency (NASA) slowed its frenzied expansion in the wake of the fervor of the 1960s Apollo program, which resulted in thousands of unemployed engineers and technicians unable to make mortgage payments on their suburban bungalows, rapidly built in the previous decade. But the acquisition of more than 140,000 acres by the federal government during the creation of the Kennedy Space Center would have the greatest effect on the Indian River.

The vast stretches of land acquired by NASA to provide a buffer between launch activities and populated areas required ending public access to popular beaches and hunting grounds. Faced with local backlash, NASA arranged for the creation of the Merritt Island National Wildlife Refuge in 1963, which included most of the Banana River but did not include Mosquito Lagoon. While the rest of the lagoon experienced the ill effects of a population boom, the vast stretches of mangroves in the northern Indian River remained uncut and healthy within the newly established sanctuary, which earned the Kennedy Space Center local and political support.[41]

NASA's vast eminent domain lands included over ten miles of beach north of Haulover Canal, which lay outside of the newly created Merritt Island National Wildlife Refuge. By the late 1960s the state legislature considered selling the land to developers. Nathaniel Reed, Florida governor Claude Kirk's new special assistant for the environment, received letters urging him to preserve the area (known as "Playalinda Beach") from being subjected to towering condominiums that were sprouting along much of Florida's coast. Due to the efforts of activists such as New Smyrna Beach artist Doris Leeper, the Mosquito Lagoon was included within the newly formed Canaveral National Seashore in 1975.[42]

Located within federal land claimed for the space program, the Merritt Island National Wildlife Refuge would become the oldest fully protected marine reserve in the nation. Sport fishermen caught record-size fish in the last decades of the twentieth century in the waters protected by the marine reserves in the Merritt Island National Wildlife Refuge and Canaveral National Seashore. Researchers caught more than twelve times the number of black drum fish within the reserves than in the waters adjacent to it. The bounty of other species suggested similar rates of vitality. The protected shorelines of the northern Indian River drew more than one million visitors by the first decade of the twenty-first century. The lack of development in these protected regions and the corresponding flourishing flora and fauna proved to be an economic boon to the towns of the region. Thousands of bird-watchers from across the nation annually flocked to Titusville's annual Space Coast Birding and Wildlife Festival in the first decade of the twenty-first century.[43]

Soon after acquiring 90,000 acres of land in the vicinity of Cape Canaveral, administrators at NASA became concerned that the clouds of mosquitoes produced in the Indian River's salt marshes could make life intolerable for NASA's workers. In response, the Joint Community Impact Coordination Committee (JCICC) was formed to fix problems associated with the creation of an enormous new facility in a recently empty region. The JCICC quickly became NASA's mosquito-fighting arm, a daunting task in an area in which researchers with hand nets reported that they captured four *pounds* of mosquitoes in one hour. In 1962 NASA expansion was at its most fevered pace, and concerns about mosquitoes were at their greatest, as forty-three Floridians died that year of mosquito-spread encephalitis. The JCICC instituted an ambitious plan for NASA to pay for the Brevard Mosquito Control District to build impoundments along the shores of the Indian River. Within three years, miles of low earthen embankments snaked along the mangrove shorelines of the Mosquito River and northern Indian River. The impoundments allowed engineers to keep the shoreline either permanently flooded or dry, either of which killed mosquito larvae, which hatch in the wet season after being laid on land in the dry months. In addition to the impoundments NASA tapped into its lavish congressional funding to continue its war on the pests by providing six airplanes, a helicopter, sixteen trucks, two bulldozers, and three draglines to the Brevard County's mosquito control program, which became the most impressive mosquito operation in the state.[44]

The population explosion in Titusville and other towns surrounding Cape Canaveral incentivized developers to build thousands of new suburban houses. Lax local building codes meant that roughly half of the houses built to house the new NASA workforce had septic tanks. The region's low elevation ensured that the tanks would dribble pollutants into the waters of the northern Indian River for decades, a problem that followed population growth throughout coastal Florida.[45] The scale of

NASA's workforce quickly overwhelmed the modest local infrastructure, and by 1962 federal funds paid for the massive Emory L. Bennet Causeway to be built across the lagoon, which freed aerospace workers from the standstill traffic that had initially plagued their commutes across the Indian River.

In this context of growing federal investment came the digging of the Port Canaveral Inlet between 1950 and 1954. After 400 years of frightening sailors, Cape Canaveral's inhospitable and isolated coast became somewhat tamed with the dredging of a relatively small harbor. Although it established one of only two deepwater ports in the Indian River (the other is located in Fort Pierce), the saltwater infusion from the inlet was less than other inlets because of a large lock built to block much of the water interchange between the Atlantic and the Banana River (the specific body of the Indian River system into which the inlet was dug). As a result, the Banana River is not tidal. This lagoon continued to have relatively high salinity because the rate at which water evaporates from the shallow Banana River is often greater than that at which freshwater is introduced from other parts of the lagoon system.

The inlet-based shipment of Indian River fruit spoken of by Thomas Richards at the 1892 opening of the St. Lucie Inlet only came to fruition in the decades following the completion of Port Canaveral, when it became a primary channel through which Indian River citrus and concentrated orange juice traveled to northern markets. Like other Indian River inlets, the southerly moving beach sand quickly accumulated along the northern jetty of the Port Canaveral Inlet and receded below the jetty on the cut's southern edge. Ten years after the creation of Port Canaveral, digging began for the Canaveral Barge Canal through Merritt Island, adjacent to the new inlet, to accommodate crude oil entering the inlet en route to the Indian River Generating Station (just south of Titusville), also built in 1964 to power the region's booming population and space industry.[46] In the 1980s Port Canaveral became a popular port for the growing cruise ship industry, focused in Florida due to the peninsula's proximity to the Caribbean. One hundred years after the Banana River was plied only with occasional rough-hewn catboats and

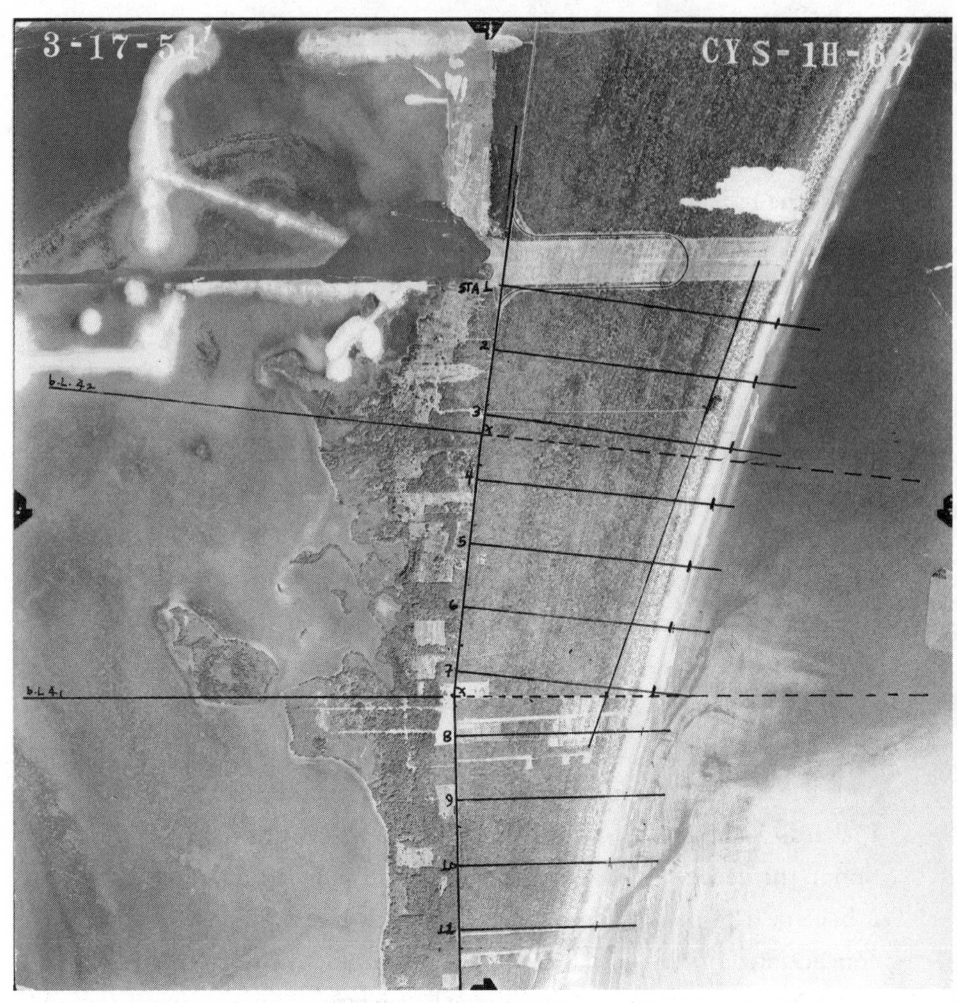

FIGURE 16. Port Canaveral under construction in 1951. The canal and harbor cut from the Banana River is visible in the upper part of the image as well as land cleared for the imminent inlet (University of Florida, "Aerial Photographs of Brevard County—Flight 1H [1951]," Map and Imagery Library, Gainesville).

sharpies carrying Douglas Dummitt's oranges, the waters became home port of mighty behemoths, such as the 1,000-foot *Disney Fantasy,* which boasted 5,336 beds and a crew of 1,450.[47]

In the years preceding World War II only small boats and ferries had access to the barrier islands of the Indian River. The infrastructure constructed to facilitate the state's postwar population boom eventually led

FIGURE 17. A 1958 aerial view of the new causeway connecting Stuart (*on left side of image*) and Sewall's Point with Hutchinson Island, just north of the St. Lucie inlet. Recently constructed spoil islands are visible in the bottom right (University of Florida, "Aerial Photographs of Martin County—Flight 1V [1958]," Map and Imagery Library, Gainesville).

to twenty-two bridges spanning the Indian River, roughly half of which were constructed in thirty years following World War II. Several of these bridges were initially wood-piling structures, including the several built before 1941. These modest, low bridges had little impact on the flora and fauna of the lagoon system, other than hosting outpost communities of fish, stone crabs, and oysters. These low-impact bridges were replaced with large causeways constructed to span the lagoon in many places in the years just before and after World War II. The popularity of low-cost causeways (which featured a swing or drawbridge in the center to accommodate boat traffic traveling north or south through the Indian River) dramatically altered the wind- and inlet-driven circulation of water in the lagoon. These long causeways effectively divided the system into segmented basins and allowed water to flow through only the narrow center under the bridge. To alleviate the increasingly clear detrimental effects of limiting the lagoon's circulation, there was modification of some causeways to include "relief bridges" that allowed a degree of water to flow from one newly segmented basin to the next through gaps at the ends of the causeways as well as under the central bridge. Long fixed bridges built to accommodate sailboat masts up to sixty-five feet (as were bridges along the whole of the Intracoastal Waterway) replaced these old causeways in the last part of the century.[48]

Fill for causeways constructed in the 1950s often came from a massive deepening of the Intracoastal Waterway canal, the same waterway originally started in 1882 by the Florida Coast Line Canal and Transportation Company. After President Truman's yacht, the USS *Sequoia,* ran aground in the Indian River near Vero Beach in the spring of 1950 en route to Key West, Congress allocated funds to deepen the Intracoastal Waterway. By 1960 the canal had been deepened to 12 feet and widened to 125 feet all the way from Trenton, New Jersey, to Fort Pierce. Over the next five years the channel south of Fort Pierce was deepened to 10 feet all the way to Key West.[49] Spoil from this canal deepening was deposited in piles in the Indian River, which ultimately created 137 spoil islands. The process of depositing the spoil covered significant areas of sea grass and created areas of significantly turbid water. The new islands quickly became inhabited by native and exotic species of flora and fauna. The proliferation of exotic species was a visible effect of how heavily altered the system had become.[50]

In addition to a deepened Indian River canal and the creation of causeway bridges, the relative national affluence in the years following World War II brought Sun Belt states like Florida a steady stream of winter tourists and retirees. Beginning in 1958 the General Development Corporation (GDC) created the community of Port St. Lucie on eighty square miles divided into 80,000 lots on wetlands and pine forest near the north fork of the St. Lucie Estuary. Along with other successful "Port" cities such as Port Charlotte, Port LaBelle, North Port, Port St. John, and Port Malabar, the Indian River's Port St. Lucie epitomized the lure of 1960s Florida. Advertisements in national magazines lured thousands of buyers with photos of smiling sunbathers and a $10 per month payment plan. Port St. Lucie's land was drained with the canalization of creeks connected to the north fork of the St. Lucie River. "The land is high and dry-studded with stately pines," boasted a typical GDC advertisement. Although it never carried the cargo or tourists envisioned by its boosters, the Okeechobee waterway was a selling point by postwar developers who claimed that residents would enjoy "miles of water to explore—wonderful boating on the St. Lucie River, Intracoastal Waterway, Atlantic Ocean, and on the Cross State Canal to Florida's West Coast."[51]

So successful were advertisements such as this that by 1970 the Indian River region hosted over 300,000 residents and was subjected to the related increase in storm-water runoff and wastewater treatment runoff, reduced estuarine habitat quality, and a lowering of the groundwater table. In the next twenty years the population underwent another significant increase, to nearly 700,000. The most significant postwar growth has often been in areas away from the Indian River's original towns and cities, and instead has focused on "mail order" developments, such as GDC's Port Malabar in the northern Indian River and Port St. Lucie in the lower. As with much of the peninsula, the growth of agricultural lands has been steadily slowing, while the decentralized nature of preplanned communities, parking lots, and urban sprawl has covered a dramatically increasing portion of the Indian River system. For example, urban land area increased 895 percent between 1940 and 1987.[52]

Air-conditioning and aggressive mosquito-control measures pacified two of the chief ecological hindrances that had kept many people

FIGURE 18. A 1969 photo of Merritt Island urbanization in the northern Indian River. The many small sea-walled canals were previously the site of mangrove coastlines (University of Florida, "Aerial Photographs of Brevard County—Flight 1KK [1969]," Map and Imagery Library, Gainesville).

from moving to the peninsula. Although the Indian River never suffered a yellow fever outbreak as did several other sections of the peninsula, the Spanish, French, English, and Americans all told stories of vicious mosquitoes that required people to spend their days in the water or covered with beach sand. In the first decades of the twentieth century the Indian River was the site of three of the state's five mosquito-control districts. In 1925 the Florida legislature created the Indian River Mosquito Control District (followed soon after by the lower Indian River's St. Lucie and Martin Mosquito Control Districts) to tame the nuisance that threatened to undermine the era's Florida fever. This was followed by decades of very limited success through spraying and dumping poisons (chiefly DDT) in standing bodies of water along the shores of the Indian River system.

The Indian River continued to be the center of the state's mosquito-control efforts when, in 1953, Vero Beach (located in the central Indian River) became the site of the newly created Entomological Research Center (later Florida Medical Entomology Laboratory [FMEL]).[53] This agency encouraged and directed the Indian River's mosquito-control districts to build hundreds of miles of mosquito impoundments. The mosquito impoundments consisted of small earthen dikes built around mangroves with the purpose of being artificially flooded during the Indian River's wet summer months, which coincides with the mosquito season. Because mosquitoes only lay their eggs in moist soil, flooding prevents mosquitoes from depositing their eggs and effectively eliminates mosquitoes without pesticides. Pumps and spillways moved water into and out of the diked areas as desired. Like the watershed of the Indian River, the coast of the lagoon itself was largely transformed into an artificial human-made system. Indian River County and the FMEL took the initiative in instituting impoundments, followed by other Indian River counties in the late 1950s. Under the FMEL, more than three-quarters of the mangrove marsh coast of the Indian River has been destroyed by hundreds of miles of impoundments. More than 40,000 acres of Indian River wetlands have been converted into mosquito impoundments. Most of these impoundments were wholly separated from the lagoon itself and kept flooded year-round, separating the critical mangroves within the impoundments from the Indian River ecosystem. Long mangrove roots that dangled into the water functioned as nurseries for a bewildering range of fish species before impoundments blocked access. This unnecessarily high flooding also killed all wetland vegetation and marshlands within many of the impoundments.

In a state in which water levels define a wide array of habitats, from wetlands to estuaries, human-manipulated water levels had immediate and devastating consequences, both in inland glades and coastal estuaries.

Although the dramatic population increase in the region is evidence of the effectiveness of the impoundments to kill mosquitoes, the impoundments have separated the mangroves and shore from fish and crabs that rely on the subtropical "walking trees" and other vegetation. The manipulation also negatively affected the water quality. In addition, the inability of the short aboveground roots of the Indian River's black mangroves to withstand prolonged flooding led to widespread death. Among the fish most adversely affected by the impounding were those considered a "transient species" because they live in the lagoon for only part of their life, including snook, tarpon, ladyfish, and mullet, all of which are crucial to the region's recreational and commercial fisheries.[54]

There were modest attempts in the last decades of the twentieth century to reconnect some of the impounded areas with the larger Indian River system by building small culverts in order to only seasonally flood the impoundment and allow the wetlands to resort to a tidal nature for the remainder of the year. This technique, known as Rotational Impoundment Management (RIM), proved to be extremely effective in both controlling mosquito reproduction and preserving key vegetation (chiefly black mangroves) and permitting fish and water to flow between the larger lagoon and impoundment.[55]

The growing environmental consensus sparked by declining water quality in many of the waterways across the country led to a series of conservation programs that benefited the Indian River, in addition to the previously discussed 1970 Clean Water Act and 1972 Water Resources Act of Florida. The 1969 Environmental Protection Act required the Army Corps of Engineers and the CSFFCD (for the first time) to consider the negative effects of their projects on receiving bodies of water, such as the Indian River.[56] Less than ten years after the doubling in size and capacity of the C-23 and C-24 canals, the alarmingly rapid mudiness and decline of the St. Lucie led to the declaration of the north fork of the estuary as an aquatic preserve in 1972.[57] Also established in

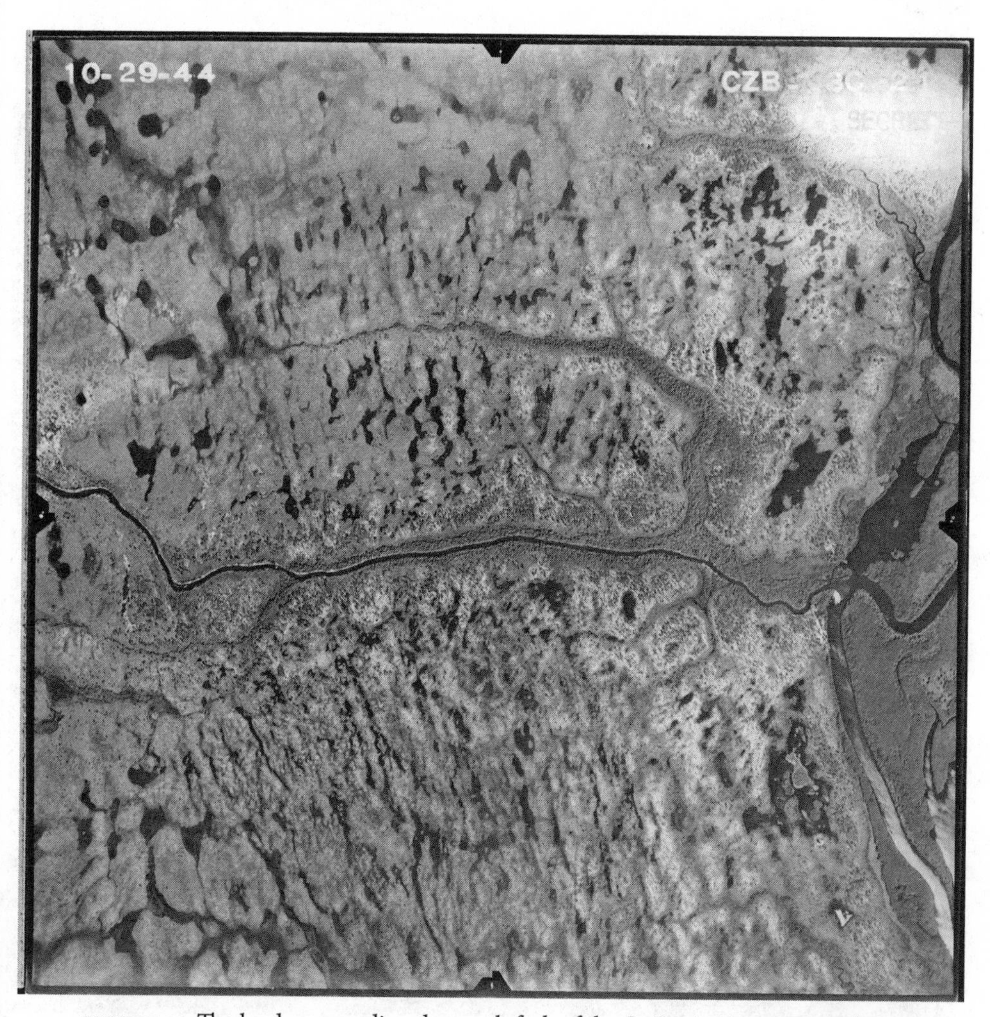

FIGURE 19. The land surrounding the north fork of the St. Lucie Estuary provides a useful study of development trends that occurred throughout the Indian River region. This 1944 aerial photo documents little more than wetlands (University of Florida, "Aerial Photographs of St. Lucie County—Flight 3C [1944]," Map and Imagery Library, Gainesville).

this period were six other aquatic preserves, which covered much of the remaining Indian River system, ultimately put under the management of the Florida Department of Natural Resources.[58]

As the population of the Indian River continued to increase in the 1990s, five counties and the St. Johns Water Management District and the South Florida Water Management District collaborated to create

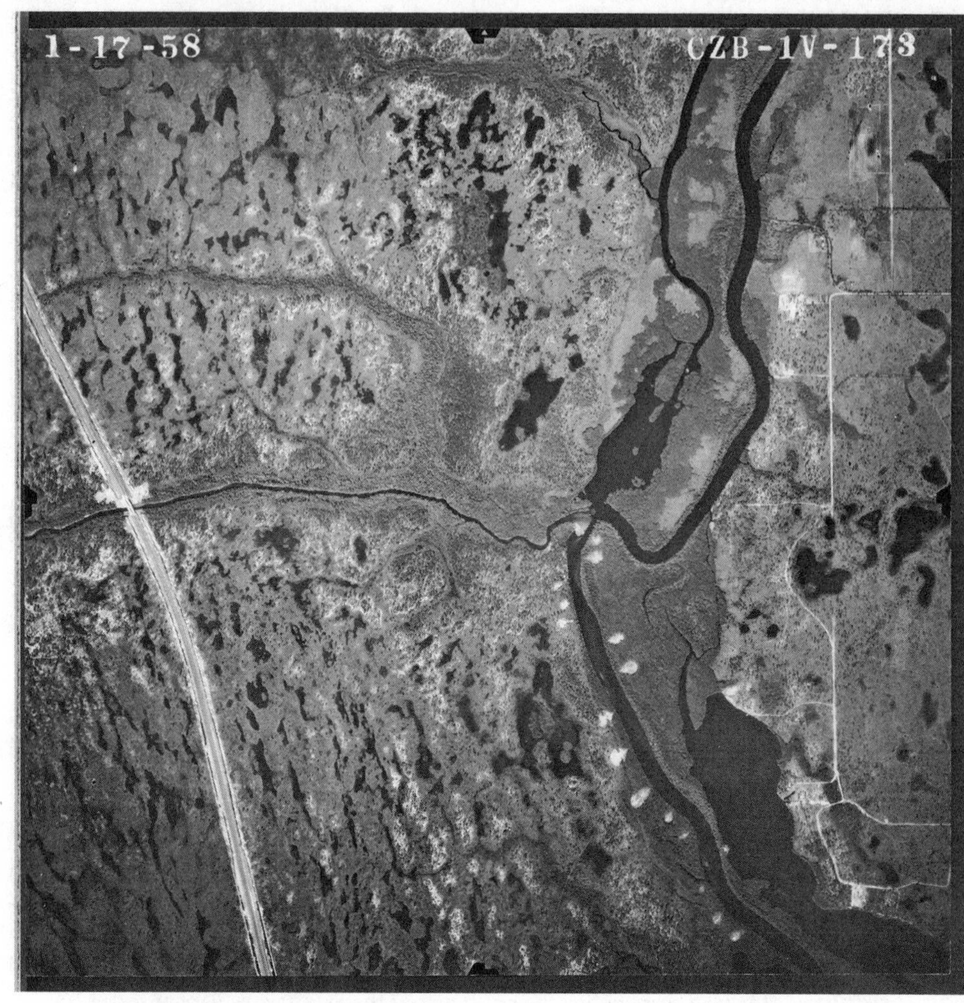

FIGURE 20. By 1958 the north fork of the St. Lucie had been dredged, and spoil deposits are clear (University of Florida, "Aerial Photographs of St. Lucie County—Flight 1V [1958]," Map and Imagery Library, Gainesville).

"Indian River Lagoon Blueway," a string of preserves intended to provide a continuous path of public areas along the length of the river's string of water bodies. By 2007 only 4,400 acres of the planned 27,000 acres had been purchased. The protected land included coves, pine flatwoods, and wetlands scattered across dozens of spots along the lagoon's shoreline.[59]

FIGURE 21. This 1970 photo shows three of the features that would become emblematic of contemporary Florida: the decentralized suburban sprawl of Port St. Lucie at the top of the image, the canalization of a small natural river into the flood control and irrigation C-24 canal, and a prominent golf course (on the right side of the image) (University of Florida, "Aerial Photographs of St. Lucie County—Flight 2MM [1970]," Map and Imagery Library, Gainesville).

In the three decades following the Clean Water Act of 1970, Florida established a number of land-acquisition plans with the purpose of protecting water quality, including the Conservation and Recreational Lands Program (1979), Save Our Rivers (1981), Florida Communities Trust (1985), Preservation 2000 (1991), and Florida Forever (1998).[60] The two most significant examples of conservation legislation that benefited the Indian River were Florida's Surface Water Improvement and Management (SWIM) program (1987) and the 1991 Indian River Lagoon National Estuary Program, established as a result of the federal Water Quality Act (1987), which included a special emphasis on estuaries of national significance. The SWIM program changed the mandate of the water management districts to assess restoration needs and implement restoration policies in six critical state water bodies, including the Indian River.[61]

In addition to federal and state programs, voters in several counties along the Indian River approved land acquisition programs to fight lagoon pollution. Among the most ambitious was Brevard County's 1990 Environmentally Endangered Lands Program, which established a twenty-year tax to raise $55 million. The Indian River County Conservation Lands Program was established in 1992 with a $26 million bond referendum, which was dwarfed by a $50 million referendum approved by voters twelve years later. St. Lucie County voters created the Environmentally Sensitive Lands Program, which would come to manage twenty-seven preserves in the Indian River watershed. More than 38,000 acres were protected in Volusia County after voters there established the Volusia Forever program in 2000.[62] In the years following these new conservation efforts, some damaged areas of the lagoon saw modest improvements. These programs and others (most importantly the Florida Forever Program, which began in 2001) purchased thousands of ecologically sensitive acres within the system watershed and scooped out significant deposits of muck at the mouths of several canalized rivers, including Turkey Creek, Crane Creek, and the St. Sebastian River.[63] Funding for Florida Forever was slashed by the state legislature in the wake of the 2008 recession. Three of four voters responded in

2014 by voting to change the state's constitution to create a robust dedicated stream of revenue (nearly $20 billion over a thirty-year period) to continue funding environmentally sensitive land purchases. The "grandfathering in" of mid-twentieth-century development and the rapidly growing regional population often mitigated the ambitious goals of these programs to reduce pollutants in the system. Unlike Gilded Age and Progressive-era settlers who had an economic and cultural reliance on the lagoon, late twentieth-century residents lived largely economically separated from the lagoon. Local ire was not raised because pollution threatened livelihoods but because of national trends that raised the profile of the problems associated with poor water quality.

Because the St. Lucie canal (C-44) yoked the Indian River to the larger Everglades ecosystem, it fell under late twentieth-century public/private programs to restore the famed "River of Grass," most notably the Comprehensive Everglades Restoration Program (CERP). Programs such as CERP called for the Army Corps of Engineers to construct more canals, holding reservoirs, levees, and pumps with an aim of reducing the amount of freshwater discharged into the system by the canals earlier constructed by the agency.[64]

The immense scale of CERP made it the world's largest ecosystem remediation project. Roughly $1 billion (of the estimated $7.8 billion price tag) would be spent on a bewildering series of increasingly complex projects, with the intention of stopping much of the damage done to the Indian River by the Central and South Florida System of the mid-twentieth century. CERP was designed with a thirty-year timeline with more than sixty major components. The undertaking relied on the cooperation of countless local, state, and federal agencies, as well as the fickle winds of local and national politics to fund each step. Encompassing 18,000 acres and sixteen counties, the component of CERP that most directly affected the lagoon was the Indian River Lagoon–South Project, which was scheduled for completion in 2017. The project did not close the C-44 canal through which Lake Okeechobee discharge flowed, but redirected much of the water to newly constructed reservoirs and flooded "Storm Treatment Areas" to hold and filter the water before it was released into the St. Lucie. The plan also called for removing a portion of the several feet of muck that lay on the bottom of the St. Lucie, which had grown deeper with each discharge and smothered a series of modest attempts to reintroduce the oyster, which had largely disappeared from much of the Indian River.[65]

Despite the lofty political rhetoric surrounding President George H. W. Bush's 1990 announcement that the federal government would give more than $1 million annually for remediation of the Indian River (as part of the new National Estuary Program), residents in the region saw no change in the steady deterioration of the system.[66] Although the National Estuary Program allocated federal funds to protect or enhance roughly 7,000 acres (of mostly wetlands) in the Indian River and waged a notable effort to remove invasive plants in the region, the two decades following federal recognition of the Indian River's plight failed to produce significant improvements discernable to the lagoon residents. The glacial pace of progress and the byzantine network of faceless agencies involved in "restoration" efforts ensured that increasingly frustrated residents along the shores of the Indian River became vocal when algae blooms and fish kills continued to return many summers.[67] An algae superbloom grew to cover much of the Banana River in the spring of 2011, and ultimately spread into the northern Indian River proper and the neighboring Mosquito Lagoon. At the same time, a separate large bloom stretched from Melbourne south to Fort Pierce, a distance of some fifty miles. The deaths of more than 300 pelicans and seventy-six dolphins preceded a steady stream of sharply elevated animal deaths over the next several years. In 2012 the Banana River experienced a ferocious "Brown Tide," a type of algae bloom that was correlated with the deaths of 135 manatees and killed a stunning 60 percent of the Indian River's crucial sea grass beds.[68]

Local concern about continued declining water quality ebbed and flowed as rainy summers were followed by Lake Okeechobee discharges into the St. Lucie Estuary. On April 22, 1970 (the first Earth Day), high school students held a funeral service for the river at the C-44 locks, where Lake Okeechobee discharges occur. In 1983 faculty members of the Florida Institute of Technology (located in the central Indian River city of Melbourne) formed the Marine Resources Council to promote the plight of the embattled lagoon. In 1989 thousands of residents of the northern Indian River stood arm-in-arm in response to the call of Marine Resources Council director Diane Barile to join the first "hands across the lagoon" protest. Similarly, citizens in the southern part of the system formed the St. Lucie River Initiative in 1991 to document and publicize declining water quality.[69] Continued concern with the chronically brown waters of the once-clear Indian River led to the creation of many grassroots organizations, including Rivers Coalition (a collection of over seventy nonprofits and other community organizations) formed in the wake of algae blooms in the summer of 1998. A Rivers Coalition spinoff, the youth-oriented River Kidz, grew from a 2011 lemonade stand fund-raiser by Sewall's Point elementary school students Naia Mader and Evie Flaugh to include hundreds of local youths. Additionally, the Indian Riverkeeper organization was established in 1993, part of the larger Water Keeper Alliance, which had its roots in the 1960s movement to clean the Hudson River in New York.

An increasingly upset public was able to understand the scope of damage done to the Indian River thanks to intensified regional media coverage, especially the "Our Indian River Lagoon" series by Scripps Treasure Coast Newspapers created in the wake of the Okeechobee discharges in the summer of 2013. Local journalists were able to convey reasonably precise details (such as the number of dead manatees and acres of sea grasses lost) in what they dubbed "The Lost Summer" of 2013 partly thanks to researchers at Florida Atlantic University's Harbor Branch Oceanographic Institute (located in Fort Pierce), who established a series of significant programs dedicated to studying the health of the Indian River.[70] Over the course of several summers, thousands of people marched to the Okeechobee canal locks in Stuart to protest the foaming brown water discharged from Lake Okeechobee in the weeks following summer afternoon rainstorms. The deluges of 2013 were not unprecedented, but the Indian River's increased fragility meant that it was harmed by discharges that would have caused less damage in earlier decades. Very few of the angry marchers voiced concern that the decline of the Indian River threatened their livelihoods, but instead they focused on the quality of recreation that they enjoyed. No longer home to schooners and stern-wheelers hauling sea turtles, the Indian River had become host to hordes of buzzing jet skis and fishing skiffs. Local residents of the late nineteenth and late twentieth centuries shared a disdain for the freshwater nature of the St. Lucie River. Victorian pineapple growers complained about the freshwater vegetation that stank, while later recreational anglers decried the fishless flats that followed lost sea grasses in the weeks following summer freshwater deluges from the Okeechobee canal.[71]

Although it was originally romantically envisioned to be a region of independent truck farmers, the hundreds of thousands of acres of land drained south of Lake Okeechobee became dominated by multinational sugar companies. The choice fields became very attractive to Cuban sugar growers who fled to Florida after losing their political clout in the wake of the 1959 Cuban Revolution. By the last decades of the twentieth century Florida politicians of both major parties relied heavily on campaign contributions from sugar corporations. Plans to stop Lake Okeechobee discharges into the Indian River by restoring the southerly flow of water met resistance from the politically powerful sugar industry, whose cane fields occupied vast stretches of the Everglades Agricultural Area (the official name of the drained lands immediately south of the lake). Public opposition to politicians chiefly concerned with the interests of the sugar industry grew as the industry's dozens of lobbyists successfully fought modest state efforts to tax the industry to cover the cost of cleaning its polluted water.[72]

In addition to tourism, citrus remained a significant part of the economy of the region throughout the twentieth century. Centered in St. Lucie and Indian River counties, the Indian River's seventy-eight million boxes of citrus accounted for over 38 percent of the state's citrus crop, and 7 percent of the global citrus produced in the late twentieth century.[73] The renown enjoyed by Indian River citrus is a result of the ecology and geography of the thin lagoon. The proximity of the lagoon to the Gulf Stream brought not only shipwrecks to eager inhabitants of the region but also the mediating effects of warm air in the winter. The Indian River has at many times been spared the brunt of hard frosts inflicted on growers in the state's interior.

Agricultural uses of land within the watershed for noncitrus produce was dwarfed by the mighty Indian River orange and occupied less than 3 percent of the land devoted to citrus. Cattle operations in the southern Indian River counties were mostly based outside of the system watershed, as are vegetable farms, which are overwhelmingly in Palm Beach County and nearly absent from lands within the system itself.[74] Until the perfection of concentration processing in 1945, oranges were shipped to northern markets fresh. In the last decade of the twentieth century, the convenience and quality associated with "not from concentrate" led to an increase in demand for fresh orange juice.[75]

While buyers loved the sweetness of the Indian River's oranges, commercial growers and concentrators could scientifically measure the superiority of the lagoon's fruit. Over 90 percent of an orange is water, and the remaining portion of an orange's juice is composed of "total soluble solids," namely sugar, organic acids, vitamins, potassium, and very small amounts of inorganic salts and organic compounds that are the cause of flavor variations. The primary way to measure juice density is in the Brix scale, which measures the weight of sugar per volume. The relatively high groundwater table in the Indian River ensured that the roots of citrus trees were shorter than those of trees planted inland. This characteristic allowed the trees to devote more energy to their limbs, leaves, and fruit, which resulted in a denser concentration of total soluble solids.[76] This increased Brix count was reflected in market demand for the lagoon's fruit. In 1991 the market rate for a box of Indian River citrus was $9.10, while a box from the interior of Florida sold for $6.60.[77] In the last decades of the twentieth century vast tracts of citrus land were bulldozed into bare fields in the wake of the dual afflictions of citrus canker and citrus greening, each of which attacked the region's once-mighty industry. "The loss of the citrus industry is tragic," observed Nathaniel Reed. "But the ability to acquire that land and change the one-way canal system into the Lagoon into huge man-made wetlands is necessary to save the system."[78]

Where once it was the center of culture and the economy to American settlers in the nineteenth century, the lagoon became increasingly peripheral to growth that was originally based on its attributes. While developers boasted of the lagoon's warm waters and balmy breezes, the low-cost housing they created grew into an industrial-housing behemoth that became increasingly divorced from the thin body of water. As the lagoon's urban centers stretched westward and ultimately had virtually no cultural or economic effect on the sprawling exurbs, the Indian River became increasingly available only to the wealthy as its long stretches of mangrove-lined shores became divided into lots upon which people built increasingly expensive houses. By the end of the twentieth century very few residents of the 153-mile-long system were employed in jobs directly related to the lagoon. As commercial fishing declined, recreational fishing increased. The Indian River had become once again commodified; this time its value came not from the market price of its fish and plumes but from the division of its shore and surrounding watershed region into thousands of lots. The transformation of the lagoon from a place of labor to a place of leisure was complete.

6

Conclusion

"It is a delight merely to view the river from the shore," wrote a travel writer of the central Indian River region in 1918. "As you look off across the blue water from the mainland you see the islands dim in dreamy haze on the other side. Schools of fishes flash their silvery sides to the sun in the shallows; farther out frolicsome mullet leap high into the air and fall back with a resounding splash."[1] This writer's description came twenty-four years after a freeze in the same lagoon killed tens of thousands of fish in such quantities that local residents shoveled them into wagons for fertilizer. The stench from the fish kill lingered for more than one year.[2] The same freeze nearly wiped out the Indian River's entire citrus and pineapple industry.[3] The same lagoon ecosystem often lauded for its fertility was at other times extremely inhospitable to the flora and fauna living within it. Historically, prolonged summer heat has often become trapped within the shallow water in the northern Indian River. With no significant inlets in the vicinity within the last several hundred years, this heated water suppressed dissolved oxygen concentrations and created anaerobic conditions with too little oxygen to support most fish life. Species able to adapt to the altered conditions became the new symbols of a brown lagoon. Anglers found that their hooks attracted smaller numbers of silvery snook and increasing numbers of muddy catfish.[4] One might be tempted to ask which of these descriptions of the east coast lagoon is accurate. Any nuanced understanding of the silver ribbon of water must recognize that the lagoon is historically both a place of biophysical diversity unsurpassed in the United States and the scene of naturally occurring dead zones, largely inhospitable to life. The complexity and productivity created in the bi-climate body, which hosts a hybrid ecosystem in which plants and animals from two distinct climate zones interact, is not one thing. It is simultaneously an ecosystem of breathtaking beauty and cringe-inducing carnage. Just as it is neither wholly fresh nor wholly salt, it is neither land nor open water. For every sensational description of an exotic creature or plant written by a nineteenth-century settler, there was one that detailed the horrors of mosquito swarms or the intolerable banality of loneliness and isolation.

The liminality of the lagoon was the secret of its significance. By existing in a permanent state of transition, and always in the process of becoming something else, it came to host both the temperate summer flounder, which swims no farther south than the Indian River, and the tropical mangrove, which grows no farther north than the lagoon.[5] The lagoon existed geographically near the Bahamas and Caribbean, but was tied by land to the distant United States. This proximity created a nineteenth-century culture that combined a reliance on imported Caribbean seeds, plants, and shipwrecks with the northern sensibilities of its new residents and appropriated southern social norms to form a culture as transitional and amalgamated as the lagoon itself. Explorers of the lagoon found the northernmost thermal effects of the warm waters of the Gulf Stream on the North American coastline before its path to northern Europe. Just as the "river in the ocean" carried wrecked Spanish treasure fleets and pre-Columbian and Cuban fishermen to the lagoon, it would bring political and economic refugees from Cuba and Haiti to the Indian River in the twentieth century. The same ecosystem that allowed its Glades culture indigenous peoples to survive without the agriculture relied upon by all other cultures on the continent also enticed Spanish, British, and American settlers, who were often just as thrilled by its teeming fish and turtle stocks and agricultural fertility as they were disappointed by its isolation from northern markets for these exotic commodities. The warm, humid climate that was reputed to heal countless maladies also bred shocking clouds of malarial mosquitoes.

The transitional nature of the Indian River presents difficulties for contemporary policy makers. Any attempt to "restore" the lagoon will by necessity declare the lagoon's state at a particular historical period to be the standard. The lagoon's complex liminality suggests that such a goal is impossible. As long as human-made inlets, impoundments, locks, and canals (and urbanization broadly) remain in the system, politicians, conservationists, and environmentalists must settle for a lagoon ecosystem that cannot be extricated from the humans who inhabit the region. Within this framework, however, it is possible to make much progress to increase species diversity through efforts to increase sea grass coverage and the reduction of siltation, particulates, and agricultural and storm water runoff. Promising efforts such as Rotational Impoundment Management (RIM) suggest that improvement in biophysical vitality is possible while maintaining the hybrid built environment–nature of the lagoon created in the twentieth century. Activists in the Indian River were encouraged in 2014 when voters approved a state constitutional amendment that would force politicians to use state funds to purchase lands for environmental protection. Many expressed hope that these funds would be used to create wetlands in the Indian River watershed so that water could be stored and filtered before it reaches the lagoon.

However, essential questions remain unanswered. Who will pay for the installation of sewer lines and sewage treatment plants to replace the leaking septic tanks in the region? Lax oversight by local governments (which did not dare to interfere with the perceived benefits of exploding development and sprawl) in the 1960s through 1990s resulted in hundreds of thousands of septic tanks, many of which were intended to be in place only until developers installed sewage lines. When many developers went bankrupt or left the region, sewers were left unbuilt, and the septic tanks they left behind would present perhaps the single greatest threat to the declining Indian River.

Many uncertainties remain about the management of the lagoon's complex network of human-made changes. If one supposes that decreasing the footprint of humans is the goal, then what should we make of instances when more human manipulation would appear to support biodiversity? Maintaining artificially flooded mosquito impoundments segmented from the larger Indian River system may at times provide more food for bird rookeries within the impoundment. Some impoundments receive stormwater runoff, and it would appear to be in the best interests of the larger system to keep this water contained. Historical events in other areas of the peninsula provide examples of environmental manipulation creating positive externalities. For example, an unexpectedly rich ecosystem quickly developed in the Rodman Dam Reservoir, created as part of the partially constructed Cross Florida Barge Canal. Similarly, a cohesive Miccosukee culture and economy was heavily influenced by the creation of the infamous Tamiami Trail. With this in mind, the Indian River's artificially opened and maintained inlets at St. Lucie and Fort Pierce, as well as the Haulover Canal, which connects the Mosquito Lagoon and Indian River proper, have led to increased biodiversity. Similarly, many of the Indian River's mid-twentieth-century spoil islands hosted vibrant rookeries and mangrove forests within several decades of their decidedly unnatural construction.

The Indian River Lagoon stood at a crossroads in the second decade of the twenty-first century. Longtime observers wondered if the lagoon had reached a tipping point and would collapse, as had central Florida's Lake Apopka. "If you simply want water on which to zoom up and down in a boat, then that is easy to have. If you want a living system, then that is much harder," observed lagoon activist Maggy Hurchalla.[6] "As horrible as the algal blooms [of 2011–13] were, they awoke a sleeping giant," observed lifelong Indian River resident Nathaniel Reed. Recent public outrage at the prospect of fishing and swimming in dark green algae blooms has begun to pressure Florida politicians to address the Indian River's increasingly visible distress. "For the first time in a long time, I am optimistic," said Reed. "The future is that with good land management and with good science to prove where the nutrients are coming from . . . we should be able to address the hotspots [where nutrient pollution enters the lagoon]." Continued Reed, "the Indian River Lagoon must be kept free of all manmade freshwater discharges from canals and sewage connections. If we are willing to do that, the future of the lagoon is bright."[7]

Environmental historians have long sought to understand the complex relationship between humans and the environment. Yearning for a natural world wholly divorced from humanity is not only impractical, it is historically uninformed. Being subject to the same physical and environmental forces ensures that it is often impossible to say what nature (including the Indian River) is or should be.[8] A goal of a wholly fixed, stationary system that would best suit the desires of many of the lagoon's inhabitants would be consistent with the yearnings of Gilded Age settlers such as pineapple grower Thomas E. Richards, who longed for a river free from the instability of opening and shoaling inlets to meet the needs of a developing market economy. As long as the Indian River exists in the context of larger ecological forces, it will remain a (partially) transitional body. The creation of several new storm-created inlets in 1896, 1948, and 1961 is evidence that the historical forces that formed and shaped the lagoon will continue to thwart attempts at stabilization.[9]

The most significant human-made change that damaged the lower Indian River, the St. Lucie canal (C-44), failed to live up to the economic dreams of its early twentieth-century boosters. Many residents of little Stuart (built on the St. Lucie) dreamed of their city becoming a major urban center overlooking a major deepwater port. The new canal was never used as a significant commercial freight route, throngs of wealthy yachting tourists did not appear, nor was their vaunted deepwater port built. Instead, the canal accomplished only the purpose for which it was originally proposed by the Everglades Drainage District, as a vehicle for draining the Everglades and regulating the level of Lake Okeechobee. The subsequent filling of the estuary with muck from the interior of central Florida robbed the region of its most touted asset, its fishing.[10]

Instead of a clear zone of cultural exchange, the largely depopulated nature of the nineteenth-century Indian River frontier allowed

American settlers to (inaccurately) describe the region in virginal, untouched terms. The physical traces of earlier peoples were less noticeable than in many other regions as the inhabitants cleared their lands, built mounds, and discarded pottery in relatively small amounts. Unlike in the American West, the Indian Wars and the removal of Indians from peninsular Florida occurred before significant numbers of Anglo Americans came to the land, which precluded the development of a lingering cultural memory of the Ais (or, to a lesser extent, Seminole) peoples and reinforced the fiction of an untouched lagoon.[11] The Indian River's Gilded Age sailing pineapple planters, turtlers, fishermen, and deer, bear, and manatee hunters were the first to divorce flora and fauna from their natural environment and commodify them. Manatees, for example, were not perceived as a cog in a complex organic machine of nature, but instead as something closer to an item on the shelf in a watery warehouse, which awaited plucking and shipment. The value of the Indian River was in its marketable goods, including the marketability of "beauty." The Indian River's ecosystem was often perceived as having little intrinsic value other than as an incubator into which commercial crops could be introduced and produced.

In addition to literal alterations, the settlers' understanding of the Indian River's identity as a "place" changed in the minds of its inhabitants. While its natural beauty was long lauded, its primary function and value were derived from its utility as a source of resources. By the late twentieth century the Indian River reflected national trends as its waterfront commercial communities (such as commercial fishing, boatbuilding, and related industries) gave way to exclusive residential neighborhoods. By 2000 the Indian River had largely ceased to be a place of labor, as its identity had overwhelmingly become one of recreation. While the Indian River's unstable nature and long, narrow coastal form largely determined and isolated the sailing and steam culture that developed in the nineteenth century, it became increasingly peripheral to a society once trains and cars usurped the role once held by the liquid highway. The image of a land of wafting orange blossom scents and balmy, fish-filled waters first promoted by Gilded Age Indian River settlers would prove to have remarkable potency and continued to shape the national consciousness of the peninsula throughout the twentieth century. Upon the softening of some of the ecosystem's more inhospitable elements by air-conditioning and mosquito impoundments in the mid-twentieth century, the lagoon's swooning descriptions from the 1870s and 1880s would be appropriated by developers to entice newly affluent Americans. It was the commodification of warm weather that largely drove the region's postwar population boom. These new increasingly westward sprawling suburbs of affordable condos and bungalows rendered the lagoon largely obsolete in an economy driven by cheap housing and service sector fields only loosely connected to the water. The story of the Indian River is one of a changing ecosystem and a changing human society. Native American peoples (and to a lesser extent Spanish and British) and Americans shaped the lagoon to fit their perceived needs, and found themselves in turn deeply changed by the lagoon.

Notes

Chapter 1. Introduction

1. Herman Herold, "Logbook of Trip to Jupiter Inlet, Transcript," 1884, 39, P. K. Yonge Library of Florida History, University of Florida Special Collections, Gainesville.

2. Michael Grunwald, *The Swamp: The Everglades, Florida, and the Politics of Paradise* (New York: Simon & Schuster, 2007), 317.

3. Woodward-Clyde Consultants et al., *Physical Features of the Indian River Lagoon* (Tampa, Fla.: Woodward-Clyde Consultants, 1994), 4-10, 4-22–25.

4. Woodward-Clyde Consultants et al., *Uses of the Indian River Lagoon* (Tampa, Fla.: Woodward-Clyde Consultants, 1994), 2-14.

5. Indian River Lagoon National Estuary Program, *Indian River Lagoon Comprehensive Conservation and Management Plan* (Palm Bay, Fla.: St. Johns River Water Management District, 2008) 40–41.

6. Jerald Milanich, *Archaeology of Precolumbian Florida* (Gainesville: University Press of Florida, 1994), 70–75.

7. Francis Ranna Stebbins and Carolyn Baker Lewis, *The Winter Sailor: Francis R. Stebbins on Florida's Indian River, 1878–1888* (Tuscaloosa: University of Alabama Press, 2004), 3.

8. Carol Sheriff, *The Artificial River: The Erie Canal and the Paradox of Progress, 1817–1862* (New York: Hill and Wang, 1997).

9. Mohammed N. Almasi, "The Importance of Inlets and Sea Level in the Development of Hutchinson Island and Indian River Lagoon, Florida," in *The Indian River Lagoon: Proceedings of the Indian River Resources Symposium,* ed. Diane D. Barile (Melbourne: Marine Resource Council of East Central Florida, 1983), 10.

10. Ibid., 15.

Chapter 2. Early Geologic History and Human Habitation to 1842

1. William Stork and Denys D. Rolle, *An Extract from the Account of East Florida* (London, 1766), 3; Florida Everglades Engineering Commission, *Report of Florida*

Everglades Engineering Commission (Washington, D.C.: Government Printing Office, 1914).

2. Alan Brech, "Neither Ocean nor Continent: Correlating the Archaeology and Geomorphology of the Barrier Islands of East Central Florida" (Master's thesis, University of Florida, 2004), 50.

3. Harrison Rhodes, *A Guide to Florida for Tourists, Sportsmen and Settlers* (New York: Dodd, Mead, 1912), 157.

4. Woodward-Clyde Consultants et al., *Physical Features of the Indian River Lagoon*, 1-2, 2-8.

5. Clifton Johnson, *Highways and Byways of Florida* (New York: MacMillan, 1918), 77.

6. Woodward-Clyde Consultants et al., *Physical Features of the Indian River Lagoon*, 6-23, 2-25.

7. Ibid., 8-3, 3-1, 3-4; Duane E. DeFreese, "The Indian River Lagoon: Connecting People to the Sea"; M. T. Brown, "Influence of Humanity on the Coastal Landscape of Florida: The Indian River as a Case Study," in *Wetlands General Research Collections*, ed. Diane D. Barile (Melbourne: Marine Resources Council of East Central Florida, 1985), 1–13.

8. "United States Map of Köppen Geiger Classification," University of Veterinary Medicine, Vienna; Robe B. Carson, "The Florida Tropics," *Economic Geography* 27, no. 4 (October 1951): 321–39.

9. In recent years the warming effects of climate change appear to have increased the northern range of some tropical species in the lagoon, such as the red mangrove. "Global Forest Resources Assessment 2000," Food and Agriculture Organization of the United Nations.

10. University of Maryland Center for Environmental Science, "Tropic Zone Tropical Connections"; Smithsonian Marine Station at Fort Pierce.

11. Johnson, *Highways and Byways of Florida*, 78.

12. The Indian River inlet was located in what is now Pepper Park, just north of the contemporary human-opened Fort Pierce inlet. Similarly, the current Jupiter inlet was dug by humans just north of where it was often located, near what is today DuBois Park.

13. Almasi, "Importance of Inlets and Sea Level," 8–11.

14. Woodward-Clyde Consultants et al., *Physical Features of the Indian River Lagoon*, 2-24; Almasi, "Importance of Inlets and Sea Level," 8.

15. Woodward-Clyde Consultants et al., *Physical Features of the Indian River Lagoon*, 3-22.

16. Brech, "Neither Ocean nor Continent," 79, 87.

17. John J. Ewel and Ronald L. Myers, *Ecosystems of Florida* (Orlando: University of Central Florida Press, 1990), 561; Woodward-Clyde Consultants et al., *Historical Imagery Inventory and Sea Grass Assessment Indian River Lagoon* (Tampa, Fla.:

Woodward-Clyde Consultants, 1994), 1-1; St. Johns Water Management District, "Indian River Lagoon."

18. Brech, "Neither Ocean nor Continent," 79.

19. Jerald T. Milanich, *Frolicking Bears, Wet Vultures, and Other Oddities: A New York City Journalist in Nineteenth-Century Florida* (Gainesville: University Press of Florida, 2005), 166.

20. Ibid., 167; Walter R. Hellier, *Indian River: Florida's Treasure Coast* (Coconut Grove, Fla.: Hurricane House, 1965), 37.

21. Woodward-Clyde Consultants et al., *Uses of the Indian River Lagoon*, 2-1.

22. Ibid., 2-3, 2-9; Brech, "Neither Ocean nor Continent," 114; Woodward-Clyde Consultants et al., *Physical Features of the Indian River Lagoon*, 3-13; Florida Department of Environmental Protection, "Florida's Geologic History"; Ginger M. Allen and Martin B. Main, "Florida's Geologic History."

23. Aleš Hrdlička, "Preliminary Report on Finds of Supposedly Ancient Human Remains at Vero, Florida," *Journal of Geology* 25, no. 1 (January–February 1917): 43–51; Milanich, *Archaeology of Precolumbian Florida*, 8; Brech, "Neither Ocean nor Continent," 105.

24. Barbara Purdy et al., "Earliest Art in the Americas: Incised Image of a Proboscidean on a Mineralized Extinct Animal Bone from Vero Beach, Florida," *Journal of Archaeological Science* 38 (2011): 2908–13.

25. Milanich, *Archaeology of Precolumbian Florida*, 72–75; Tammy T. Stone, David N. Dickel, and Glen H. Doran, "The Preservation and Conservation of Waterlogged Bone from the Windover Site, Florida: A Comparison of Methods," *Journal of Field Archaeology* 17 (1990): 177–83.

26. Brech, "Neither Ocean nor Continent," 111–22.

27. Jerald T. Milanich, *Florida Indians and the Invasion from Europe* (Gainesville: University Press of Florida, 1995), 20.

28. Ibid., 21; Hrdlička, "Preliminary Report," 43–51.

29. Milanich, *Florida Indians*, 81.

30. It is unclear whether the contact-era peoples of the southern Mosquito Lagoon, the Surroques, were affiliated with the Timucua or Ais. Brech, "Neither Ocean nor Continent," 12; John H. Hann, *A History of the Timucua Indians and Missions* (Gainesville: University Press of Florida, 1996), 170.

31. Herold, "Logbook of Trip to Jupiter Inlet," 22; Stebbins and Lewis, *Winter Sailor*, 179; Florida Department of State, Division of Historical Resources, Archaeological Site Data Supplement, Florida Master Site File, VO00109.

32. Florida Department of State, Division of Historical Resources, Archaeological Site Data Supplement, Florida Master Site File, VO00124; Florida Department of State, Division of Historical Resources, Archaeological Site Data Supplement, Florida Master Site File, VO00109; Susan Parker, *Historic Resource Study* (Atlanta: National Park Service, Cultural Resources, 2008), 39.

33. Jerald Milanich, "Frolicking Bears, Wet Vultures, and Other Mysteries: Amos Jay Cummings' Description of Mounds in East-Central Florida," *Florida Historical Quarterly* 80, no. 3 (Winter 2002): 365–66.

34. On the Castle Windy mounds of the southern Mosquito Lagoon, Daytona Beach mayor "Dr. Wallace . . . made a residence on one of these mounds, on the other he has a blacksmith's shop." Similarly, pioneer Henry DuBois built his home in 1898 on a mound on the shores of the Jupiter inlet. Parker, *Historic Resource Study*.

35. Paul A. Hoffman, *Florida's Frontiers* (Bloomington: Indiana University Press, 1994), 54, 56; Milanich, *Florida Indians*, 108–11; Robert S. Weddle, *Spanish Sea: The Gulf of Mexico in North American Discovery* (College Station: Texas A&M University Press, 1985), 41–42.

36. Milanich, *Florida Indians*, 114.

37. Sandra Henderson Thurlow, *Stuart on the St. Lucie* (Stuart, Fla.: Sewall's Point, 2001), 1; Mark Derr, *Some Kind of Paradise: A Chronicle of Man and the Land in Florida* (Gainesville: University Press of Florida, 1998), 219.

38. Brech, "Neither Ocean nor Continent," 55; Alan Brech and J. F. Lanham, "The Destruction of the Ais Chiefdom and Other Overlooked Ethnographic and Ethnological Information from Jonathan Dickinson's 1699 Shipwreck Journal," paper presented at the annual meeting of the Florida Historical Society, Pensacola, May 23, 2009.

39. Charles D. Higgs, "Contacts with the Ais Indian River Country," *Florida Historical Quarterly* 21, no. 1 (July 1942): 25–39.

40. Florida Department of State, Division of Historical Resources, Archaeological Site Data Supplement, Florida Master Site File, VO00131.

41. Milanich, *Florida Indians*, 34.

42. Far from recording a culture in its pre-Columbian form, Jonathan Dickinson's 1696 journal recounted a people who had been subjected to varying degrees of Spanish influence for roughly 150 years, and only decades before their extinction.

43. Milanich, *Florida Indians*, 156–58, 60, 65; Woodward-Clyde Consultants et al., *Uses of the Indian River Lagoon*, 2-4; Charlton W. Tebeau and Ruby Leach Carson, *Florida from Indian Trail to Space Age: A History* (Delray Beach, Fla.: Southern Publishing, 1965), 25–26.

44. Milanich, *Florida Indians*; Tebeau and Carson, *Florida from Indian Trail to Space Age*.

45. J. F. Lanham and Alan Brech, "Locating the Ais Indian Town of Pentoaya along the Indian River Lagoon, Florida," *Brevard Journal* 7, no. 1 (Spring/Summer 2008): 5.

46. Marion Clayton Link, "The Spanish Camp Site and the 1715 Plate Fleet Wreck," *Tequesta* 26 (1966): 22, 26.

47. The Indians showed no interest in taking the liquor or molasses from the wreck, which some have claimed is evidence of political complexity (speculating that there was a prearrangement that the chief of the Ais was entitled to claim all liquor) and others see as evidence of intentional cultural preservation, through resistance

to "two items of white culture that often corrupted or weakened North American aboriginal cultures." Ibid., 58, 66; Brech, "Neither Ocean nor Continent," 15.

48. Brech and Lanham, "Destruction of the Ais Chiefdom"; Charles Blacker Vignoles, *Observations upon the Floridas* (1823; reprint, Gainesville: University Press of Florida, 1977), 43.

49. Milanich, *Florida Indians*, 66.

50. Ibid., 57.

51. Ibid., 58.

52. Derr, *Some Kind of Paradise*, 219.

53. Alan Gallay, *The Indian Slave Trade: The Rise of the English Empire in the American South, 1670–1717* (New Haven, Conn.: Yale University Press, 2002), 295.

54. Sherry Johnson, *Climate and Catastrophe in Cuba and the Atlantic World in the Age of Revolution* (Chapel Hill: University of North Carolina Press, 2011), 60–68; Milanich, *Florida Indians*, 248.

55. Frederick George Mulcaster, "Letter to James Grant." 1772. *Florida History Online*, University of North Florida.

56. Ibid.

57. Jane G. Landers, *Colonial Plantations and Economy in Florida* (Gainesville: University Press of Florida, 2000), 40–42.

58. Carita Doggett Corse, *Dr. Andrew Turnbull and the New Smyrnea Colony of Florida* (Jacksonville, Fla.: Drew Press, 1919), 68.

59. Patricia C. Griffin recounted how one driver forced a slow-working, sick ten-year-old boy to be stoned to death in the field by his coworkers, who were also boys. Landers, *Colonial Plantations*, 53; Corse, *Dr. Andrew Turnbull*, 76.

60. Andrew Turnbull to Sir William Duncan, Smyrnéa, December 3, 1770, *Florida History Online*, University of North Florida.

61. Ibid.

62. William Bartram, *Travels through North and South Carolina, Georgia, East and West Florida, the Cherokee Country* (Dublin: J. Moore, W. Jones, R. McAllister, and J. Rice, 1793).

63. The largely undisturbed remains of the settlement would later be described as "one of the most significant properties in North America" by archaeologist Margo Shwadron, of the National Park Service. Similarly, the miles of slave-built canals and cleared fields would be hailed as "one of the most significant African American landscapes known." Florida Department of State, Division of Historical Resources, Archaeological Site Data Supplement, Florida Master Site File, VO009407; Daniel L. Schafer, "St. Augustine's British Years, 1763–1783," *El Escribiano: The Journal of the St. Augustine Historical Society* 38 (2001): 44–65; Parker, *Historic Resource Study*, 2008.

64. Vignoles, *Observations upon the Floridas*, 41–42.

65. "Spanish Land Grant for Hutchinson, James," 1803, Spanish Land Grant Claims, State Library and Archives of Florida, Tallahassee.

66. Tim Robinson, *A Tropical Frontier: Pioneers and Settlers of Southeast Florida, 1800–1890* (Port Salerno, Fla.: Port Sun, 2005), 283–84.

67. Woodward-Clyde Consultants et al., *Uses of the Indian River Lagoon*, 2-5; Robinson, *Tropical Frontier*, 162.

68. Vignoles, *Observations upon the Floridas*, 14.

69. Ibid., 41.

70. The relationship between the historically decentralized Seminole and Miccosukee peoples (not to mention African Americans who joined them) is complex, the strands of which have at various times merged and separated. John Missall and Mary Lou Missall, *The Seminole Wars: America's Longest Indian Conflict* (Gainesville: University Press of Florida, 2004), 94–97; James W. Covington, "The Armed Occupation Act of 1842," *Florida Historical Quarterly* 40, no. 1 (July 1961): 41–52.

71. Woodward-Clyde Consultants et al., *Physical Features of the Indian River Lagoon*, 2-5; Jacob Rhett Motte, *Journey into Wilderness: An Army Surgeon's Account of Life in Camp and Field during the Creek and Seminole Wars, 1836–1838* (Gainesville: University of Florida Press, 1953), 176.

72. Motte, *Journey into Wilderness*, 177.

73. Ibid., 186–87; Woodward-Clyde Consultants et al., *Biological Resources of the Indian River Lagoon* (Tampa, Fla.: Woodward-Clyde Consultants, 1994), 2-5, 2-6.

74. Motte, *Journey into Wilderness*, 187.

75. Vignoles, *Observations upon the Floridas*, 47.

76. Ibid.

Chapter 3. Mosquitoes and Kegs of Manatee Meat, 1842–1892

1. Robinson, *Tropical Frontier*, 75; Edward Caleb Coker and Daniel L. Schafer, "A New Englander on the Indian River Frontier: Caleb Lyndon Brayton and the View from Brayton's Bluff," *Florida Historical Quarterly* 70, no. 3 (January 1992): 312, 324.

2. Coker and Schafer, "New Englander on the Indian River Frontier," 316–17, 323–31.

3. Eckhardt Fuchs and Benedikt Stuchtey, eds., *Across Cultural Borders* (New York: Rowman and Littlefield, 2002); Richard Slotkin, *Regeneration through Violence: The Mythology of the American Frontier 1600–1860* (Norman: University of Oklahoma Press, 2000).

4. Covington, "Armed Occupation Act of 1842," 42.

5. Edward E. Baptist, *Creating an Old South: Middle Florida's Plantation Frontier before the Civil War* (Chapel Hill: University of North Carolina Press, 2002), 17.

6. Ibid., 64–65; Covington, "Armed Occupation Act of 1842," 41–52; Robinson, *Tropical Frontier*, 433; Joe Knetsch and Paul S. George, "A Problematical Law: The Armed Occupation Act of 1842 and Its Impact on Southeast Florida," *Tequesta* 53 (1993): 64–65.

7. "Proceedings in Congress, Mar 19, 1844," *New York Times*; *The Army and Navy Chronicle, and Scientific Repository. Being a Continuation of Homans' "Army and Navy Chronicle" (1843–1844)*, (Washington, D.C., 1844) 13.

8. U.S. Department of the Treasury, *Report of the President of the Light-House Board, in Relation to Re-Establishing the Light-Houses at Cape Florida, Jupiter Inlet and Cape Canaveral* (Washington, D.C.: Government Printing Office, 1865), 1.

9. Charles W. Bockelman, *Six Columns and Fort New Smyrna* (New Smyrna, Fla.: Halifax Historical Society, 1985).

10. The hasty nature of Confederate operations in rural areas has resulted in no written record of the saltworks. This has led some researchers to speculate that the "Confederate" saltworks actually date to the British period. If the ruins were from the Civil War, they would be perhaps the only Florida East Coast Confederate saltworks. See Parker, *Historic Resource Study*, 47; Paul Taylor, *Discovering the Civil War in Florida* (Sarasota, Fla.: Pineapple Press, 2001), 10–12; Zelia W. Sweet, *New Smyrna, Florida, in the Civil War* (New Smyrna, Fla.: Volusia County Historical Commission, 1963); Florida Department of State, Division of Historical Resources, Archaeological Site Data, VO00130, 23; VO00124, 17–18.

11. Tom Chaffin, *Fatal Glory: Narciso Lopez and the First Clandestine United States War against Cuba* (Charlottesville: University Press of Virginia, 1996); Alejandro B. Geyer, *Favored of the Gods: Biography of William Walker* (Masaya, Nicaragua: privately printed, 2002), 126–27; William Walker, *The War in Nicaragua* (1860; reprint, Tucson: University of Arizona Press, 1985), 340.

12. U.S. Naval War Records Office, *Official Record of the Union and Confederate Navies in the War of the Rebellion* (Washington, D.C.: Government Printing Office, 1903), 369–75.

13. None of the Union dispatches from this area mention Confederate saltworks in the area, and subsequent archaeological observations of the remains of the saltworks suggest that they were never found. See Florida Department of State, Division of Historical Resources, Archaeological Site Data Supplement, Florida Master Site File VO00130; U.S. Naval War Records Office, *Official Record*, 369–75; Taylor, *Discovering the Civil War*, 161–63; Sweet, *New Smyrna*.

14. Charles William Pierce and Donald Walter Curl, *Pioneer Life in Southeast Florida* (Coral Gables, Fla.: University of Miami Press, 1970), 50.

15. Woodward-Clyde Consultants et al., *Uses of the Indian River Lagoon*, 2-7; Robinson, *Tropical Frontier*, 6.

16. Anna Pearl Leonard Newman, *Stories of Early Life Along Beautiful Indian River* (Stuart, Fla.: Stuart Daily News, 1953), 6.

17. Milanich, *Frolicking Bears*, 123.

18. Curt Schroeder, "Ernest Stypmann," *Stuart News*, November 9, 1950, sec. D, 7.

19. Stebbins and Baker Lewis, *Winter Sailor*, 1.

20. Johnson, *Highways and Byways of Florida*, 82.

21. "Manatee Exhibited in New York," *Forest and Stream*, Vol. 31, 1888.

22. Sandra Henderson Thurlow, "Lonely Vigils: Houses of Refuge on Florida's East Coast, 1876–1915," *Florida Historical Quarterly* 76, no. 2 (Fall 1997): 169.

23. Hellier, *Indian River*, 34.

24. "Florida Resorts," *Forest and Stream*, Vol. 18, 1882.

25. Brown, "Influence of Humanity," 35, 39, 78, 82.

26. Pierce and Curl, *Pioneer Life in Southeast Florida*, 54.

27. Emily Lagow Bell, *My Pioneer Days in Florida, 1876–1898* (Miami: McMurray Printing, 1928), 36.

28. Thurlow/Runke Collection, Sewall's Point, Fla.; Lucy Richards LeTourneau, *Stuart Messenger/Stuart Times/Stuart News*, Box 1–6, Blake Library, Stuart, Fla.

29. Milanich, *Frolicking Bears*, 24, 26.

30. Stebbins and Lewis, *Winter Sailor*, 59.

31. Brown, "Influence of Humanity," 18.

32. "Indian River, of Florida," *Forest and Stream*, Vol. 1, 1873.

33. Charles Hallock, *Camp Life in Florida: A Handbook for Sportsmen and Settlers* (New York: Forest and Stream, 1876).

34. D. P. P., "The Indian River Region of Florida," *Friends' Intelligencer*, 1891, 14.

35. Milanich, *Frolicking Bears*, 100.

36. Ibid., 120.

37. Stebbins and Lewis, *Winter Sailor*, 59.

38. B. W. Mulford, *Little Journeys to Salerno and the Famous St. Lucie Inlet Farms* (1915), 4, 12.

39. Woodward-Clyde Consultants et al., *Uses of the Indian River Lagoon*, 6-2; U.S. Fish Commission, *The Fisheries of Indian River, Florida* (Washington, D.C.: Government Printing Office, 1897), 2.

40. Daniel F. Austin, "The Glades Indians and the Plants They Used: Ethnobotany of a Lost Culture," *Palmetto* 17, no. 2 (Summer/Fall 1997): 7–11.

41. Hellier, *Indian River*, 64.

42. Milanich, *Frolicking Bears*, 139; Hallock, *Camp Life in Florida*.

43. Bell, *My Pioneer Days*, 52; Newman, *Stories of Early Life*, 19.

44. In 1890 Titusville shipped 1,072,355 pounds, and only 409,710 in 1895. U.S. Fish Commission, *Fisheries of Indian River*, 27–28.

45. Sandra Henderson Thurlow, *Historic Jensen and Eden on Florida's Indian River* (Stuart, Fla.: Sewall's Point, 2004), 59–61; Newman, *Stories of Early Life*, 21.

46. Curt Schroeder, "Commercial Fishing," unpublished manuscript, 2, Sandra Henderson Thurlow Collection, Stuart, Fla.

47. Thurlow, *Stuart on the St. Lucie*, 47.

48. U.S. Fish Commission, *Fisheries of Indian River*, 3.

49. Hellier, *Indian River*, 81.

50. Schroeder, "Commercial Fishing," 2; U.S. Fish Commission, *Fisheries of Indian River*, 2.

51. Thurlow, *Historic Jensen*, 136.

52. A catboat sailing rig consisted of a single mast and sail. This simple traditional type was associated with Cape Cod and was familiar to the many New Englanders who moved to the Indian River. A kraal (or "krall") was a watery pen for keeping live

turtles. Burnham's kraal was probably similar to that of St. Lucie Estuary resident Otto Stypmann, who built his kraal under his dock with poles forming a rudimentary cage. Robinson, *Tropical Frontier*, 101; Schroeder, "Ernest Stypmann" (see n. 18); James A. Henshall, *Camping and Cruising in Florida* (Cincinnati: R. Clarke 1884), 72.

53. "Papers of the Port of New Smyrnea, 1849–1858," Microfilm, P. K. Yonge Library of Florida History, University of Florida Special Collections, Gainesville.

54. Milanich, *Frolicking Bears*, 195.

55. Lucy Richards LeTourneau, *Stuart Messenger/Stuart Times/Stuart News*, Box 1–6, Blake Library, Stuart, Fla.

56. Schroeder, "Ernest Stypmann," 7 (see n. 18).

57. Bell, *My Pioneer Days*, 52.

58. U.S. Fish Commission, *Fisheries of Indian River*, 31.

59. Schroeder, "Commercial Fishing," 10.

60. Stebbins and Lewis, *Winter Sailor*, 173.

61. U.S. Fish Commission, *Fisheries of Indian River*, 31.

62. A manatee hunting lance inscribed with the name of notable Indian River resident, explorer, and aviation pioneer Hugh L. Willoughby is on display at the House of Refuge Museum, Hutchinson Island, Florida; Newman, *Stories of Early Life*, 47; Milanich, *Frolicking Bears*, 144.

63. Schroeder, "Commercial Fishing," 3–5.

64. Gilbert L. Voss, "The Orange Grove House of Refuge no. 3," *Tequesta* 28 (1968): 3–18.

65. "Disasters at Sea," *The Sailors' Magazine and Seamen's Friend*, 1871, 392; Pierce and Curl, *Pioneer Life in Southeast Florida*, 36–38.

66. Pierce and Curl, *Pioneer Life in Southeast Florida*, 203–4; Newman, *Stories of Early Life*, 26.

67. Milanich, *Frolicking Bears*, 38–39.

68. Ibid., 42.

69. Bell, *My Pioneer Days*, 34.

70. Newman, *Stories of Early Life*, 37; Brech and Lanham, "Destruction of the Ais Chiefdom."

71. Rosalyn Howard, "The 'Wild Indians' of Andros Island: Black Seminole Legacy in the Bahamas," *Journal of Black Studies* 37, no. 2 (November 2006): 287.

72. Thurlow, *Stuart on the St. Lucie*, 57.

73. Brech and Lanham, "Destruction of the Ais Chiefdom."

74. Milanich, *Frolicking Bears*, 44.

75. Ibid., 44–45.

76. Stephen Kerber, "The United States Life-Saving Service and the Florida Houses of Refuge" (Master's thesis, Florida Atlantic University, 1971), 21.

77. Ibid., 141.

78. Thurlow/Runke Collection, Sewall's Point, Fla.; Lucy Richards LeTourneau, *Stuart Messenger/Stuart Times/Stuart News*, Box 1–6, Blake Library, Stuart, Fla.

79. Kimberly G. Smith, "100 Years Ago in the American Ornithologist's Union," *Auk* 122, no. 4 (2004): 1311; Stuart McIver, *Death in the Everglades: The Murder of Guy Bradley, America's First Martyr to Environmentalism* (Gainesville: University Press of Florida, 2003); "Biological Status Review Report for the Roseate Spoonbill," *Florida Fish and Wildlife Conservation Commission*, March 31, 2011.

80. Grunwald, *Swamp*, 120, 125.

81. U.S. Department of Agriculture, *Laws Applicable to the United States Department of Agriculture* (Washington, D.C.: Government Printing Office, 1912), 210, 214.

82. Derr, *Some Kind of Paradise*, 137–40.

83. Brech, "Neither Ocean nor Continent," 125; Austin, "Glades Indians," 7–11.

84. Milanich, *Frolicking Bears*, 38.

85. Mulcaster, "Letter to James Grant."

86. Pierce and Curl, *Pioneer Life in Southeast Florida*, 257.

87. Henshall, *Camping and Cruising in Florida*, 114; Charles Pierce made note of H. F. Hammon's sharpie "of about twenty feet"; Hendrickson's sixty-foot schooner-rigged sharpie *Bessie B.* regularly sailed through the Indian River while delivering goods between Lake Worth and Jacksonville and was wrecked on a reef south of the Lake Worth inlet in 1892. See Pierce and Curl, *Pioneer Life in Southeast Florida*, 175.

88. Bell, *My Pioneer Days*, 44.

89. Pierce and Curl, *Pioneer Life in Southeast Florida*, 44.

90. Ibid., 245.

91. "Interview with Mrs. J. E. Taylor," November 28, 1972, Samuel Proctor Oral History Program, University of Florida, Gainesville, 7.

92. Newman, *Stories of Early Life*, 12.

93. Thurlow/Runke Collection, Sewall's Point, Fla.; Lucy Richards LeTourneau, *Stuart Messenger/Stuart Times/Stuart News*, Box 1–6, Blake Library, Stuart, Fla.

94. Hellier, *Indian River*, 38.

95. Thurlow, *Historic Jensen*, 60.

96. Milanich, *Frolicking Bears*, 118.

97. Bell, *My Pioneer Days*, 45.

98. Robinson, *Tropical Frontier*, 13–14.

99. Ibid., 14.

100. St. George Rathbone, "Up and Down the Indian River, Florida," *Outing*, 1890, 3.

101. Robinson, *Tropical Frontier*, 218.

102. U.S. Congress, *Letter from the Chief of Engineers, a Report of the Preliminary Examination of Indian River, Florida*, 51st Cong., 2d Sess., 1891, Doc. 168; "Santa Lucia Inlet," *Indian River Advocate*, October 21, 1892, 1.

103. "Future of the E.C.T. Co.," *East Coast Advocate*, January 30, 1891, 4; William G. Crawford Jr., *Florida's Big Dig: The Atlantic Intracoastal Waterway from Jacksonville to Miami, 1881 to 1935* (Cocoa: Florida Historical Society Press, 2006), 38, 40.

104. William G. Crawford Jr., "A History of Florida's East Coast Canal," *Broward Legacy* (Summer/Fall 1997): 9.

105. Crawford, *Florida's Big Dig*, 95.

106. Ibid., 110.

107. Why the headless body of Old Cuba was found on his land soon after this incident was the cause of much speculation by the homesteaders of the lower Indian River. In the words of Eden resident Lucy Richards (whose father, Thomas, found the body): "They never could understand how the Cuban lost his head. They supposed an alligator must have bitten it off as we had no sharks or barracuda in fresh water." His land was purchased by Thomas Richards, who gave it to local character and widely reputed lazy thief "Portuguese Joe" (Joseph Parata), who stayed in the lagoon after being shipwrecked in New Smyrnea. The lifeless body of Portuguese Joe was also found sometime later by local resident Alfred Lagow. Lucy Richards LeTourneau, *Stuart Messenger/Stuart Times/Stuart News*, Box 3, Blake Library, Stuart, Fla.; Bell, *My Pioneer Days*, 33.

108. Robinson, *Tropical Frontier*, 100.

109. Hellier, *Indian River*, 33; Thurlow, *Historic Jensen*, 123–24.

110. Thurlow/Runke Collection, Sewall's Point, Fla.; Lucy Richards LeTourneau, *Stuart Messenger/Stuart Times/Stuart News*, Box 1–6, Blake Library, Stuart, Fla.

111. Lucy Richards LeTourneau, *Stuart Messenger/Stuart Times/Stuart News*, Box 1–6, Blake Library, Stuart, Fla.

112. Rhodes, *Guide to Florida*, 34. Commodore Ralph Munroe, of Coconut Grove, dismissed Richards's "Pinapin" as "some sort of 'live forever' cordial" and recounted that Richards was at one time among many desperate Indian River settlers who delayed returning tourists by sailing to Rockledge or Titusville so as to extract as much money as possible from these visiting tenants. See Ralph Middleton Munroe and Vincent Gilpin, *The Commodore's Story* (1930; reprint, Coconut Grove, Fla.: Barnacle Society, 2010), 129.

113. Johnson, *Highways and Byways of Florida*, 80.

114. Rhodes, *Guide to Florida*, 159.

115. Thurlow/Runke Collection, Sewall's Point, Fla.; Lucy Richards LeTourneau, *Stuart Messenger/Stuart Times/Stuart News*, Box 1–6, Blake Library, Stuart, Fla.

116. Thomas E. Richards, "Letter to Editor," *Florida Star*, July 5, 1888, 1. Within four years Richards was no longer satisfied with the Indian River Steamboat Company and would help organize the opening of the St. Lucie inlet, near Eden, to promote competition with the firm.

117. The daughter of Peter Cobb, whose Fort Pierce dock had become the second-most busy port-of-call for steamboats (second to Titusville), publicly performed the tune "When Cuba Gains Her Victory Under the American Flag." Bell, *My Pioneer Days*, 31.

118. The train was derisively referred to as the "Cuban Fruit Express" by Indian River growers. Schroeder, "Commercial Fishing," 6.

119. U.S. Congress, *St. Lucia (Lucie), Florida*, 60th Cong., 2d Sess., 1909, Doc. 1312.

120. Woodward-Clyde Consultants et al., *Uses of the Indian River Lagoon*, 2-9.

121. Johnson, *Highways and Byways of Florida*, 80.

122. Florida governor Sidney J. Catts boasted in 1920, "I am not in favor of allowing the Railroads to haul fruits and vegetables, raised by Cubans and negroes in Cuba, through Florida, while the Senate and Congress allow the Florida fruits and vegetables to rot in our fields and groves. I will see that the Florida citizen has a better chance than the Cuban to sell his fruits and vegetables." "Hon. Sidney J. Catts, Candidate for Office of United States Senator, Subject to Democratic Primary (1920)," State Library and Archives of Florida, Tallahassee.

123. Richards, "Letter to Editor" (see n. 116).

124. Dummitt's oranges had been laboriously paddled by canoe to St. Augustine.

125. Andrew P. Canova, *Life Adventures in South Florida* (Palatka, Fla.: Southern Sun Publishing House, 1885), 97.

126. Bell, *My Pioneer Days*, 19; J. W. Hawks, *The East Coast of Florida* (Wynn, Mass.: Lewis and Wynnship, 1887; reprint, New Smyrna Beach, Fla.: E. O. Painter Printing, 1995), 112. The presence of the Indian River in the public mind increased dramatically with the post–Civil War population influx and the oranges that they shipped to northern markets. References to "Indian River" in published material increased tenfold in 1865 and 1886. "Google Books Ngram Viewer."

127. Dummitt's long and colorful life included a stint as head of the "Mosquito Roarers," who searched the Indian River in canoes and sailboats for Seminoles during the Second Seminole War. Dummitt's remaining years were spent in a house 200 feet from that of his slave and mistress from Barbados, who was the mother of his three daughters. Gary Ross Mormino, *Land of Sunshine, State of Dreams: A Social History of Modern Florida* (Gainesville: University Press of Florida, 2005), 204, 206; Robinson, *Tropical Frontier*, 162; Derr, *Some Kind of Paradise*, 78–79.

128. Milanich, *Frolicking Bears*, 26.

129. Hellier, *Indian River*, 5.

130. Milanich, *Frolicking Bears*, 27.

131. Robinson, *Tropical Frontier*, 9.

132. "Down the Indian River: Close Quarters in the Jupiter Narrows," *New York Times*, June 1889, 12.

133. Pierce and Curl, *Pioneer Life in Southeast Florida*, 201.

134. Milanich, *Frolicking Bears*, 118.

135. Newman, *Stories of Early Life*, 37.

136. Ernest Lyons, "Charm of the Indian River," *Stuart News*, January 12, 1956; Coker and Schafer, "New Englander on the Indian River Frontier," 305–32.

137. U.S. Congress, *Copy of a Report from Lieut. Col. Q. A. Gilmore, Corps of Engineers, upon a Survey of the Indian River, Florida, with a View to Opening a Passage to Mosquito Lagoon, by Way of the Haulover*, 47th Cong., 1st Sess., 1882, Doc. 33; U.S.

Congress, *Preliminary Examination of Indian River, Florida*, 51st Cong., 2d Sess., 1891, Doc. 168.

138. U.S. Congress, *St. Lucia (Lucie), Florida*; Florida Congress, *Acts and Resolutions Adopted by the State of Florida*, 1901, 209.

139. Milanich, *Frolicking Bears*, 118.

140. U.S. Congress, *St. Lucia (Lucie), Florida*.

141. Robinson, *Tropical Frontier*, 216.

142. Gary Roderick, personal communication, Stuart, Fla., 2011.

143. Johnson, *Highways and Byways of Florida*, 81.

144. U.S. Fish Commission, *Fisheries of Indian River*.

Chapter 4. Atlantic Gateway to the Gulf of Mexico, 1881–1941

1. The digger who awoke his fellow workers was Ossian Hart, twenty-nine years before he would become a Reconstruction governor of the state. William Henry Peck, "How and by Whom Gilbert's Bar Was Opened in 1844," *Florida Star* (Titusville), May 5, 1886; Thurlow, *Historic Jensen*, 127–29.

2. Thurlow, *Historic Jensen*, 127–29.

3. Peck's inlet was located in the area known as "Gilbert's Bar," named for the pirate Don Pedro Gilbert, who was reputed to have operated in the area in the 1830s. Thurlow, *Historic Jensen*, 127–29.

4. "Historical Census Browser," University of Virginia, Geospatial and Statistical Data Center.

5. Florida Museum of Natural History, *Exhibit: South Florida: People & Environments* (Gainesville: University of Florida, 2011); Lanham and Brech, "Locating the Ais Indian Town of Pentoaya," 5–22.

6. Crawford, *Florida's Big Dig*, 1–2.

7. The dynamic forces of the Indian River's water flow collapsed a portion of the canal during years of neglect due to the Civil War. Reconstruction-era politician and Indian River settler William Gleason observed in 1869, "We had no difficulty in finding the canal, but the entrance to it was so shallow that we had to unload our boat and drag it through into the canal, where there was deeper water. It took us two hours to get our boat through into Indian River." The state's post–Civil War government chartered five companies tasked with digging navigable canals along the east coast, including Gleason's own Southern Inland Navigation Company, which received 1.4 million acres of public land before a federal judge ended the unscrupulous Reconstruction-era scheme. By 1884 the walls of the 2,043-foot canal had collapsed in several places, and the current that passed through the two lagoons caused the bottom to vary between only 1.7 and 3.8 feet, making it of "no practical use for navigation," although the water on the Mosquito Lagoon side of the canal itself "does not exceed 2 ½ feet." U.S. Congress, *Letter from the Secretary of War Transmitting a Letter from the Chief of Engineers, Submitting Copies of Reports from Colonel Gilmore Containing Plans*

and Estimates for the Improvement of the Saint Johns River, Florida, &c, with Accompanying Maps, 48th Cong., 1st Sess., 1884, Doc. 65.

8. Ibid.; Crawford, *Florida's Big Dig,* 9–10.

9. Crawford, *Florida's Big Dig,* 9–10.

10. Ibid., 8; "St. Johns–Indian River Canal Is Discussed," *Daytona Beach Morning Journal,* August 21, 1946, 4.

11. Robinson, *Tropical Frontier,* 233; Derr, *Some Kind of Paradise,* 307.

12. "The Southern Harbors of the United States," *Merchants' Magazine and Commercial Review* 45, no. 1 (1861): 17.

13. Robinson, *Tropical Frontier,* 228.

14. "Yachting and Boating," *Forest and Stream,* Vol. 5, 1876.

15. W. H. Gleason, "Florida Internal Navigation," *Semi-Tropical,* July 1877, 419–21.

16. "Prospectus of the Florida Coast Line Canal and Transportation Company," 1891, P. K. Yonge Library of Florida History, University of Florida Special Collections, Gainesville.

17. Crawford, *Florida's Big Dig,* 17.

18. Ibid., 30.

19. "Down the Indian River," *New York* Times, June 9, 1889, 12.

20. "Future of the E.C.T. Co.," 4 (see n. 103, chapter 3); Robinson, *Tropical Frontier,* 58; Crawford, *Florida's Big Dig,* 58.

21. "Future of the E.C.T. Co.," 4 (see n. 103, chapter 3).

22. U.S. Congress, *Intracoastal Waterway from Jacksonville, Florida to Miami, Florida,* 69th Cong., 2d Sess., 1926, Doc. 586, 2.

23. Crawford, *Florida's Big Dig,* iv–v, 334; Thurlow, *Historic Jensen,* 120.

24. Woodward-Clyde Consultants et al., *Physical Features of the Indian River Lagoon,* 2-13.

25. South Florida Ecosystem Restoration Task Force, *South Florida Ecosystem Restoration: Scientific Information Needs,* 158, U.S. Geological Survey, 1996.

26. Thurlow/Runke Collection, Sewall's Point, Fla.; Lucy Richards LeTourneau, *Stuart Messenger/Stuart Times/Stuart News,* Box 1–6, Blake Library, Stuart, Fla.

27. The site of the 1844 inlet would later be known as Peck's Lake.

28. Thurlow, *Historic Jensen,* 130.

29. Ibid.

30. Ibid.; Almasi, "Importance of Inlets and Sea Level," 8.

31. Curt Schroeder, "Santa Lucie—First Opening of the St. Lucie Inlet," *Stuart News,* January 18, 1945.

32. Milanich, *Frolicking Bears,* 27.

33. Thurlow, *Historic Jensen,* 119.

34. Thurlow/Runke Collection, Sewall's Point, Fla.; Lucy Richards LeTourneau, *Stuart Messenger/Stuart Times/Stuart News,* Box 1–6, Blake Library, Stuart, Fla.

35. U.S. Congress, *Survey of the Santa Lucie Inlet and River, Florida,* 10, 55th Cong., 2d Sess., 1898, Doc. 548; U.S. Congress, *Letter from the Chief of Engineers, a Report of*

the Preliminary Examination of Indian River, Florida, 51st Cong., 2d Sess., 1891, Doc. 168, 3.

36. This location is two or three miles north of the inlet opened by the Armed Occupation Act settlers, known as Gilbert's Bar. U.S. Congress, *Survey of the Santa Lucie Inlet and River.*

37. Thurlow, *Historic Jensen*, 131; Schroeder, "Santa Lucie" (see n. 31).

38. *Indian River Advocate*, December 9, 1892, 1.

39. *Indian River Advocate*, November 25, 1892, 1; *Indian River Advocate*, December 9, 1892, 1.

40. Lawrence Goodwyn, *The Populist Moment: A Short History of Agrarian Revolt in America* (New York: Oxford University Press, 1978), 55, 172.

41. Just south of the Indian River, Lake Worth also experienced a very similar human alteration in the 1890s. Like the Indian River, northern Lake Worth was freshwater in the nineteenth century until the East Coast Canal and Transportation Company dug a canal between the lake and Jupiter's Loxahatchee River to the north, and Biscayne Bay to the south, which introduced moderate saltwater intrusion. Southern Lake Worth was sufficiently salty to support modest oyster beds. In 1877 residents of lower Lake Worth banded together to dig an inlet, just as their northern Indian River neighbors would at other times. The lake became thoroughly transformed into a salty marine system after a World War I–era inlet was dug between the lake itself and the Atlantic Ocean. Milanich, *Frolicking Bears*, 163; U.S. Congress, *Survey of the Santa Lucie Inlet and River*, 3, 10; Pierce and Curl, *Pioneer Life in Southeast Florida*, 106.

42. Pierce and Curl, *Pioneer Life in Southeast Florida*, 106.

43. Thurlow/Runke Collection, Sewall's Point, Fla.; Lucy Richards LeTourneau, *Stuart Messenger/Stuart Times/Stuart News*, Box 1–6, Blake Library, Stuart, Fla.

44. Schroeder, "Santa Lucie" (see n. 31).

45. U.S. Congress, *Survey of the Santa Lucie Inlet and River*, 3, 6–7, 10.

46. Ibid.

47. The anthropologist Alan Brech has presented considerable evidence that the Indian River inlet was not the "Barra de Ais" observed by the Spanish. Brech argued that the Barra de Ais (site of the Ais capital town of Pentoaya) was located at a now-closed inlet in the Indian River narrows, between modern-day Vero Beach and Sebastian, while the "St. a Lucia inlet" described by Jonathan Dickinson was actually the Indian River inlet, just north of the modern-day Fort Pierce inlet. Lanham and Brech, "Locating the Ais Indian Town of Pentoaya," 5–22; Brech and Lanham, "Destruction of the Ais Chiefdom." The strategic value of this inlet led the soldiers to create a small establishment, Fort Pierce, on the west shore of the lagoon several miles south of the inlet. In the years immediately following the war, Armed Occupation Act settlers, such as Caleb Brayton, cleared much of the land adjacent to the inlet and established a loose settlement known as Indian River Colony. The lower Indian River was nearly emptied of settlers once again after this colony was abandoned in

the wake of the 1849 bloodshed, recounted by Brayton. See Coker and Shafer, "New Englander on the Indian River Frontier," 317–21.

48. Stebbins and Lewis, *Winter Sailor*, 96.

49. Newman, *Stories of Early Life*, 89; Robinson, *Tropical Frontier*, 490.

50. Woodward-Clyde Consultants et al., *Physical Features of the Indian River Lagoon*, 8-4.

51. Stebbins and Lewis, *Winter Sailor*, 123.

52. Robinson, *Tropical Frontier*, 401.

53. Gibson was among the minority of the era's Indian River settlers who had not arrived from the North (he hailed from Valdosta, Georgia) and brought with him two African American women, namely a "servant-cook" named F. B. Kennedy and a "servant-laborer" named R. Hamilton. It was widely believed at the time that Gibson's peculiar hexagon-shaped building perched at the end of his dock was built to allow him to spot and fire upon the sheriff (who, like everyone, was forced to approach by boat because there was no road along the lagoon at this time) should he have attempted to arrest Gibson for practicing polygamy. Robinson, *Tropical Frontier*, 216.

54. Stebbins and Lewis, *Winter Sailor*, 134.

55. In 1926, at the height of the Florida land boom, Mosquito inlet was renamed Ponce de Leon inlet to encourage development in the region.

56. Vignoles, *Observations upon the Floridas*, 40.

57. There is conflicting evidence whether the net erosion/deposition of sand is northerly or southerly at the Mosquito (Ponce de Leon) inlet. Woodward-Clyde Consultants et al., *Physical Features of the Indian River Lagoon*, 2-26.

58. W. W. Fineren, "Early Attempts at Inlet Construction on the Florida East Coast," *Shore and Beach Magazine*, July 1938, 90.

59. Woodward-Clyde Consultants et al., *Physical Features of the Indian River Lagoon*, 2-19, 2-27.

60. Woodward-Clyde Consultants et al., *Uses of the Indian River Lagoon*, 2-11.

61. Thurlow, *Historic Jensen*, 148.

62. Woodward-Clyde Consultants, *Uses of the Indian River Lagoon*, 2-11, 2-12.

63. J. C. Ives, *Military Map of the Peninsula of Florida South of Tampa Bay, etc.*, 1856, Old Florida Maps, University of Miami Libraries.

64. Gordon Patterson, "Ditches and Dreams: Nelson Fell and the Rise of Fellsmere," *Florida Historical Quarterly* 76, no. 1 (Summer 1997): 1–19; Reclaiming the Everglades, *The Muck Soils of Fellsmere Farms, Florida* (Fellsmere, Fla.: Fellsmere Sales, 1913), 7; Gail Clement, "Everglades Timeline: Reclaiming the Everglades: Florida's Natural History, 1884 to 1934."

65. Clement, "Everglades Timeline."

66. Ibid.

67. Ibid.

68. Reclaiming the Everglades, *Muck Soils of Fellsmere Farms*, 4; Clement, "Everglades Timeline."

69. Reclaiming the Everglades, *Muck Soils of Fellsmere Farms*, 4.

70. Clement, "Everglades Timeline"; Derr, *Some Kind of Paradise*, 158.

71. "From Gulf to the Atlantic," *St. Lucie Tribune*, May 31, 1907, sec. 1.

72. Raymond T. Fernald, *Coastal Xeric Scrub Communities of the Treasure Coast Region, Florida a Summary of their Distribution and Ecology, with Guidelines for their Preservation and Management* (Tallahassee: Office of Environmental Services, Florida Game and Fresh Water Fish Commission, 1989), 94; U.S. Congress, House, Committee on Rivers and Harbors, *Caloosahatchee River, St. Lucie River, Lake Okeechobee, and Miami River, Fla.*, 71st Cong., 2nd sess., March 19 and 27, 1930, 11.

73. The south fork of the St. Lucie was called "Halpatiokee" by the Seminoles and by the area's early Anglo settlers. Thurlow, *Stuart on the St. Lucie*, 43; Derr, *Some Kind of Paradise*, 167.

74. Woodward-Clyde Consultants et al., *Physical Features of the Indian River Lagoon*, 2-39.

75. Ibid., 2-38, 2-43.

76. "Hon. Sidney J. Catts, Candidate for Office of United States Senator."

77. Similar voluntary associations were formed for related purposes throughout the state in the midst of Florida's expected 1920s rapid development. For example, supporters of improving and expanding the coastal network of canals created by the Florida Coast Line Canal and Transportation Company established the "Florida East Coast Canal Association" in the same decade. Crawford, *Florida's Big Dig*, 271.

78. Gulf, Okeechobee and Atlantic Waterway Association, "Minutes of a General Meeting of the Gulf, Okeechobee and Atlantic Waterway Association," October 27, 1926, P. K. Yonge Library of Florida History, University of Florida Special Collections, Gainesville.

79. Ibid., June 15, 1926.

80. The members of the association declared their allegiance to the Republican Party and argued that Florida and the Everglades Drainage District would "get the attention of the political leaders for appropriations within the state in a more substantial way than if the State continued to be solidly Democratic." Because western states were politically "doubtful," claimed one association member, they had received $150 million in federal funds for agricultural irrigation projects despite the fact that they were "2000 miles away from the great markets," while Florida received little "because we are too much politically." The group expressed optimism that the Democrats would nominate Roman Catholic Al Smith as their presidential candidate in 1928 because "if Smith is nominated next year, there will be a lot of Republicans in Florida." Ibid., July 24, 1926; Ibid., August 20, 1926.

81. This argument was expressed despite the era's unprecedented agricultural production and exceptionally low food prices. Ibid., August 20, 1926.

82. Schroeder, "Commercial Fishing," 11; Thurlow, *Stuart on the St. Lucie*, 46.

83. U.S. Congress, *Caloosahatchee River, St. Lucie River, Lake Okeechobee, and Miami River, Fla.*, 22–23.

84. U.S. Congress, *Survey of the Santa Lucie Inlet and River*, 6.

85. Ibid., 7.

86. Ibid., 11; U.S. Life Saving Service, *Copy of Wreck Report* (1904; reprint, Stuart, Fla.: Historical Society of Martin County, 2008).

87. Powerful progressive politicians argued in favor of the improvement at a January 1908 hearing on the matter, including presidential candidate and future secretary of state William Jennings Bryan (likely influenced by the political work of his daughter, Ruth, who was a Miami activist). U.S. Congress, *St. Lucia (Lucie), Florida*, 2–8.

88. Ibid., 9, 13.

89. U.S. Congress, *Survey of the Santa Lucie Inlet and River*, 8.

90. Newspapers of the lower Indian River boasted that this new master-planned "Port St. Lucie" (a separate plan and several miles south of the post–World War II development of the same name) would become a major port city that would boast the most modern progressive public electricity and water. Sewall's Point resident Hugh L. Willoughby succeeded in arranging for the New York Yacht Club to make the new city the club's winter headquarters: "the largest, handsomest and best boats afloat will each season be steaming in and out of the St. Lucie inlet and will when assembled in the harbor, comprise a flotilla which will be attractive in every way." The *St. Lucie Tribune* claimed that it was due to the influence of the powerful members of the New York Yacht Club that $1.4 million in federal funding was secured for improvements to the inlet in 1913. "Work at Port Santa Lucia," *St. Lucie Tribune*, June 16 1911, 1; *St. Lucie Tribune*, April 13, 1921, 1; U.S. Congress, *St. Lucia (Lucie), Florida*, 14–17.

91. Fineren, "Early Attempts at Inlet Construction," 89–90 (see n. 58).

92. "From Gulf to Atlantic," *St. Lucie Tribune*, May 3, 1907, 1.

93. Thurlow, *Stuart on the St. Lucie*, 23.

94. U.S. Congress, House, *St. Lucie River, Fla*, 77th Cong., 1st Sess., 1941, Doc. 391, 6.

95. "St. Lucie County Vote Inlet Bonds," *Stuart Daily News*, June 19, 1926, 1; "Million-Dollar Inlet Issue Endorsed," *Stuart Daily News*, April 21, 1926, 1; "First Rock in $1,250,000 St. Lucie Inlet Project Laid for Construction of Long Jetty on North Point Today," *Stuart Daily News*, June 30, 1926, 1.

96. "Ernest Lyons' Column," *Stuart News*, June 18, 1979; Thurlow, *Stuart on the St. Lucie*, 23.

97. George R. Kline, B. W. Mulford, and H. J. Quincey, "Correspondence and Printed Materials Regarding Salerno Development Company," State University Libraries of Florida; Mulford, *Little Journeys*.

98. Kline, Mulford, and Quincey, "Correspondence and Printed Materials," 8.

99. Ibid., 10; Mulford, *Little Journeys*, 3.

100. "Good News for Tarpon Fishers," *New York Times*, December 18, 1892, 8.

Chapter 5. From Labor to Leisure, 1941–Present

1. General Development Corporation, "Life in Port St. Lucie, Florida," 1961.

2. Gary R. Mormino, "Sunbelt Dreams and Altered States: A Social and Cultural History of Florida, 1950–2000," *Florida Historical Quarterly* 81, no. 1 (Summer 2002): 3.

3. Woodward-Clyde Consultants et al., *Physical Features of the Indian River Lagoon*, 2-12, 2-28.

4. "Historical Census Browser"; Thurlow, *Stuart on the St. Lucie*, 46.

5. Brown, "Influence of Humanity," 7.

6. Woodward-Clyde Consultants et al., *Physical Features of the Indian River Lagoon*, 7-2.

7. "Hurricane Highlights," *Stuart News*, September 17, 1947, 1.

8. Fernald, *Coastal Xeric Scrub Communities*, 157.

9. Ibid., 162.

10. In 1949 the enlarged canal (deepened to eight feet) could discharge at a rate of 9,000 cubic feet per second (cfs), a significant increase from the 5,000 cfs permitted after the canal was deepened to six feet in 1937. Woodward-Clyde Consultants et al., *Physical Features of the Indian River Lagoon*, 7-2.

11. Brown, "Influence of Humanity," 8.

12. St. Johns Water Management District, "Indian River Lagoon," 19, 30.

13. At the extreme north of the St. Lucie's North Fork, the small tributaries called Five Mile Creek and Ten Mile Creek were canalized and also sped water to the estuary.

14. Florida Department of Environmental Protection, "Physical Characteristics of the North Fork St. Lucie River."

15. H. W. Bearden, *Water Available in Canals and Shallow Sediments in St. Lucie County, Florida* (Tallahassee: State of Florida, Bureau of Geology, 1972), 2.

16. Specifically, 15.5 National Geodetic Vertical Datum (NGVD); Woodward-Clyde Consultants et al., *Physical Features of the Indian River Lagoon*, 2-46.

17. Not all of the Indian River's natural forces created slow change. Storm-created inlets, for example, could have an immediate and major effect on a region's flora and fauna.

18. Woodward-Clyde Consultants et al., *Physical Features of the Indian River Lagoon*, 2-47.

19. Joe Crankshaw, personal interview with author, Stuart, Fla., June 23, 2011.

20. So little was known by Europeans and Americans in the years following the cession of Florida from Spain to the United States that Vignoles speculated that the St. Lucie might "perhaps originat[e] in the much talked of lake Mayaco [Okeechobee], which like the fountain of youth has not been found." Vignoles, *Observations upon the Floridas*, 46–47.

21. Fernald, *Coastal Xeric Scrub Communities*, 162; Bruce Stephenson, "A Monstrous Desecration: Dredge and Fill in Boca Ciega Bay" in *Paradise Lost?: The Environmental History of Florida*, ed. Jack E. Davis and Raymond Arsenault (Gainesville: University Press of Florida, 2005), 326–49.

22. *Stuart News* reporter Joe Crankshaw recalled a time when editor Ernie Lyons took him on a sunrise ride in his skiff up the north fork of the St. Lucie in the 1950s. Crankshaw recounted that the river "exploded like whipped cream" as hundreds of tarpon attacked snook en masse. Lyons used his newspaper to become a leading voice against the canalization of the Kissimmee River and the construction of the C-23 and C-24 canals, which drain into the north fork of the estuary. "Remember what you've seen. It will probably never happen again. They are killing this river," Lyons told Crankshaw. Crankshaw interview; Mote Marine Laboratory, *St. Lucie Estuary Nutrient Loading Assessment* (Sarasota, Fla.: Mote Marine Laboratory, 1993), 3.

23. Over 7,500 cubic feet of water were released through the C-44 canal alone for weeks at a time in the spring of 1998. Andrew Conte, "Decades of Abuse Flow On," *Stuart News*, March 29, 1998.

24. Woodward-Clyde Consultants et al., *Physical Features of the Indian River Lagoon*, 3-22, 3-23.

25. Conte, "Decades of Abuse Flow On," 1 (see n. 23).

26. Patti Simi, "Fish Health in the St. Lucie Estuarine System," U.S. Department of the Interior, U.S. Geological Survey, Center for Coastal Geology.

27. W. E. Hameedi et al., *Sediment Contamination, Toxicity and Infaunal Community Composition in St. Lucie Estuary, Florida Based upon Measures of the Sediment Quality Triad* (Silver Spring, Md.: Center for Coastal Monitoring and Assessment, 2006).

28. J. S. Reif et al., "Lobomycosis in Atlantic Bottlenose Dolphins from the Indian River Lagoon, Florida," *Journal of the American Veterinary Medical Association* 228, no. 1 (January 1, 2006): 104–8; St. Johns Water Management District, "Indian River Lagoon," 74.

29. St. Johns Water Management District, "Indian River Lagoon," 29; Woodward-Clyde Consultants et al., *Uses of the Indian River Lagoon*, 6-2, 6-17.

30. St. Johns Water Management District, "Indian River Lagoon," 34.

31. Ibid., 2; Fernald, *Coastal Xeric Scrub Communities*, 162.

32. M. Dennis Hanisak and Mark M. Littler, *Submersed Plants of the Indian River Lagoon: A Floristic Inventory and Field Guide* (Washington, D.C.: OffShore Graphics, 2008), 9.

33. Fernald, *Coastal Xeric Scrub Communities*, 229.

34. These trends are consistent with other peninsular water bodies that have been highly urbanized in the second half of the twentieth century. Tampa Bay Estuary, for example, lost 80 percent of its sea grasses (a greater systemwide percentage than the Indian River) and 44 percent of its mangroves. Similarly, Charlotte Harbor lost

29 percent of its sea grasses but had an unusual 11 percent increase in the size of its mangrove forests. St. Johns Water Management District, "Indian River Lagoon," 49; Fernald, *Coastal Xeric Scrub Communities*, 49.

35. St. Johns Water Management District, "Indian River Lagoon," 19, 30; Woodward-Clyde Consultants et al., *Uses of the Indian River Lagoon*, 2-13, 2-16; Indian River Lagoon National Estuary Program, *Indian River Lagoon Comprehensive Conservation and Management Plan* (Palm Bay, Fla.: St. Johns River Water Management District, 2008).

36. Kenneth D. Haddad, "Habitats of the Indian River," in *The Indian River Lagoon: Proceedings of the Indian River Resources Symposium*, ed. Diane D. Barile (Melbourne: Marine Resources Council of East Central Florida, Florida Institute of Technology, 1985), 23–26.

37. *Stuart News*, July 25, 1945.

38. The lagoon in the vicinity of the Sebastian and Fort Pierce inlets also remained relatively clean, due to the flushing effects of the inlets. Fernald, *Coastal Xeric Scrub Communities*, 229.

39. Robert L. Nabors, ed., "Countdown in History: Titusville Centennial: Historical Booklet and Program" (1967), North Brevard Historical Society and Museum/North Brevard Business Directory.

40. Sallie Middleton, "Space Rush: Local Impact of Federal Aerospace Programs on Brevard and Surrounding Counties," *Florida Historical Quarterly* 87, no. 2 (Fall 2008): 260–61.

41. Ibid., 281

42. Residents of Jupiter Island in the lower Indian River, Nathaniel Reed's family was instrumental in creating a winter community for affluent northerners on the barrier island, a small part of the larger trend of the Indian River transitioning from a source of food and labor to one of rest and play. See Middleton, "Space Rush," 284–85; Nathaniel P. Reed, personal interview with author, Jupiter Island, Fla., October 29, 2013; Nathaniel P. Reed, *A Different Vision: The History of the Hobe Sound Company and the Jupiter Island Club* (Hobe Sound, Fla.: Reed, 2010).

43. Callum M. Roberts et al., "Effects of Marine Reserves on Adjacent Fisheries," *Science* 295, no. 5548 (November 30, 2001): 1920–23.

44. Gordon Patterson, *The Mosquito Crusades* (New Brunswick, N.J.: Rutgers University Press), 201–2; Middleton, "Space Rush," 265–66.

45. Middleton, "Space Rush," 266

46. Despite the growth of the Indian River's industry, agriculture, and population, the ports at Fort Pierce and Canaveral handled only 2.7 percent of Florida's imports and exports in 1984 ($12 million in Fort Pierce and $357 million in Port Canaveral). http://www.genon.com/company/stations/indianriver.aspx; Woodward-Clyde Consultants et al., *Uses of the Indian River Lagoon*, 6-27; Woodward-Clyde Consultants et al., *Physical Features of the Indian River Lagoon*, 2-26, 4-26.

47. Disney Cruise Lines, "Disney Fantasy."

48. Woodward-Clyde Consultants et al., *Uses of the Indian River Lagoon*, 2-14; Woodward-Clyde Consultants et al., *Physical Features of the Indian River Lagoon*, 2-13.

49. Crawford, *Florida's Big Dig*, 336–37.

50. Nearly all of the Indian River's 137 spoil islands were owned by the state, with the exception of several that were owned by the federal government (such as the Pelican Island National Wildlife Refuge discussed in chapter 2) and several by Martin County. Two islands near the St. Lucie inlet were sold by the state to private individuals soon after some of them were created, but a public outcry in August 1946 led by *Stuart News* editor Ernie Lyons led to the end of the practice. *Stuart News*, August 3 and 22, 1946; Florida Department of Environmental Protection, "Spoil Island Project—Indian River Lagoon," http://www.spoilislandproject.org/contact.htm; St. Johns Water Management District, "Indian River Lagoon"; "Stop the Grabbers! Save Our Islands for Use by Public!," *Stuart News*, August 3, 1946; "Public Protests Halt Islands Sale Attempt," *Stuart News*, August 22, 1946.

51. General Development Corporation, "Life in Port St. Lucie."

52. Woodward-Clyde Consultants et al., *Uses of the Indian River Lagoon*, 2-17, 3-17, 4-12.

53. "Florida Mosquito Control," Florida Medical Entomology Laboratory, University of Florida.

54. Jorge R. Rey and C. Roxanne Rutledge, "Mangroves," Institute of Food and Agricultural Sciences, University of Florida; Jorge R. Rey and C. Roxanne Rutledge, "Mosquito Control Impoundments," University of Florida.

55. Among the strategies used by the SWIM program was the reconnection of fixed impoundments to the larger estuary by making them RIM impoundments by installing culverts and pumps. Rey and Rutledge, "Mosquito Control Impoundments"; Indian River Lagoon National Estuary Program, "Indian River Lagoon: Introduction to a National Treasure" (Palm Bay, Fla.: St. Johns River Water Management District, 2007), 41; Indian River Lagoon National Estuary Program, *Indian River Lagoon Comprehensive Conservation and Management Plan*. The difficulties associated with removing impoundments are explored in Randall W. Parkinson, "Tuning Surface Water Management and Wetland Restoration Programs with Historic Sediment Accumulation Rates: Merritt Island National Wildlife Refuge, East-Central Florida, U.S.A.," *Journal of Coastal Research* 22, no. 5 (September 2006): 1268–77.

56. Fernald, *Coastal Xeric Scrub Communities*, 165.

57. Florida Department of Environmental Protection, "Physical Characteristics of the North Fork St. Lucie River."

58. Woodward-Clyde Consultants et al., *Physical Features of the Indian River Lagoon*, 2-17.

59. Florida Department of Environmental Protection, "Indian River Blueway," http://www.dep.state.fl.us/lands/FFAnnual/Indian%20River%20Lagoon%20Blueway.pdf.

60. James A. Farr and O. Greg Brock, "Florida's Landmark Programs for Conservation and Recreation Land Acquisition"; St. Johns Water Management District, "Indian River Lagoon."

61. Fernald, *Coastal Xeric Scrub Communities*, 164.

62. Florida Department of Education, "Conservation Land Acquisition Programs of Local Governments," http://www.dep.state.fl.us/lands/FFAnnual/Conservation_Land_Programs_of_Local_Governments.pdf; Indian River Land Trust, "A Brief History of IRLT: Highlights," http://www.indianriverlandtrust.org/cfiles/about_history.cfm.

63. Indian River Lagoon National Estuary Program, "Indian River Lagoon: Introduction to a National Treasure" (Palm Bay, Fla.: St. Johns River Water Management District, 2007).

64. *Independent Scientific Review of the Indian River Lagoon—South Project Implementation Report* (Jacksonville, Fla.: U.S. Army Corps of Engineers/South Florida Water Management District, 2004).

65. Vincent Encomio, personal interview with author, Stuart, Fla., August 23, 2012.

66. George Bush, "Remarks at a Republican Party Fundraising Dinner in Orlando, Florida," George Bush Presidential Library and Museum, http://bushlibrary.tamu.edu/research/public_papers.php?id=1783.

67. U.S. Army Corps of Engineers, "CERP: The Plan in Depth," Comprehensive Everglades Restoration Plan; Everglades Foundation, "Indian River Lagoon South—C-44"; Gary Goforth, personal interview with author, Hobe Sound, Fla., December 2, 2013.

68. Margaret A. Lasi et al., "Investigating the Causes of the 2011 IRL Superbloom—A Water Quality Analysis," paper presented at 2013 Indian River Lagoon Symposium, Harbor Branch Oceanographic Institute, Fort Pierce, Fla.; St. Johns River Water Management District, "It's Your Lagoon," http://floridaswater.com/itsyourlagoon/index.html; Jim Waymer, "What Went Wrong?," *Florida Today*, July 31, 2014; Christopher Buzelli, "Modelling and Monitoring of *Syringodium filiforme* (Manatee Grass) in the Southern Indian River Lagoon," *Estuaries and Coasts* 35, no. 6 (November 2012): 1401–15; Vincent Encomio, personal interview with author, Stuart, Fla., August 5, 2012.

69. "Activists Hope 'Hands Across the Lagoon' Puts Focus on Waterways Plight," *Florida Today*, September 25, 2013; St. Lucie River Initiative, *De-Ooze It or Lose It! Save the St. Lucie River and Estuary: A Citizen's Report to Congress* (Stuart, Fla.: St. Lucie River Initiative, 1995); Marine Resources Council, "About Us."

70. Mark Tomasik, "Covering Our Indian River Lagoon Is Our Commitment, Our Responsibility," TCPalm.com, June 30, 2013; Brian Lapointe et al., "Effects of Hurricanes, Land Use, and Water Management on Nutrient and Microbial Pollution: St. Lucie Estuary, South East Florida," *Journal of Coastal Research* 28, no. 6 (November 2012): 1345–61; "Indian River Lagoon Observatory: Biodiversity and Ecosystem Function of an Estuary in Transition," Harbor Branch Oceanographic Institute;

Diane S. Littler et al., *Submersed Plants of the Indian River Lagoon: A Floristic Inventory and Field Guide* (Boca Raton, Fla.: Offshore Graphics, 2008).

71. Forty-two years after the first "funeral" for the St. Lucie, local activists held a similar funeral and expressed frustration at the lack of progress. "High School Students Refuse to Give Up on Polluted River," *Stuart News*, April 26, 2014; Nicole Mader, personal interview with author, Stuart, Fla., June 23, 2014; Marty Baum, personal interview with author, Stuart, Fla., April 2, 2014; Kelly Tyko, "Rally Protests Water Discharges," *Sun Sentinel* (Fort Lauderdale), September 28, 2003; Laurie K. Blandford and Tyler Treadway, "Thousands Attend Rally for Indian River Lagoon in Stuart," *Stuart News*, August 3, 2013; Jackie Holfelder, "Indian Riverkeeper Advocating for Lagoon," *Stuart News*, December 6, 2012; Max Quackenbos Collection, George A. Smathers Libraries, University of Florida, Gainesville.

72. John Kenney, "Florida Sugar Growers Win House Vote on Everglades Pollution Payout," *Palm Beach Post*, March 7, 2013; Lori Morris et al., "The Bloomin' Lagoon—Bloom and Bust of Indian River Lagoon Sea Grasses," paper presented at 2013 Indian River Lagoon Symposium, Harbor Branch Oceanographic Institute, Fort Pierce, Fla.

73. In 1991 St. Lucie produced more citrus than any other Florida county. Indian River was the third most productive county. Woodward-Clyde Consultants et al., *Uses of the Indian River Lagoon*, 5-7. Most of Florida's oranges are now grown in the interior of the state, and St. Lucie and Indian River counties produce primarily grapefruit. Frederick S. Davies and Larry K. Jackson, *Citrus Growing in Florida* (Gainesville: University Press of Florida, 2009).

74. Woodward-Clyde Consultants et al., *Uses of the Indian River Lagoon*, 5-9.

75. Davies and Jackson, *Citrus Growing in Florida*, 19.

76. Robert M. Hutchings, "From Oranges to Orange Juice: A Transformation in Florida Agriculture, 1945–1965" (Stuart, Fla.: Pioneer America Society, October 14, 2011).

77. Woodward-Clyde Consultants et al., *Uses of the Indian River Lagoon*, 5-7.

78. Nathaniel Reed, personal interview, Jupiter Island, Fla., December 12, 2014.

Chapter 6. Conclusion

1. Johnson, *Highways and Byways of Florida*.

2. Newman, *Stories of Early Life*, 19.

3. Crawford, *Florida's Big Dig*, 141.

4. Woodward-Clyde Consultants et al., *Physical Features of the Indian River Lagoon*, 3-21, 3-22.

5. K. Hill, "Paralichthys Dentatus," Smithsonian Marine Station at Fort Pierce; Rey and Rutledge, "Mangroves."

6. Maggy Hurchalla, personal interview, Port Salerno, Fla., December 19, 2014.

7. Reed interview, December 12, 2014.

8. Sarah T. Phillips, "Environmental History," in *American History Now*, ed. Eric Foner and Lisa McGirr (Philadelphia: Temple University Press, 2011), 286.

9. "High Seas Carved New Inlet through Back of Sea Island," *Stuart News*, March 1961; Sandra Henderson Thurlow, *Sewall's Point: The History of a Peninsular Community on Florida's Treasure Coast* (Stuart, Fla.: Sewall's Point, 1992), 19.

10. Gulf, Okeechobee and Atlantic Waterway Association, "Minutes"; U.S. Congress, *Caloosahatchee River, St. Lucie River, Lake Okeechobee, and Miami River, Fla.*

11. Milanich, *Archaeology of Precolumbian Florida*, 40.

Bibliography

Primary Sources

The Army and Navy Chronicle, and Scientific Repository. Being a Continuation of Homans' "Army and Navy Chronicle" (1843–1844). Washington, D.C., 1844.

Barbour, George M. *Florida for Tourists, Invalids and Settlers*. New York: Appleton, 1882.

Bartram, William. *Travels through North and South Carolina, Georgia, East and West Florida, the Cherokee Country*. Dublin: J. Moore, W. Jones, R. McAllister, and J. Rice, 1793.

———. *Travels through North and South Carolina, Georgia, East and West Florida*. Philadelphia: James and Johnson, 1791. The Open Library. https://openlibrary.org/books/OL23530384M/Travels_through_North_and_South_Carolina_Georgia_East_and_West_Florida_the_Cherokee_country_the_exte.

Bell, Emily Lagow. *My Pioneer Days in Florida, 1876–1898*. Miami: McMurray Printing, 1928.

"Canaveral Post Office Ledger, 1891–1895." Ledgers 2. University of Florida Special Collections, P. K. Yonge Library of Florida History, Gainesville.

Canova, Andrew P. *Life Adventures in South Florida*. Palatka, Fla.: Southern Sun Publishing House, 1885.

Cohen, M. M., and O. Z. Tyler Jr. *Notices of Florida and the Campaigns*. 1836. Reprint, Gainesville: University of Florida Press, 1964.

Crankshaw, Joe. Personal interview with author. Stuart, Fla., June 16, 2011.

de Laet, Joannes. *Florida et Regiones Vicinae*. 1630. Old Florida Maps. University of Miami Libraries. http://scholar.library.miami.edu/floridamaps/view_image.php?image_name=dlp0002000020001001&group=sp.

de Solis, Juan Diaz. *British East Florida*. 1764. Old Florida Maps. University of Miami Libraries. http://scholar.library.miami.edu/floridamaps/view_image.php?image_name=dlp0002000600001001&group=spanish.

Dickinson, Jonathan, *Jonathan Dickinson's Journal: Or, God's Protecting Providence. Being the Narrative of a Journey from Port Royal in Jamaica to Philadelphia between August 23, 1696 and April 1, 1697*. Reprint, Stuart, Fla.: Valentine Books, 1975.

East Coast Railway Maps. Ft. Pierce to Perrine Grant (Dade and Brevard Counties). Map ed. Box 1, Folder Railroads. University of Florida Special Collections, Gainesville. http://ufdc.ufl.edu/UF00095315/00005.

Ferguson, C. *Sketch of Indian River Florida*. U.S. Coast Survey. 1:10,000. Washington, D.C., 1861.

Florida Congress. *Acts and Resolutions Adopted by the State of Florida*, 1901.

Florida Everglades Engineering Commission. *Report of Florida Everglades Engineering Commission*. Washington, D.C.: Government Printing Office, 1914.

Gauld, George. *Chart of the Gulf of Florida Or New Bahama Channel Commonly Called the Gulf Passage, etc.* London: 1794. Old Florida Maps. University of Miami Libraries. http://scholar.library.miami.edu/floridamaps/view_image.php?image_name=dlp00020000720001001&group=spanish.

General Development Corporation. "Life in Port St. Lucie, Florida." 1961. http://www.pslhistory.org/images/gallery/lifeinPSL61.jpg.

Gregg, William H. *Where, When, and How to Catch Fish on the East Coast of Florida*. Buffalo, N.Y.: Matthews-Northrup Works, 1902.

Gulf, Okeechobee and Atlantic Waterway Association. "Minutes of a General Meeting of the Gulf, Okeechobee and Atlantic Waterway Association." 1926. Meeting Minutes. P. K. Yonge Library of Florida History, University of Florida Special Collections, Gainesville.

Hallock, Charles. *Camp Life in Florida: A Handbook for Sportsmen and Settlers*. New York: Forest and Stream, 1876.

Hawks, J. W. *The East Coast of Florida*. Wynn, Mass.: Lewis and Wynnship, 1887. Reprint, New Smyrna Beach, Fla.: E. O. Painter Printing, 1995.

Henshall, James A. *Camping and Cruising in Florida*. Cincinnati: R. Clarke, 1884.

Herold, Herman. "Logbook of Trip to Jupiter Inlet, Transcript." 1884. P. K. Yonge Library of Florida History, University of Florida Special Collections, Gainesville.

"Hon. Sidney J. Catts, Candidate for Office of United States Senator, Subject to Democratic Primary (1920)." State Library and Archives of Florida, Tallahassee. http://www.floridamemory.com/items/show/212324.

Indian River Steamboat Company. "Pursers Ticket." 1893. University of Florida Special Collections, Gainesville.

"Interview with Mrs. J. E. Taylor." November 28, 1972. Samuel Proctor Oral History Program, University of Florida, Gainesville. http://ufdc.ufl.edu/UF00007961/00001/2j.

Ives, J. C. *Military Map of the Peninsula of Florida South of Tampa Bay, etc.* 1856. Old Florida Maps. University of Miami Libraries. http://scholar.library.miami.edu/floridamaps/view_image.php?image_name=dlp00020001270001001&group=statehood.

Johnson, Clifton. *Highways and Byways of Florida.* New York: MacMillan, 1918.

Kline, George R., B. W. Mulford, and H. J. Quincey. "Correspondence and Printed Materials Regarding Salerno Development Company." State University Libraries of Florida. http://digitool.fcla.edu/R/9J1NSPC8FQ284YEH1VPBVKQF1UJY5K8VR7DJHGYGJC2XVIE3TP-00798?func=dbin-jump-full&object_id=2633574&local_base=GEN01&pds_handle=GUEST.

Lanier, Sidney. *Florida: Its Scenery, Climate, and History, with an Account of Charleston, Savannah, Augusta, and Aiken, a Chapter for Consumptives, various Papers on Fruit-Culture, and a Complete Hand-Book and Guide.* Philadelphia: J. B. Lippincott, 1876.

Le Conte, John Eatton, and Richard Adicks. *Le Conte's Report on East Florida.* Gainesville: University Presses of Florida, 1978.

LeTourneau, Lucy Richards. *Stuart Messenger/Stuart Times/Stuart News.* Box 1–6, Blake Library, Stuart, Fla.

Mackay, John, and J. E. Blake. *Map of East Florida.* Boston: Thayer, 1840.

Menninger, Edwin Arnold. *From the Atlantic to the Gulf of Mexico.* Stuart, Fla.: Edwin A. Menninger, 1937. University of Florida Special Collections, Gainesville.

Motte, Jacob Rhett. *Journey into Wilderness: An Army Surgeon's Account of Life in Camp and Field during the Creek and Seminole Wars, 1836–1838.* Gainesville: University of Florida Press, 1953.

Mulcaster, Frederick George. "Letter to James Grant." 1772. *Florida History Online,* University of North Florida. http://www.unf.edu/floridahistoryonline/BiscayneBay/biscaynebay1772.html.

Mulford, B. W. *Little Journeys to Salerno and the Famous St. Lucie Inlet Farms* (1915).

Munroe, Ralph Middleton, and Vincent Gilpin. *The Commodore's Story.* 1930. Reprint, Coconut Grove, Fla.: Barnacle Society, 2010.

Museum Exhibit: Manatee Hunting Lance of Hugh L. Willoughby (Circa 1890s). Stuart, Fla.: House of Refuge Museum, Historical Society of Martin County, Florida.

National Oceanic and Atmospheric Administration. "Sailfish Point, Florida." National Oceanic and Atmospheric Administration. http://oceanexplorer.noaa.gov/explorations/05deepcorals/logs/nov7/media/stlucie_600.html.

Newman, Anna Pearl Leonard. *Stories of Early Life Along Beautiful Indian River.* Stuart, Fla.: Stuart Daily News, 1953.

"One of the Dredges—It Excavated 475,000 Cubic Yards of Earth in One Month." University of Florida, University Archives Photograph Collection. http://ufdc.ufl.edu/UF00034421/00001.

"Papers of the Port of New Smyrnea, 1849–1858." Microfilm, P. K. Yonge Library of Florida History, University of Florida Special Collections, Gainesville.

"Photograph of the Main Entrance to the Indian River Hotel, Rockledge, Florida." Photograph, University of Florida Digital Collections, Gainesville. http://ufdc.ufl.edu/UF00028756/00001.

"Prospectus of the Florida Coast Line Canal and Transportation Company." 1891.

University of Florida Special Collections, P. K. Yonge Library of Florida History, Gainesville.

Quackenbos, Max, Collection. Special and Area Studies Collections, George A. Smathers Libraries, University of Florida, Gainesville.

Reclaiming the Everglades. *The Muck Soils of Fellsmere Farms, Florida*. Fellsmere, Fla.: Fellsmere Sales, 1913.

Rhodes, Harrison. *A Guide to Florida for Tourists, Sportsmen and Settlers*. New York: Dodd, Mead, 1912.

Roberts, William, and Thomas Jefferys. *An Account of the First Discovery, and Natural History of Florida: With a Particular Detail of the several Expeditions and Descents Made on that Coast*. 1763. Reprint, Gainesville: University Press of Florida, 1976.

Rockledge Hotel: Souvenir Album. 1891. University of Florida Special Collections, P. K. Yonge Library of Florida History, Gainesville.

Romans, Bernard, and William Brown. *A Concise Natural History of East and West Florida*. New York: R. Aitken, 1775.

Schroeder, Curt. "Commercial Fishing." Unpublished manuscript. Sandra Henderson Thurlow Collection, Stuart, Fla.

Simmons, William H. *Notices of East Florida*. 1822. Reprint, Gainesville: University of Florida Press, 1973.

"The Southern Harbors of the United States." *Merchants' Magazine and Commercial Review* 45, no. 1 (1861): 17–24.

"Spanish Land Grant for Delespine, Joseph." Land Grant. State Library and Archives of Florida, Tallahassee. http://www.floridamemory.com/items/show/232594?id=1.

"Spanish Land Grant for Hutchinson, James." 1803. Spanish Land Grant Claims. State Library and Archives of Florida, Tallahassee. http://www.floridamemory.com/items/show/232742?id=1.

"'St. Sebastian' and 'St. Augustine' Deteriorating in the Loxahatchee River." State Library and Archives of Florida, Tallahassee. http://www.floridamemory.com/PhotographicCollection/displayphoto.cfm?IMGTITLE=RC09314.

Stebbins, Francis Ranna, and Carolyn Baker Lewis. *The Winter Sailor: Francis R. Stebbins on Florida's Indian River, 1878–1888*. Tuscaloosa: University of Alabama Press, 2004.

Stork, William, and Denys D. Rolle. *An Extract from the Account of East Florida*. London, 1766.

Thurlow/Runke Collection. Sewall's Point, Fla.

Turnbull, Andrew to Sir William Duncan, Smyrnéa, December 3, 1770. *Florida History Online*, University of North Florida. http://www.unf.edu/floridahistoryonline/Turnbull/letters/July-Dec1770.htm.

U.S. Army Corps of Engineers. "SAJSP Permit (2443)."

U.S. Coast and Geodetic Survey. *Inside Route Pilot: New York to Key West*. Washington, D.C.: Government Printing Office, 1920.

U.S. Congress. House. Committee on Rivers and Harbors. *Caloosahatchee River, St.*

Lucie River, Lake Okeechobee, and Miami River, Fla. 71st Cong., 2nd sess., March 19 and 27, 1930.

———. *Copy of a Report from Lieut. Col. Q. A. Gilmore, Corps of Engineers, upon a Survey of the Indian River, Florida, with a View to Opening a Passage to Mosquito Lagoon, by Way of the Haulover.* 47th Cong. 1st Sess., 1882, Doc. 33.

———. *Intracoastal Waterway from Jacksonville, Florida to Miami, Florida.* 69th Cong., 2d Sess., 1926, Doc. 586.

———. *Letter from the Chief of Engineers, a Report of the Preliminary Examination of Indian River, Florida.* 51st Cong., 2d Sess., 1891, Doc. 168.

———. *Letter from the Secretary of War Transmitting, with the Chief of Engineers, Report of Examination and Survey of Sebastian Inlet, Indian River, Florida.* 59th Cong., 1st Sess., 1906, Doc. 858.

———. *Letter from the Secretary of War Transmitting, with a Letter from the Chief of Engineers, Reports of Examination and Survey of St. Lucie Inlet, Florida.* 61st Cong., 1st Sess., 1909, Doc. 75.

———. *St. Lucia (Lucie), Florida.* 60th Cong., 2d Sess., 1909, Doc. 1312.

———. *St. Lucie River, Fla.* 77th Cong., 1st Sess., 1941, Doc. 391.

———. *Survey of the Santa Lucie Inlet and River, Florida.* 55th Cong., 2d Sess., 1898, Doc. 548.

U.S. Congress. Senate. Committee on Commerce. *Waterway from Punta Rasa to Fort Pierce and Stuart, Florida.* U.S. Congress. 47th Cong. 1st Sess., 1882, Doc. 33.

———. *Letter from the Secretary of War Transmitting a Letter from the Chief of Engineers, Submitting Copies of Reports from Colonel Gilmore Containing Plans and Estimates for the Improvement of the Saint Johns River, Florida, &c, with Accompanying Maps.* 48th Cong., 1st Sess., 1884, Doc. 65.

U.S. Department of Agriculture. *Laws Applicable to the United States Department of Agriculture.* Washington, D.C.: Government Printing Office, 1912.

U.S. Department of the Treasury. *Report of the President of the Light-House Board, in Relation to Re-Establishing the Light-Houses at Cape Florida, Jupiter Inlet and Cape Canaveral.* Washington, D.C.: Government Printing Office, 1865.

U.S. Fish Commission. *The Fisheries of Indian River, Florida.* Washington, D.C.: Government Printing Office, 1897.

U.S. Life Saving Service. *Copy of Wreck Report.* 1904. Reprint, Stuart, Fla.: Historical Society of Martin County, 2008.

U.S. Naval War Records Office. *Official Record of the Union and Confederate Navies in the War of the Rebellion.* Washington, D.C.: Government Printing Office, 1903.

Vignoles, Charles. *Map of Florida.* 1823. University of Florida Digital Collections, Gainesville. http://ufdc.ufl.edu/UF00005241/00001.

———. *Observations upon the Floridas.* 1823. Reprint, Gainesville: University Press of Florida, 1977.

Walker, William. *The War in Nicaragua.* 1860. Reprint, Tucson: University of Arizona Press, 1985.

Williams, John Lee. *Map of Florida*. New York: Greene & McGowran, 1837.
———. *The Territory of Florida: Or, Sketches of the Topography, Civil and Natural History, of the Country, the Climate, and the Indian Tribes, from the First Discovery to the Present Time, with a Map, Views, etc.* New York: A. T. Goodrich, 1837.
"Work Train Laying Track when the Florida East Coast Railroad was Built through Fort Pierce, Saint Lucie County, 1894." Photograph. University of Florida Digital Collections, Gainesville. http://ufdc.ufl.edu/UF00072289/00001.

Secondary Sources

Allen, Ginger M., and Martin B. Main. "Florida's Geologic History." http://edis.ifas.ufl.edu/uw208.
Almasi, Mohammed N. "The Importance of Inlets and Sea Level in the Development of Hutchinson Island and Indian River Lagoon, Florida." In *The Indian River Lagoon: Proceedings of the Indian River Resources Symposium,* edited by Diane D. Barile, 8–16. Melbourne: Marine Resource Council of East Central Florida, 1983.
Arnade, Charles W. "Cattle Raising in Spanish Florida, 1513–1763." *Agricultural History* 35, no. 3 (July 1961): 116–24.
Attaway, John A. *A History of Florida Citrus Freezes*. DeLeon Springs, Fla.: E. O. Painter Printing, 1997.
Auchincloss, Louis. *Theodore Roosevelt*. New York: Times Books, 2002.
Austin, Daniel F. "The Glades Indians and the Plants They Used: Ethnobotony of a Lost Culture." *Palmetto* 17, no. 2 (Summer/Fall 1997): 7–11.
Baptist, Edward E. *Creating an Old South: Middle Florida's Plantation Frontier before the Civil War*. Chapel Hill: University of North Carolina Press, 2002.
Bearden, H. W. *Water Available in Canals and Shallow Sediments in St. Lucie County, Florida*. Tallahassee: State of Florida, Bureau of Geology, 1972.
"Biological Status Review Report for the Roseate Spoonbill." *Florida Fish and Wildlife Conservation Commission,* March 31, 2011. http://myfwc.com/media/2273376/Roseate-Spoonbill-BSR.pdf.
Bockelman, Charles W. *Six Columns and Fort New Smyrna*. New Smyrna, Fla.: Halifax Historical Society, 1985.
Brech, Alan. "Neither Ocean nor Continent: Correlating the Archaeology and Geomorphology of the Barrier Islands of East Central Florida." Master's thesis, University of Florida, 2004.
Brech, Alan, and J. F. Lanham. "The Destruction of the Ais Chiefdom and Other Overlooked Ethnographic and Ethnological Information from Jonathan Dickinson's 1699 Shipwreck Journal." Paper presented at the annual meeting of the Florida Historical Society, Pensacola, May 23, 2009.
Brown, M. T. "Influence of Humanity on the Coastal Landscape of Florida: The Indian River as a Case Study." In *Wetlands General Research Collections,* edited by Diane D. Barile, 1–13. Melbourne: Marine Resources Council of East Central Florida, 1985. http://ufdc.ufl.edu/UF00017049/00001.

Brown, William E., Jr., and Karen Hudson. "Henry Flagler and the Model Land Company." *Tequesta* 56 (1996): 47–78.

Bullen, Ripley P., and Frederick W. Sleight. *Archaeological Investigations of the Castle Windy Site*. William L. Bryant Foundation American Studies Report 1, 1959.

Bush, George. "Remarks at a Republican Party Fundraising Dinner in Orlando, Florida," George Bush Presidential Library and Museum. http://bushlibrary.tamu.edu/research/public_papers.php?id=1783.

Buzelli, Christopher. "Modelling and Monitoring of *Syringodium filiforme* (Manatee Grass) in the Southern Indian River Lagoon." *Estuaries and Coasts* 35, no. 6 (November 2012): 1401–15.

Carson, Robe B. "The Florida Tropics." *Economic Geography* 27, no. 4 (October 1951): 321–39.

Chaffin, Tom. *Fatal Glory: Narciso Lopez and the First Clandestine United States War against Cuba*. Charlottesville: University Press of Virginia, 1996.

Clement, Gail. "Everglades Timeline: Reclaiming the Everglades: Florida's Natural History, 1884 to 1934." http://everglades.fiu.edu/reclaim/timeline/timeline6.htm.

Cline, Howard Francis, and United States Indian Claims Commission. *Provisional Historical Gazeteer with Locational Notes on Florida Colonial Communities*. American Indian Ethnohistory: Southern and Southeast Indians. New York: Garland, 1974.

Coker, Edward Caleb, and Daniel L. Schafer. "A New Englander on the Indian River Frontier: Caleb Lyndon Brayton and the View from Brayton's Bluff." *Florida Historical Quarterly* 70, no. 3 (January 1992): 305–32.

Coker, William S., and Thomas D. Watson. *Indian Traders of the Southeastern Spanish Borderlands: Panton, Leslie & Company and John Forbes & Company, 1783–1847*. Gainesville: University Press of Florida, 1986.

Corliss, Carlton J. "Henry M. Flagler: Railroad Builder." *Florida Historical Quarterly* 38, no. 3 (January 1960): 195–205.

Corse, Carita Doggett. *Dr. Andrew Turnbull and the New Smyrnea Colony of Florida*. Jacksonville, Fla.: Drew Press, 1919.

Covington, James W. "The Armed Occupation Act of 1842." *Florida Historical Quarterly* 40, no. 1 (July 1961): 41–52.

Crawford, William G., Jr. "A History of Florida's East Coast Canal." *Broward Legacy* (Summer/Fall 1997): 2–27.

———. *Florida's Big Dig: The Atlantic Intracoastal Waterway from Jacksonville to Miami, 1881 to 1935*. Cocoa: Florida Historical Society Press, 2006.

Cronon, William. *Changes in the Land: Indians, Colonists, and the Ecology of New England*. New York: Hill and Wang, 1983.

Davies, Frederick S., and Larry K. Jackson. *Citrus Growing in Florida*. Gainesville: University Press of Florida, 2009.

DeFreese, Duane E. "The Indian River Lagoon: Connecting People to the Sea." http://www.myregion.org/clientuploads/pdfs/ncfl_Indian River.pdf.

Derr, Mark. *Some Kind of Paradise: A Chronicle of Man and the Land in Florida.* Gainesville: University Press of Florida, 1998.

"Diagram Tropic Zone Tropical Connections." University of Maryland Center for Environmental Science. http://ian.umces.edu/imagelibrary/albums/userpics/84469/normal_iil_diagram_tropic_zone_tropical_connections.png.

Disney Cruise Lines. "Disney Fantasy." http://disneycruise.disney.go.com/ships-activities/ships/fantasy/.

"Dr. Andrew Turnbull and the Mediterranean Settlement at New Smyrnea and Edgewater, Florida, 1766–1777." *Florida History Online,* University of North Florida. http://www.unf.edu/floridahistoryonline/Turnbull/images/map-combo.jpg.

"The 1880s." Indian River County Library, Vero Beach, Fla. http://www.irclibrary.org/sebastianlibrary/george/1880.html.

Everglades Foundation. "Indian River Lagoon South—C-44." http://content.protectourrivers.com/pdf/c44.pdf.

Ewel, John J., and Ronald L. Myers. *Ecosystems of Florida.* Orlando: University of Central Florida Press, 1990.

Farr, James A., and O. Greg Brock. "Florida's Landmark Programs for Conservation and Recreation Land Acquisition." Florida Department of Environmental Protection. http://www.dep.state.fl.us/lands/AcqHistory.htm.

Fernald, Raymond T. *Coastal Xeric Scrub Communities of the Treasure Coast Region, Florida a Summary of their Distribution and Ecology, with Guidelines for their Preservation and Management.* Tallahassee: Office of Environmental Services, Florida Game and Fresh Water Fish Commission, 1989.

Florida Department of Education. "Conservation Land Acquisition Programs of Local Governments." http://www.dep.state.fl.us/lands/FFAnnual/Conservation_Land_Programs_of_Local_Governments.pdf.

Florida Department of Environmental Protection. "Florida's Geologic History." http://www.dep.state.fl.us/geology/geologictopics/geohist-2.htm.

———. "Historic and Altered Rivercourse of North Fork St. Lucie River." http://www.dep.state.fl.us/coastal/sites/northfork/pub/NF_Map06_Rivercourse.pdf.

———. "Indian River Blueway." http://www.dep.state.fl.us/lands/FFAnnual/Indian%20River%20Lagoon%20Blueway.pdf.

———. "Natural Resources of North Fork St. Lucie River Aquatic Preserve." http://www.dep.state.fl.us/coastal/sites/northfork/resources/.

———. "Physical Characteristics of the North Fork St. Lucie River." http://www.dep.state.fl.us/coastal/sites/northfork/resources/physical.htm.

———. "Spoil Island Project—Indian River Lagoon." http://www.spoilislandproject.org.

Florida Department of State, Division of Historical Resources. Archaeological Site Data Supplement. Florida Master Site File.

"Florida Mosquito Control." Florida Medical Entomology Laboratory, University of Florida. http://mosquito.ifas.ufl.edu/Florida_Mosquito_Control.htm.

Florida Museum of Natural History. *Exhibit: South Florida: People & Environments.* Gainesville: University of Florida, 2011.

"Fort Pierce Port Plan." St. Lucie County Government. http://www.stlucieco.gov/port/Background.htm.

Fuchs, Eckhardt, and Benedikt Stuchtey, eds. *Across Cultural Borders.* New York: Rowman and Littlefield, 2002.

Gallay, Alan. *The Indian Slave Trade: The Rise of the English Empire in the American South, 1670–1717.* New Haven, Conn.: Yale University Press, 2002.

Geyer, Alejandro B. *Favored of the Gods: Biography of William Walker.* Masaya, Nicaragua: privately printed, 2002.

"Global Forest Resources Assessment 2000." Food and Agriculture Organization of the United Nations. http://www.fao.org/3/a-y1997e/y1997e12.htm.

Godfrey, Matthew C., and Theodore Catton. *River of Interests: Water Management in South Florida and the Everglades, 1948–2010.* Washington, D.C.: Government Printing Office, 2012.

Goodwyn, Lawrence. *The Populist Moment: A Short History of the Agrarian Revolt in America.* New York: Oxford University Press, 1978.

Grunwald, Michael. *The Swamp: The Everglades, Florida, and the Politics of Paradise.* New York: Simon & Schuster, 2007.

Haddad, Kenneth D. "Habitats of the Indian River." In *The Indian River Lagoon: Proceedings of the Indian River Resources Symposium,* edited by Diane D. Barile, 23–26. Melbourne: Marine Resources Council of East Central Florida, Florida Institute of Technology, 1985.

Hameedi, M. J., W. E. Johnson, K. L. Kimbrough, and J. A. Browder. *Sediment Contamination, Toxicity and Infaunal Community Composition in St. Lucie Estuary, Florida Based upon Measures of the Sediment Quality Triad.* Silver Spring, Md.: Center for Coastal Monitoring and Assessment, 2006. http://ccma.nos.noaa.gov/publications/sle_report.pdf.

Hanisak, M. Dennis, and Mark M. Littler. *Submersed Plants of the Indian River Lagoon: A Floristic Inventory and Field Guide.* Washington, D.C.: OffShore Graphics, 2008.

Hann, John H. *A History of the Timucua Indians and Missions.* Gainesville: University Press of Florida, 1996.

Hellier, Walter R. *Indian River: Florida's Treasure Coast.* Coconut Grove, Fla.: Hurricane House, 1965.

Higgs, Charles D. "Contacts with the Ais Indian River Country." *Florida Historical Quarterly* 21, no. 1 (July 1942): 25–39.

Hill, K. "Paralichthys Dentatus." Smithsonian Marine Station at Fort Pierce. http://www.sms.si.edu/Indian Riverspec/parali_dentat.htm.

"Historical Census Browser." University of Virginia, Geospatial and Statistical Data Center. http://fisher.lib.virginia.edu/collections/stats/histcensus/index.html.
Hoffman, Paul A. *Florida's Frontiers*. Bloomington: Indiana University Press, 1994.
Hopwood, Fred A. *The Golden Era of Steamboating on the Indian River, 1877–1900*. 1985. Reprint. Cocoa: Florida Historical Society Press, 1998.
Howard, Rosalyn. "The 'Wild Indians' of Andros Island: Black Seminole Legacy in the Bahamas." *Journal of Black Studies* 37, no. 2 (November 2006): 275–98.
Hrdlička, Aleš. "Preliminary Report on Finds of Supposedly Ancient Human Remains at Vero, Florida." *Journal of Geology* 25, no. 1 (January–February 1917): 43–51.
Hutchings, Robert M. "From Oranges to Orange Juice: A Transformation in Florida Agriculture, 1945–1965." Stuart, Fla.: Pioneer America Society, October 14, 2011.
Independent Scientific Review of the Indian River Lagoon—South Project Implementation Report. Jacksonville, Fla.: U.S. Army Corps of Engineers/South Florida Water Management District, 2004.
Indian River Lagoon National Estuary Program. "Indian River Lagoon: Introduction to a National Treasure." Palm Bay, Fla.: St. Johns River Water Management District, 2007. http://www.sjrwmd.com/itsyourlagoon/pdfs/Indian River_Natural_Treasure_book.pdf.
———. *Indian River Lagoon Comprehensive Conservation and Management Plan*. Palm Bay, Fla.: St. Johns River Water Management District, 2008.
———. St. Johns Water Management District. http://floridaswater.com/itsyourlagoon/index.html.
"Indian River Lagoon Observatory: Biodiversity and Ecosystem Function of an Estuary in Transition." Harbor Branch Oceanographic Institute. http://www.fau.edu/hboi/meh/irlo.php.
Indian River Land Trust. "A Brief History of IRLT: Highlights." http://www.indianriverlandtrust.org/cfiles/about_history.cfm.
Johnson, Howard. "Bahamian Labor Migration to Florida in the Late Nineteenth and Early Twentieth Centuries." *International Migration Review* 22, no. 1 (Spring 1988): 84–103.
Johnson, Sherry. *Climate and Catastrophe in Cuba and the Atlantic World in the Age of Revolution*. Chapel Hill: University of North Carolina Press, 2011.
Kerber, Stephen. "The United States Life-Saving Service and the Florida Houses of Refuge." Master's thesis, Florida Atlantic University, 1971.
Knetsch, Joe, and Paul S. George. "A Problematical Law: The Armed Occupation Act of 1842 and Its Impact on Southeast Florida." *Tequesta* 53 (1993): 63–80.
Kruczynski, W. L., and P. J. Fletcher. *Tropical Connections: South Florida's Marine Environment*. Cambridge, Md.: Ian Press, 2012.
Landers, Jane G. *Colonial Plantations and Economy in Florida*. Gainesville: University Press of Florida, 2000.
Lang, Robert E., Deborah Epstein Popper, and Frank J. Popper. "'Progress of the

Nation': The Settlement History of the Enduring American Frontier." *Western Historical Quarterly* 26, no. 3 (Autumn 1995): 289–307.

Lanham, J. F., and Alan Brech. "Locating the Ais Indian Town of Pentoaya along the Indian River Lagoon, Florida." *Brevard Journal* 7, no. 1 (Spring/Summer 2008): 5–22.

Lapointe, Brian E., Laura W. Herren, and Bradley J. Bedford. "Effects of Hurricanes, Land Use, and Water Management on Nutrient and Microbial Pollution: St. Lucie Estuary, South East Florida." *Journal of Coastal Research* 28, no. 6 (November 2012): 1345–61.

Lasi, Margaret A, Charles A. Jacoby, Wendy A. Tweedale, Joel S. Steward, Edward J. Phlips, and Susan Badylak. "Investigating the Causes of the 2011 IRL Superbloom—A Water Quality Analysis." Paper presented at 2013 Indian River Lagoon Symposium, Harbor Branch Oceanographic Institute, Fort Pierce, Fla.

Link, Marion Clayton. "The Spanish Camp Site and the 1715 Plate Fleet Wreck." *Tequesta* 26 (1966): 21–30.

Littler, Diane S., Mark M. Littler, and M. Dennis Hanisak. *Submersed Plants of the Indian River Lagoon: A Floristic Inventory and Field Guide*. Boca Raton, Fla.: Offshore Graphics, 2008.

Marine Resources Council. "About Us." http://www.mrcirl.org/who-is-the-mrc.

McCarthy, Kevin. *African American Sites in Florida*. Sarasota, Fla.: Pineapple Press, 2007.

McHarg, Ian L. *Design with Nature*. New York: J. Wiley, 1992.

McIver, Stuart. *Death in the Everglades: The Murder of Guy Bradley, America's First Martyr to Environmentalism*. Gainesville: University Press of Florida, 2003.

Middleton, Sallie. "Space Rush: Local Impact of Federal Aerospace Programs on Brevard and Surrounding Counties." *Florida Historical Quarterly* 87, no. 2 (Fall 2008): 258–89.

Milanich, Jerald T. *Archaeology of Precolumbian Florida*. Gainesville: University Press of Florida, 1994.

———. *Florida Indians and the Invasion from Europe*. Gainesville: University Press of Florida, 1995.

———. "Frolicking Bears, Wet Vultures, and Other Mysteries: Amos Jay Cummings' Description of Mounds in East-Central Florida." *Florida Historical Quarterly* 80, no. 3 (Winter 2002): 360–374.

———. *Frolicking Bears, Wet Vultures, and Other Oddities: A New York City Journalist in Nineteenth-Century Florida*. Gainesville: University Press of Florida, 2005.

———. *Tacachale: Essays on the Indians of Florida and Southeastern Georgia during the Historic Period*. Gainesville: University Press of Florida, 1978.

Miller, James J. *An Environmental History of Northeast Florida*. Gainesville: University Press of Florida, 1998.

Missall, John, and Mary Lou Missall. *The Seminole Wars: America's Longest Indian Conflict*. Gainesville: University Press of Florida, 2004.

Mormino, Gary R. *Land of Sunshine, State of Dreams: A Social History of Modern Florida*. Gainesville: University Press of Florida, 2005.

———. "Sunbelt Dreams and Altered States: A Social and Cultural History of Florida, 1950–2000." *Florida Historical Quarterly* 81, no. 1 (Summer 2002): 3–21.

Morris, Lori J., Robert Chamberlain, and Lauren Hall. "The Bloomin' Lagoon—Bloom and Bust of Indian River Lagoon Sea Grasses." Paper presented at 2013 Indian River Lagoon Symposium, Harbor Branch Oceanographic Institute, Fort Pierce, Fla.

Mote Marine Laboratory. *St. Lucie Estuary Nutrient Loading Assessment*. Sarasota, Fla.: Mote Marine Laboratory, 1993.

Mueller, Edward A. "East Coast Florida Steamboating, 1831–1861." *Florida Historical Quarterly* 40, no. 3 (January 1962): 241–60.

Nabors, Robert L., ed. "Countdown in History: Titusville Centennial: Historical Booklet and Program" (1967). North Brevard Historical Society and Museum/North Brevard Business Directory.

Okie, Thomas. "Everything Is Peaches Down in Georgia: Culture and Agriculture in the American South." Ph.D. diss., University of Georgia, 2012.

Panagopoulos, Epaminondas P. *New Smyrnea: An Eighteenth Century Greek Odyssey*. Gainesville: University of Florida Press, 1966.

Parker, Susan. *Historic Resource Study*. Atlanta: National Park Service, Cultural Resources, 2008.

Parkinson, Randall W. "Tuning Surface Water Management and Wetland Restoration Programs with Historic Sediment Accumulation Rates: Merritt Island National Wildlife Refuge, East-Central Florida, U.S.A." *Journal of Coastal Research* 22, no. 5 (September 2006): 1268–77.

Patterson, Gordon. "Ditches and Dreams: Nelson Fell and the Rise of Fellsmere." *Florida Historical Quarterly* 76, no. 1 (Summer 1997): 1–19.

———. *The Mosquito Crusades*. New Brunswick, N.J.: Rutgers University Press, 2009.

Phillips, Sarah T. "Environmental History." In *American History Now*, edited by Eric Foner and Lisa McGirr, 285–313. Philadelphia: Temple University Press, 2011.

Pierce, Charles William, and Donald Walter Curl. *Pioneer Life in Southeast Florida*. Coral Gables, Fla.: University of Miami Press, 1970.

Pittman, Craig, and Matthew Waite. *Paving Paradise: Florida's Vanishing Wetlands and the Failure of No Net Loss*. Gainesville: University Press of Florida, 2010.

Purdy, Barbara A., Kevin S. Jones, John J. Mecholsky, Gerald Bourne, Richard C. Hulbert Jr., Bruce J. MacFadden, Krista L. Church, Michael W. Warren, Thomas F. Jorstad, Dennis J. Stanford, Melvin J. Wachowiak, and Robert J. Speakman. "Earliest Art in the Americas: Incised Image of a Proboscidean on a Mineralized Extinct Animal Bone from Vero Beach, Florida." *Journal of Archaeological Science* 38 (2011): 2908–13.

Ramey, Vic, and Jeff Schardt. "Plant Management in Florida Waters." Department of Environmental Protection, Bureau of Invasive Plant Management. http://plants.ifas.ufl.edu/guide/bodcanal2.jpg.

Reed, Nathaniel P. *A Different Vision: The History of the Hobe Sound Company and the Jupiter Island Club*. Hobe Sound, Fla.: Reed, 2010

———. Everglades Papers. Special and Area Studies Collections, George A. Smathers Libraries, University of Florida, Gainesville.

Reif, John S., Marilyn S. Mazzoil, Stephen D. McCulloch, Rene A. Varela, Juli D. Goldstein, Patricia A. Fair, and Gregory D. Bossart. "Lobomycosis in Atlantic Bottlenose Dolphins from the Indian River Lagoon, Florida." *Journal of the American Veterinary Medical Association* 228, no. 1 (January 1, 2006): 104–8.

Rey, Jorge R., and C. Roxanne Rutledge. "Mangroves." Institute of Food and Agricultural Sciences, University of Florida. http://edis.ifas.ufl.edu/in195.

———. "Mosquito Control Impoundments." University of Florida. http://edis.ifas.ufl.edu/in192.

Roberts, Callum M., J. A. Bohnsack, F. Gell, J. P. Hawkins, and R. Goodridge. "Effects of Marine Reserves on Adjacent Fisheries." *Science* 295, no. 5548 (November 30, 2001): 1920–23.

Robinson, Tim. *A Tropical Frontier: Pioneers and Settlers of Southeast Florida, 1800–1890*. Port Salerno, Fla.: Port Sun, 2005.

Schafer, Daniel L. " . . . Everything Carried the Face of Spring: Biscayne Bay in the 1770s." *Tequesta* 44 (1984): 23–31.

———. "St. Augustine's British Years, 1763–1783." *El Escribiano: The Journal of the St. Augustine Historical Society* 38 (2001): 44–65.

Sebastian Inlet District. "The History of the Sebastian Inlet." http://www.sebastianinletdistrict.com/Inlet_History.html.

"Sebastian Inlet 1886." Indian River County Library. http://www.irclibrary.org/sebastianlibrary/george/1880.html.

Shappee, Nathan D. "The Celestial Railroad to Juno." *Florida Historical Quarterly* 40, no. 4 (April 1962): 329–49.

Sheriff, Carol. *The Artificial River: The Erie Canal and the Paradox of Progress, 1817–1862*. New York: Hill and Wang, 1997.

Simi, Patti. "Fish Health in the St. Lucie Estuarine System." U.S. Department of the Interior, U.S. Geological Survey, Center for Coastal Geology. http://sofia.usgs.gov/sfrsf/rooms/coastal/stlucie/fish/.

Slotkin, Richard. *Regeneration through Violence: The Mythology of the American Frontier 1600–1860*. Norman: University of Oklahoma Press, 2000.

Smith, Kimberly G. "100 Years Ago in the American Ornithologist's Union." *Auk* 122, no. 4 (2004): 1310–11.

Smithsonian Marine Station at Fort Pierce. http://www.sms.si.edu/IRLspec/Maps.htm.

South Florida Ecosystem Restoration Task Force. *South Florida Ecosystem Restoration: Scientific Information Needs.* U.S. Geological Survey, 1996. http://www.sfrestore.org/sct/Scieneeds/front.pdf.

———. *Focus on the St. Lucie River.* South Florida Water Management District, 1999. https://my.sfwmd.gov/portal/page/portal/common/pdf/stlucie.pdf.

South Florida Water Management District. *Technical Documentation to Support Development of Minimum Flows for the St. Lucie River and Estuary.* West Palm Beach: South Florida Water Management District, 2002.

St. Johns Water Management District. "Indian River Lagoon." St. Johns Water Management District. http://www.sjrwmd.com/itsyourlagoon/.

———. "It's Your Lagoon." http://floridaswater.com/itsyourlagoon/index.html.

St. Lucie River Initiative. *De-Ooze It or Lose It! Save the St. Lucie River and Estuary: A Citizen's Report to Congress.* Stuart, Fla.: St. Lucie River Initiative, 1995.

Stephenson, Bruce. "A Monstrous Desecration: Dredge and Fill in Boca Ciega Bay." In *Paradise Lost?: The Environmental History of Florida,* edited by Jack E. Davis and Raymond Arsenault, 326–49. Gainesville: University Press of Florida, 2005.

Stone, Tammy T., David N. Dickel, and Glen H. Doran. "The Preservation and Conservation of Waterlogged Bone from the Windover Site, Florida: A Comparison of Methods." *Journal of Field Archaeology* 17 (1990): 177–83.

Sweet, Zelia W. *New Smyrna, Florida, in the Civil War.* New Smyrna, Fla.: Volusia County Historical Commission, 1963.

Sweet, Zelia Wilson, and A. W. Trainor. *Buried Treasure: New Smyrnea, Florida.* Federal Writers' Project, 1936. University of Florida Digital Collections, Gainesville. http://ufdc.ufl.edu/UF00055124/00001.

Taylor, Paul. *Discovering the Civil War in Florida.* Sarasota, Fla.: Pineapple Press, 2001.

Tebeau, Charlton W., and Ruby Leach Carson. *Florida from Indian Trail to Space Age: A History.* Delray Beach, Fla.: Southern Publishing, 1965.

Thurlow, Sandra Henderson. *Historic Jensen and Eden on Florida's Indian River.* Stuart, Fla.: Sewall's Point, 2004.

———. "Lonely Vigils: Houses of Refuge on Florida's East Coast, 1876–1915." *Florida Historical Quarterly* 76, no. 2 (Fall 1997): 152–73.

———. *Sewall's Point: The History of a Peninsular Community on Florida's Treasure Coast.* Stuart, Fla.: Sewall's Point, 1992.

———. *Stuart on the St. Lucie.* Stuart, Fla.: Sewall's Point, 2001.

"United States Map of Köppen Geiger Classification." University of Veterinary Medicine, Vienna. http://koeppen-geiger.vu-wien.ac.at/pics/KG_USA.jpg.

University of Maryland Center for Environmental Science. "Tropic Zone Tropical Connections." http://ian.umces.edu/imagelibrary/albums/userpics/84469/normal_iil_diagram_tropic_zone_tropical_connections.png.

U.S. Army Corps of Engineers. "CERP: The Plan in Depth." Comprehensive Ev-

erglades Restoration Plan. http://www.evergladesplan.org/about/rest_plan_pt_01.aspx.
U.S. Imaging, Inc. "Sebastian Inlet." http://www.usimaging.com/images/digital3_002.jpg.
Voss, Gilbert L. "The Orange Grove House of Refuge no. 3." *Tequesta* 28 (1968): 3–18.
Weber, David J. "The Spanish Borderlands of North America: A Historiography." *Magazine of History* 14, no. 4 (2000): 5–11.
Weddle, Robert S. *Spanish Sea: The Gulf of Mexico in North American Discovery*. College Station: Texas A&M University Press, 1985.
Whitfield, Stephen J. "Florida's Fudged Identity." *Florida Historical Quarterly* 71, no. 4 (April 1993): 413–35.
Woodward-Clyde Consultants, Marshall McCully & Associates, Inc., and Natural Systems Analysts, Inc. *Biological Resources of the Indian River Lagoon*. Tampa, Fla.: Woodward-Clyde Consultants, 1994.
———. *Historical Imagery Inventory and Sea Grass Assessment Indian River Lagoon*. Tampa, Fla.: Woodward-Clyde Consultants, 1994.
———. *Physical Features of the Indian River Lagoon*. Tampa, Fla.: Woodward-Clyde Consultants, 1994.
———. *Uses of the Indian River Lagoon*. Tampa, Fla.: Woodward-Clyde Consultants, 1994.
Wrobel, David M. "Beyond the Frontier-Region Dichotomy." *Pacific Historical Review* 65, no. 3 (August 1996): 401–29.

Index

Page numbers in italics refer to illustrations.

NATHANIEL OSBORN is a member of the History Department at the Pine School in Hobe Sound, Florida. Born and raised in Santa Barbara, California, Osborn moved to the Indian River Lagoon at seventeen. He lives with his wife and three children in Jensen Beach, Florida.